D0577347

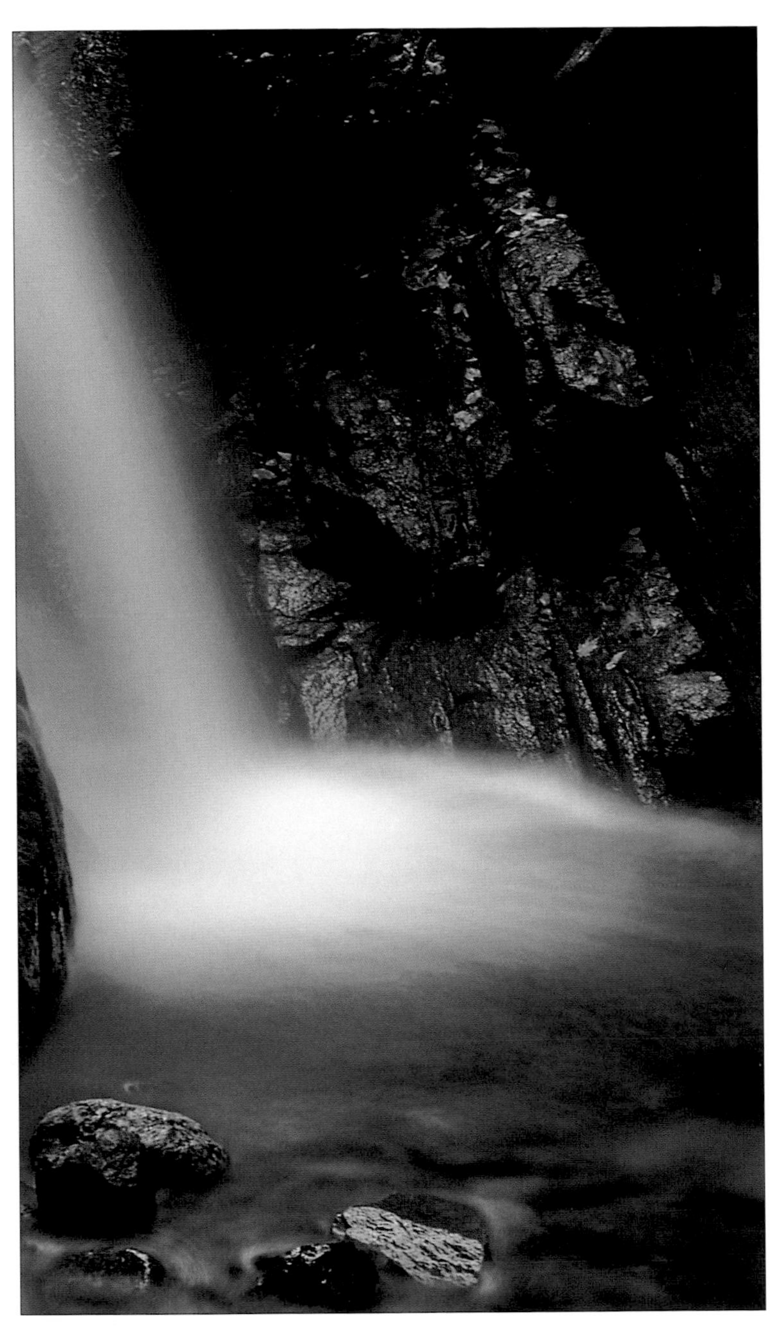

Only that day dawns to which we are awake.

—*Henry David Thoreau*

A NEW ENGLAND AUTUMN

a sentimental journey

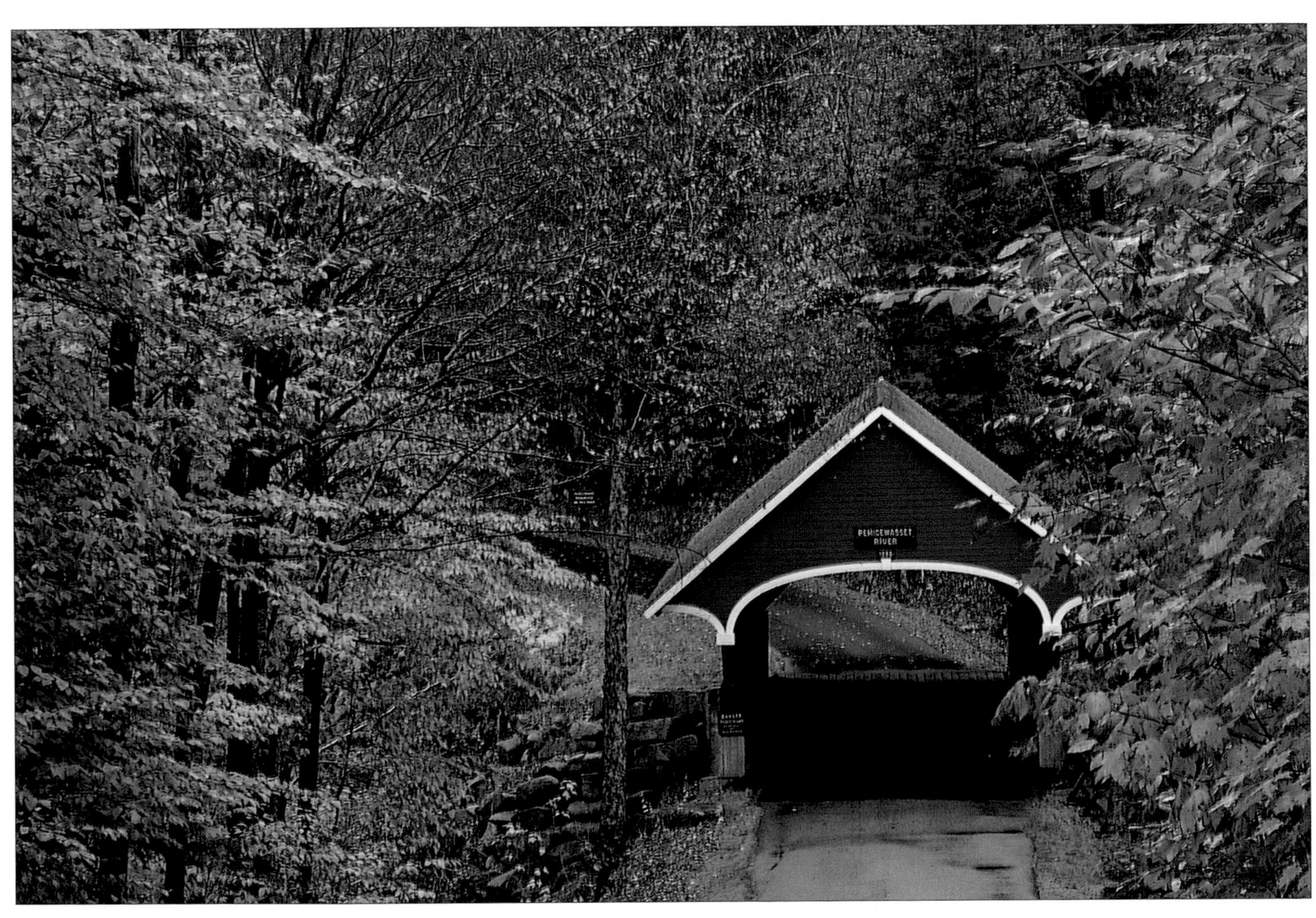

PHOTOGRAPHS BY FERENC MÁTÉ

WRITINGS BY NEW ENGLAND AUTHORS

Designed by Celine Little and Ferenc Máté
Composed in Berkeley Old Style
Printed in Italy by Mondadori Printing, Verona

Published by Albatross Books
ISBN 978-0-920256-55-8

Albatross Books
at W. W. Norton & Co.
500 Fifth Avenue. New York

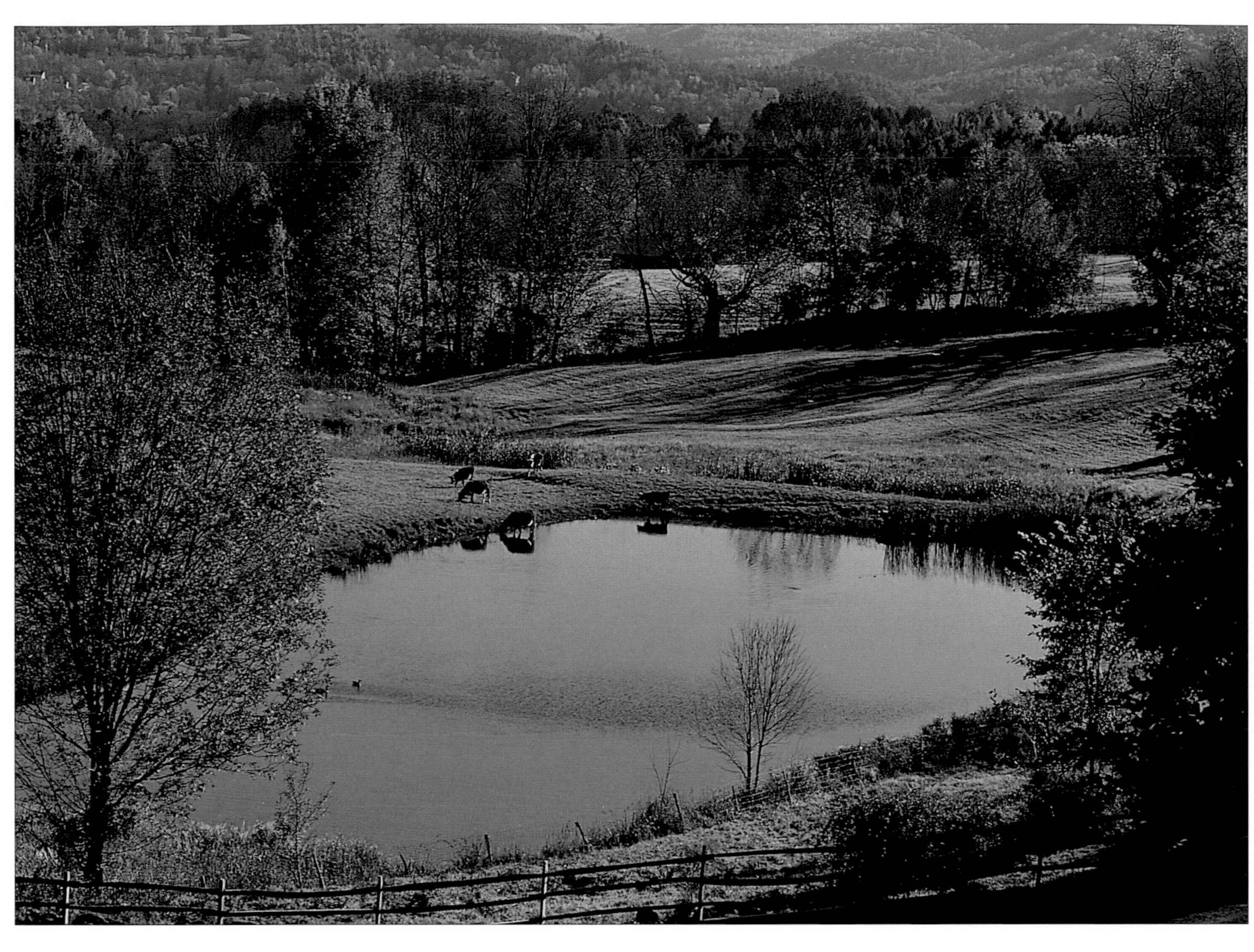

for W. F. R.

Contents

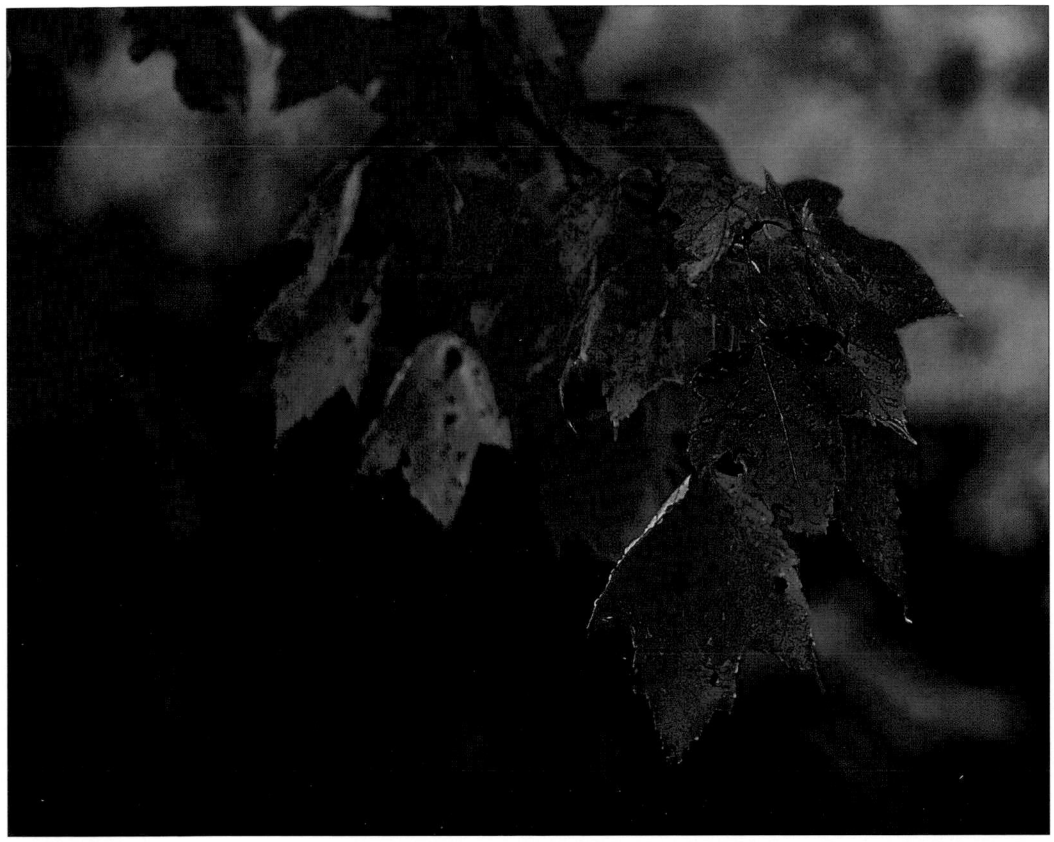

INTRODUCTION

It rained before I set out that morning. The forest floor was soft underfoot, the brook swollen, rocks gleamed and a breath of wind in the boughs above brought down a drifting shower. Beads hung from turning leaves and glistened filled with dawn light.

A mist hung over the lake, leaving only the reeds and shore.

Up the road, between a house and barn, was a table set with two baskets of apples, a few ears of corn and small jugs of maple syrup. Pigeons swooped from the hayloft down to the lake to drink and the cows ambled after them, wet grass swaying around their feet. Taking two apples, I left some money in a coffee can marked "Thank you".

Sunrise over the harbor was blinding. Among the rocks, lobster boats stirred the fog as they headed out to sea. The day slowly passed, a young man swept the fish house and gulls screeched and plunged in glee. A skiff was carried up beside the house and turned over, the oars tucked under it, protected for the winter. In the clear, hard light the white clapboard church glowed and headstones in the graveyard threw long shadows. After school, the children's voices were swallowed by leaves thick on the ground.

As the day wound down, lights were lit; it was twilight—the autumn of the day.

Ferenc Máté

A
New England Autumn

a sentimental journey

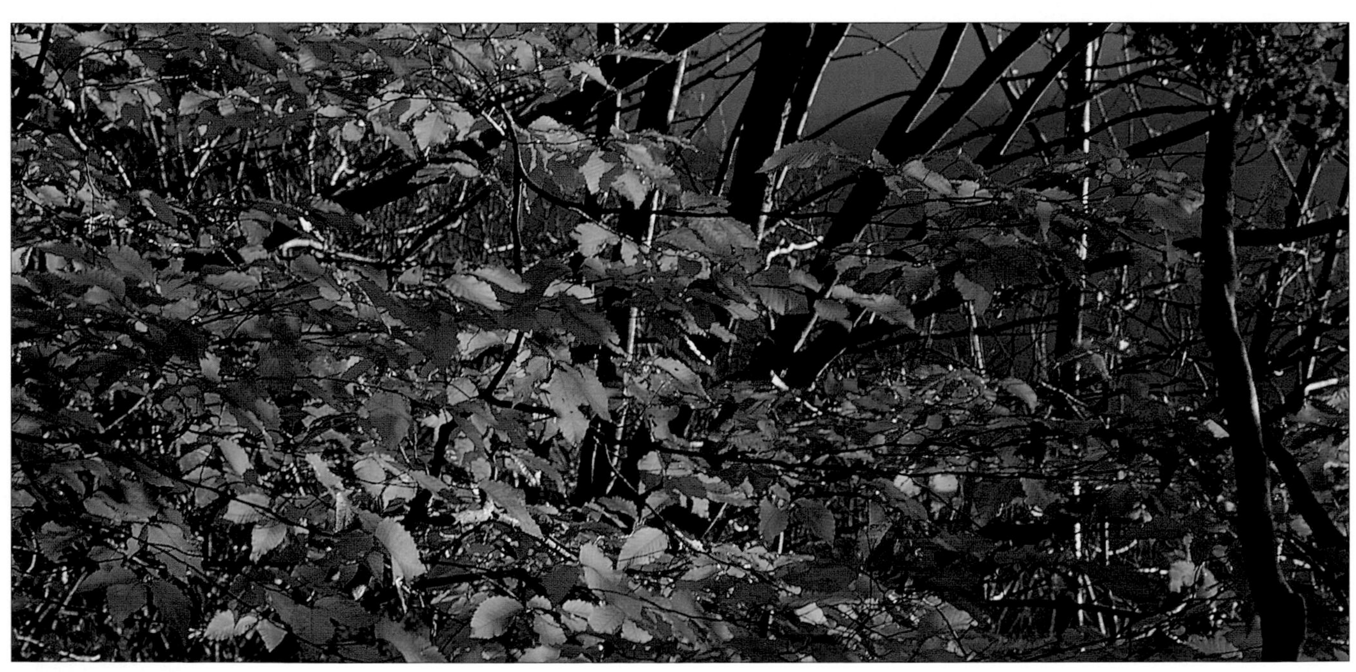

As imperceptibly as Grief
The Summer lapsed away—
Too imperceptible at last
To seem like Perfidy—
A Quietness distilled
As Twilight long begun,
Or Nature spending with herself
Sequestered Afternoon—
The Dusk drew earlier in—
The Morning foreign shone—
A courteous, yet harrowing Grace,
As Guest, that would be gone—
And thus, without a Wing
Or service of a Keel
Our summer made her light escape
Into the Beautiful.

Emily Dickinson, 1865

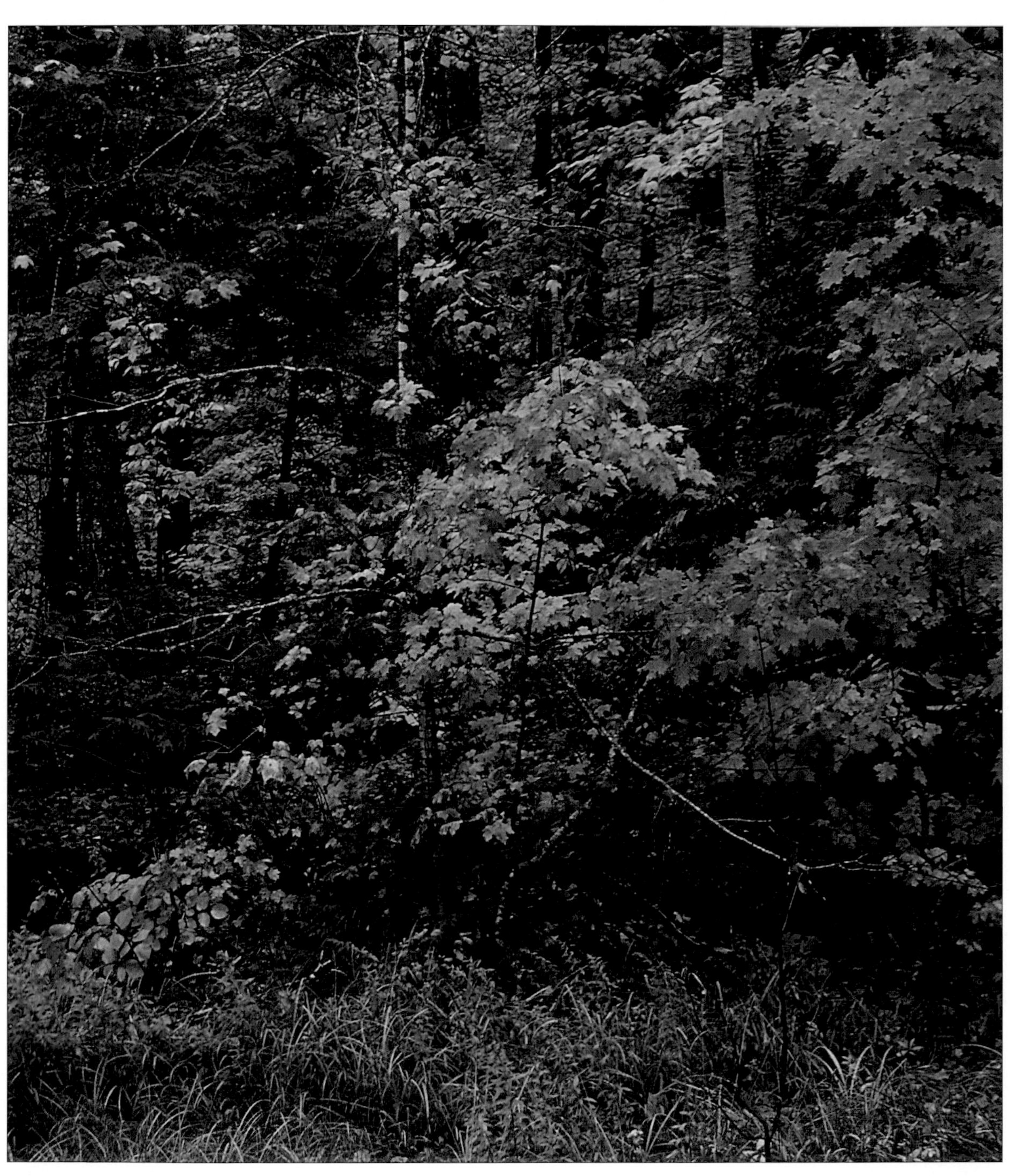

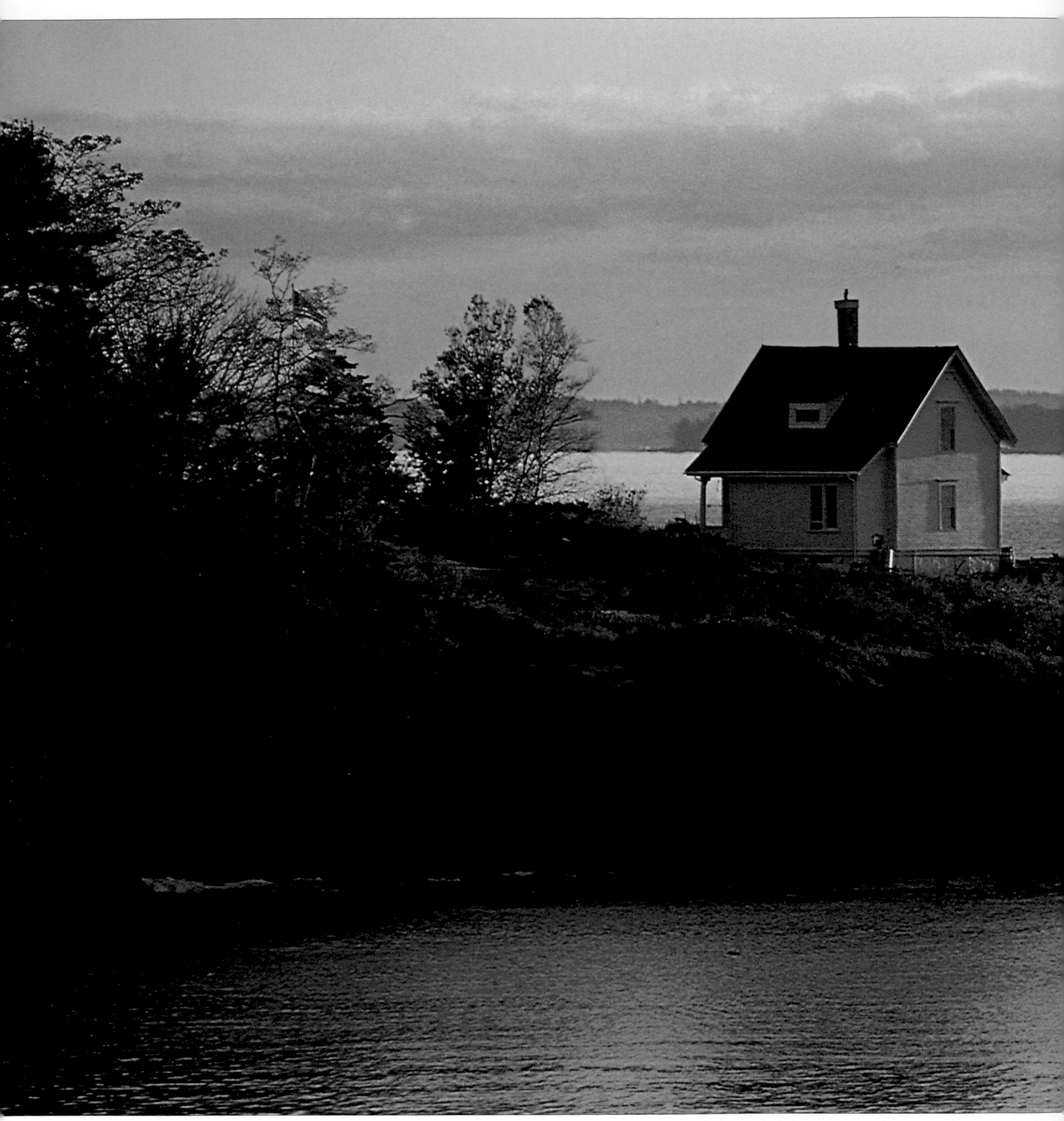

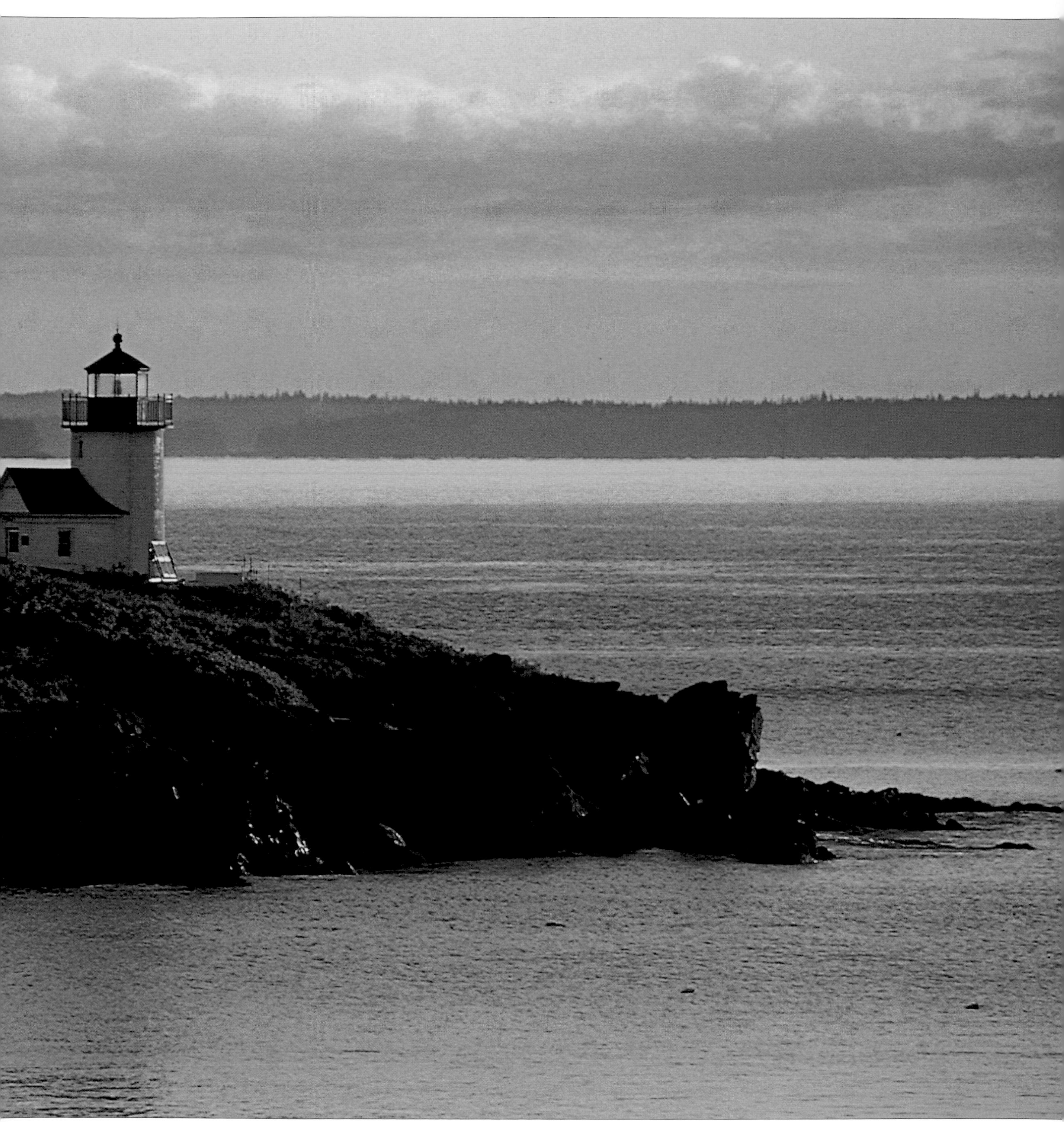

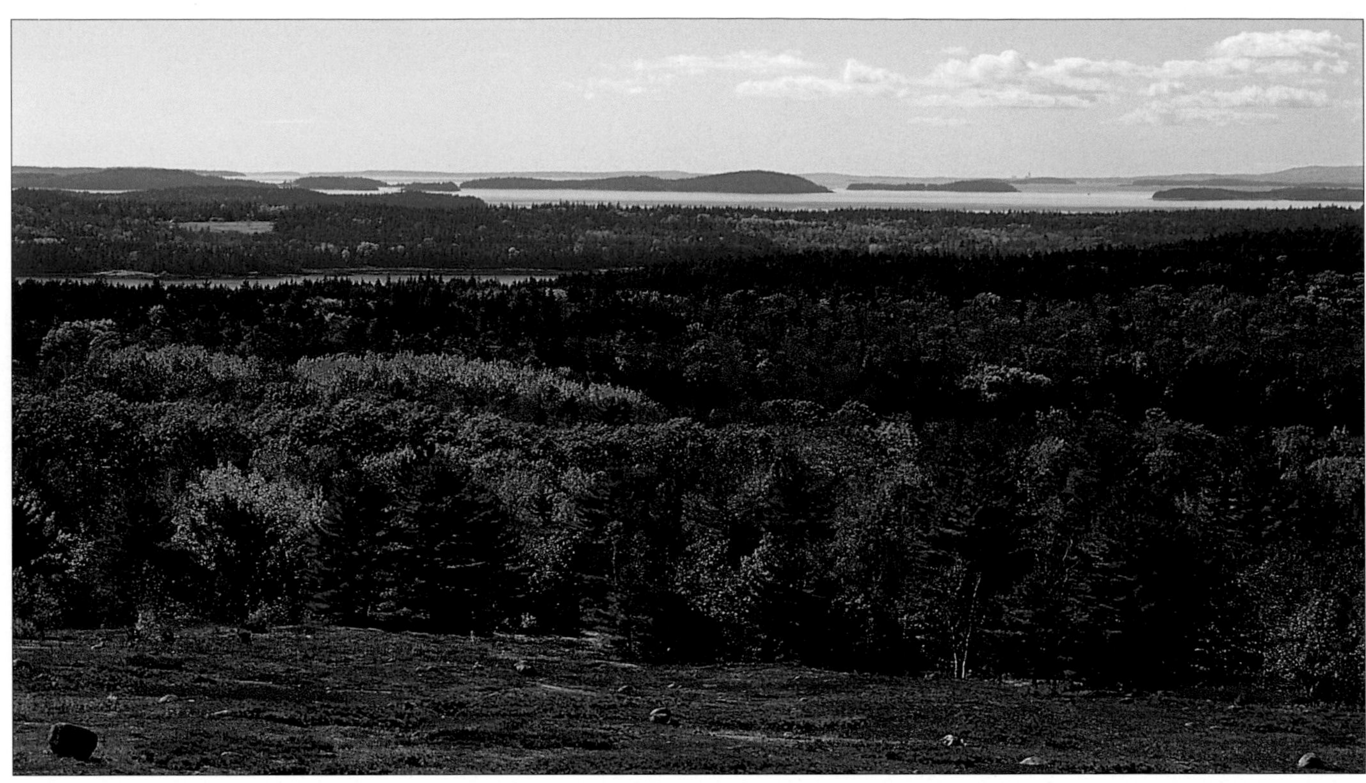

William

We went from the upper edge of the field above the house into a smooth, brown path among the dark spruces. The hot sun brought out the fragrance of the pitchy bark, and the shade was pleasant as we climbed the hill. William stopped once or twice to show me as great wasps'-nest close by, or some fishhawks'-nests below in a bit of swamp. He picked a few sprigs of late-blooming linnaea as we came out upon an open but of pasture at the top of the island, and gave them to me without speaking, but he knew as well as I that one could not say half he wished about linnaea. Through this piece of rough pasture ran a huge shape of stone like the great backbone of an enormous creature. At the end, near the woods, we could climb up on it and walk along to the highest point, there above the circle of pointed firs we could look down over all the island, and could see the ocean that circled this and a hundred other bits of island ground, the mainland shore and all the far horizons. It gave a sudden sense of space, for nothing stopped the eye or hedged one in,—that sense of liberty in space and time which great prospects always give.

From *The Country of the Pointed Firs*
Sarah Orne Jewett, 1896

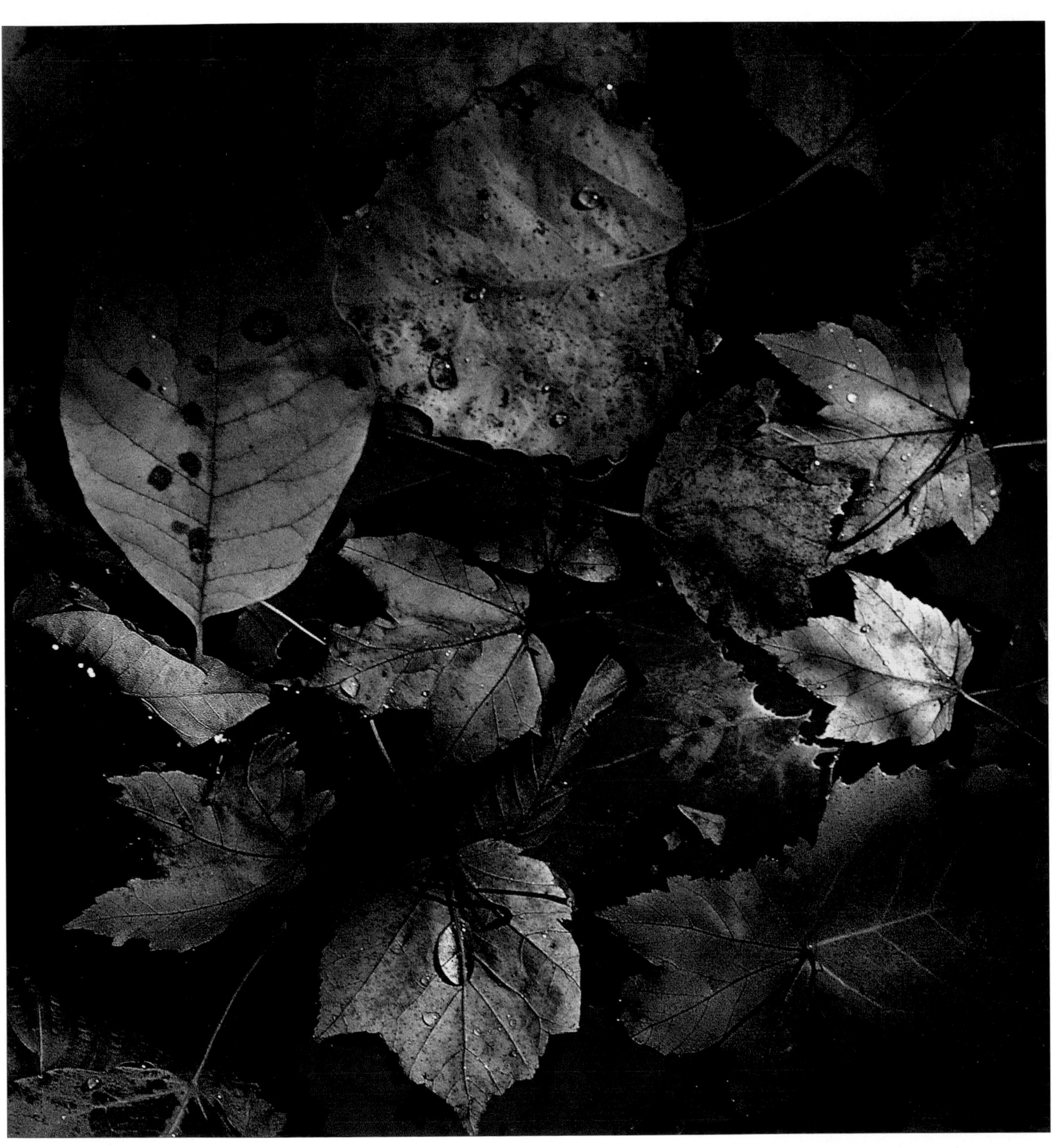

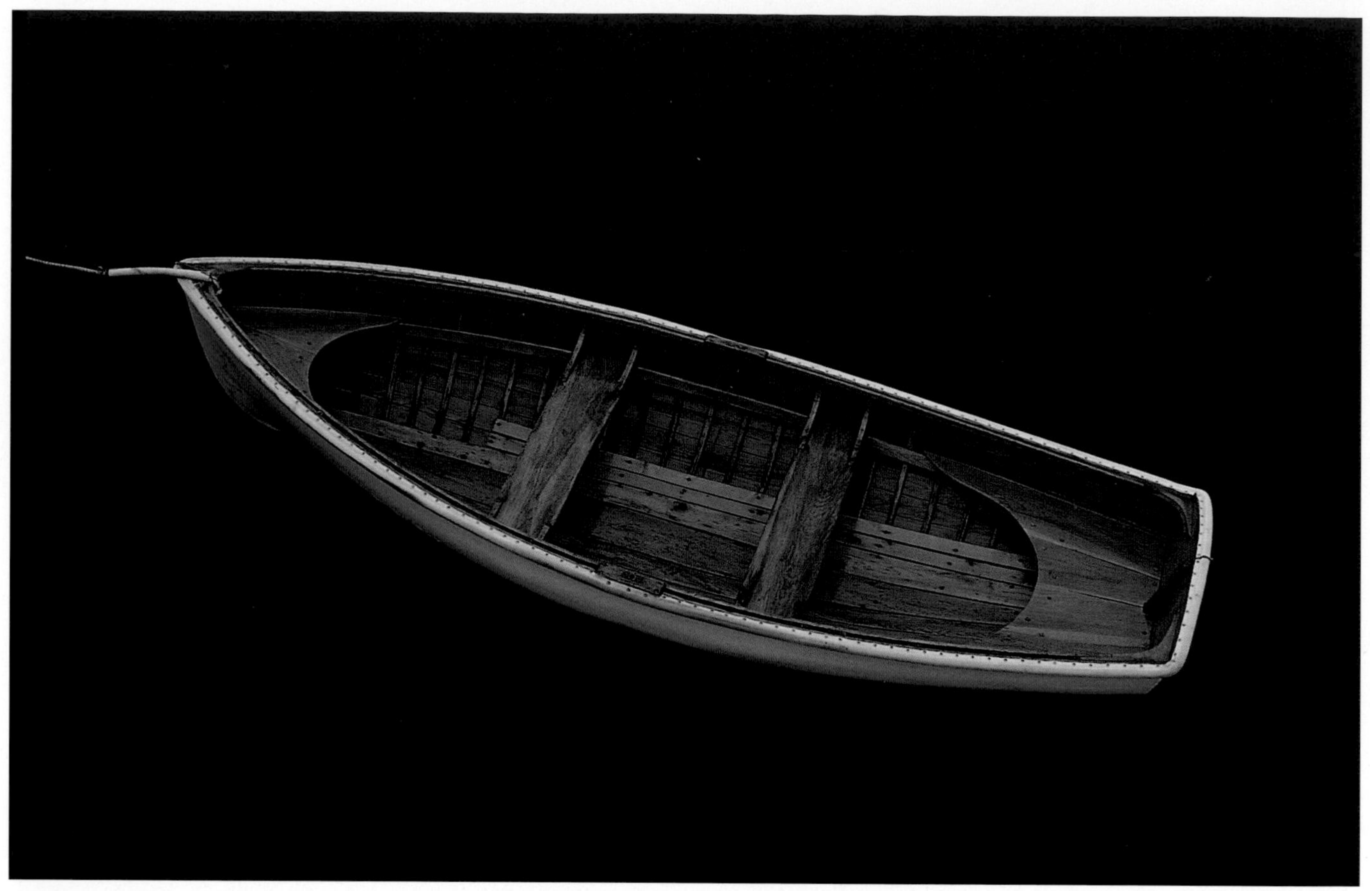

Green Island

I had become well acquainted with Mrs. Todd as landlady, herb-gatherer, and rustic philosopher, we had been discreet fellow-passengers once or twice when I had sailed up the coast to a larger town than Dunnet Landing to do some shopping; but I was yet to become acquainted with her as a mariner. An hour later we pushed off from the landing in the desired dory. The tide was just on the turn, beginning to fall, and several friends and acquaintances stood along the side of the dilapidated wharf and cheered us by their words and evident interest. Johnny Bowden and I were both rowing in haste to get out where we could catch the breeze and put up the small sail which lay clumsily furled along the gunwale. Mrs. Todd sat aft, a stern and unbending lawgiver.

"You better let her drift; we'll get there 'bout as quick; the tide'll take her right out from under these old buildin's; there's plenty of wind outside."

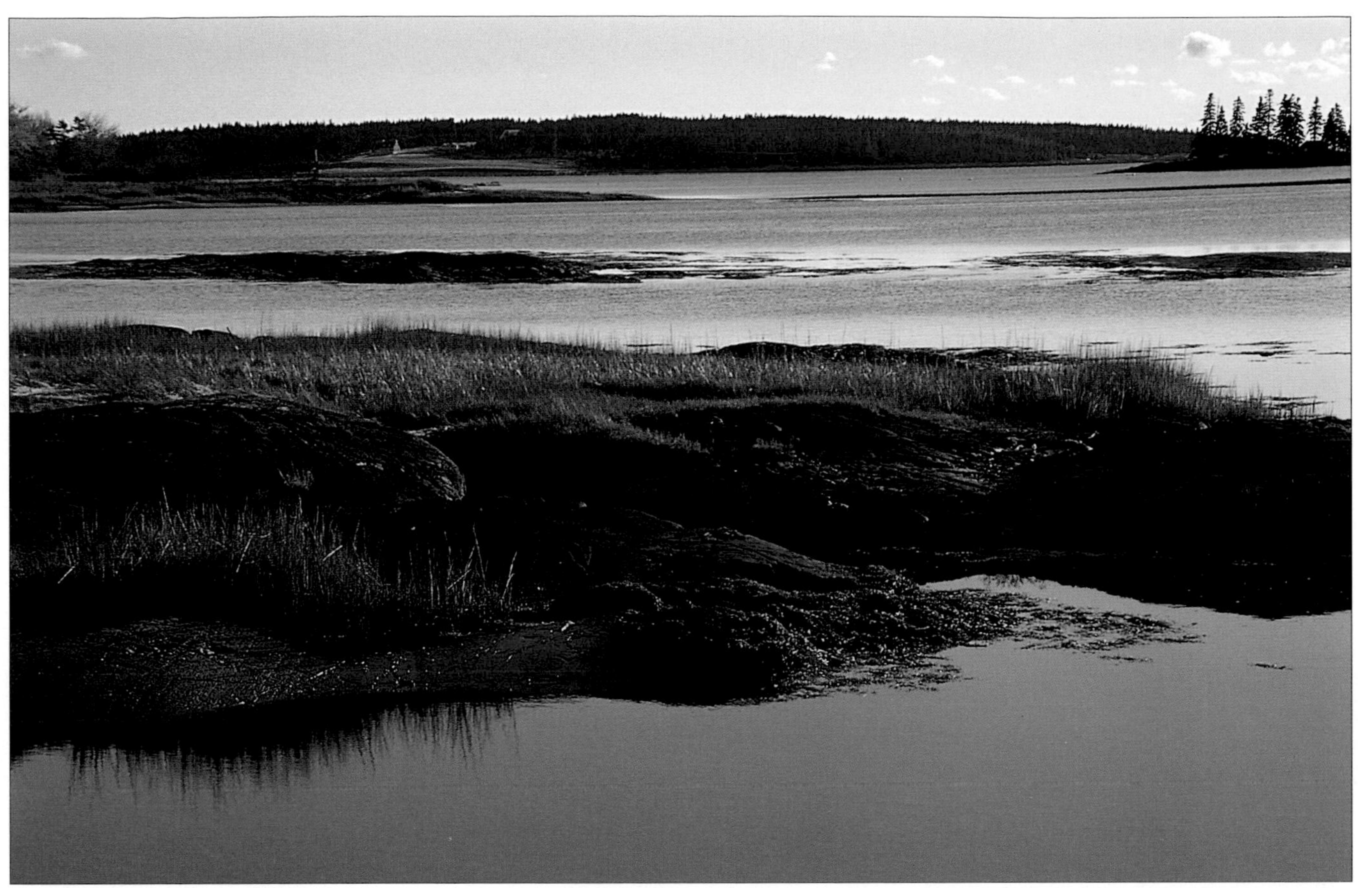

When we caught the wind we were soon on our seaward course, and only stopped to underrun a trawl, for the floats of which Mrs. Todd looked earnestly, explaining that her mother might not be prepared for three extra to dinner; it was her brother's trawl, and she meant to just run her eye along for the right sort of a little haddock. I leaned over the boat's side with great interest and excitement, while she skillfully handled the long line of hooks, and made scornful remarks upon worthless, bait-consuming creatures of the sea as she reviewed them and left them on the trawl or shook them off into the waves. At last we came to what she pronounced a proper haddock, and having taken him on board and ended his life resolutely, we went our way.

From *The Country of the Pointed Firs*
Sarah Orne Jewett, 1896

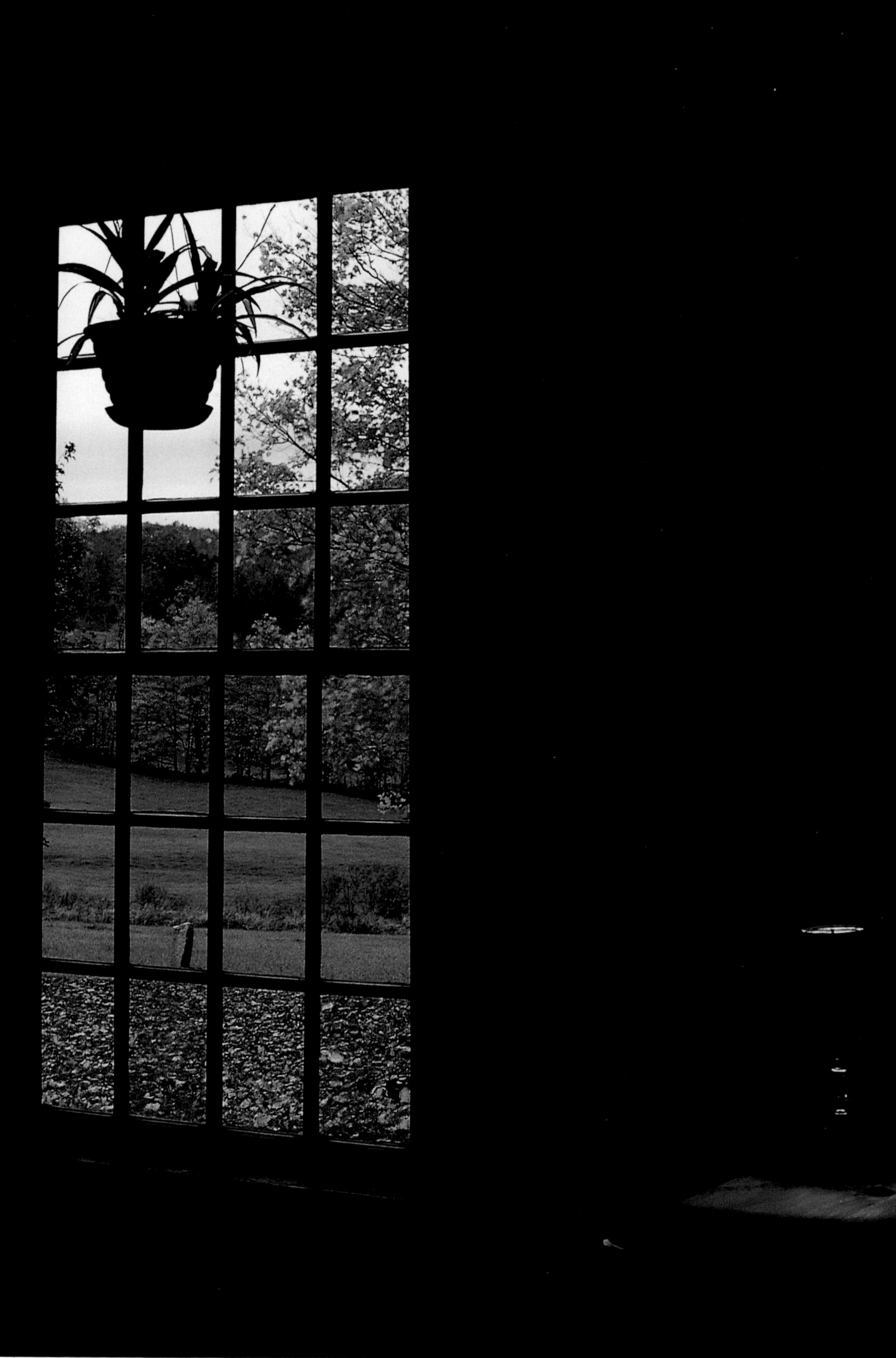

The Backward View

At last it was the time of late summer, when the house was cool and damp in the morning, and all the light seemed to come through green leaves; but at the first step out of doors the sunshine always laid a warm hand on my shoulder, and the clear, high sky seemed to lift quickly as I looked at it. There was no autumnal mist on the coast, nor any August fog, instead of these, the sea, the sky, all the long shore line and the inland hills, with every bush of bay and every fir-top, gained a deeper color and a sharper clearness. There was something shining in the air, and a kind of luster on the water and the pasture grass,—a northern look that, except at this moment of the year, one must go far to seek. The sunshine of a northern summer was coming to its lovely end.

From *The Country of the Pointed Firs*
Sarah Orne Jewett, 1896

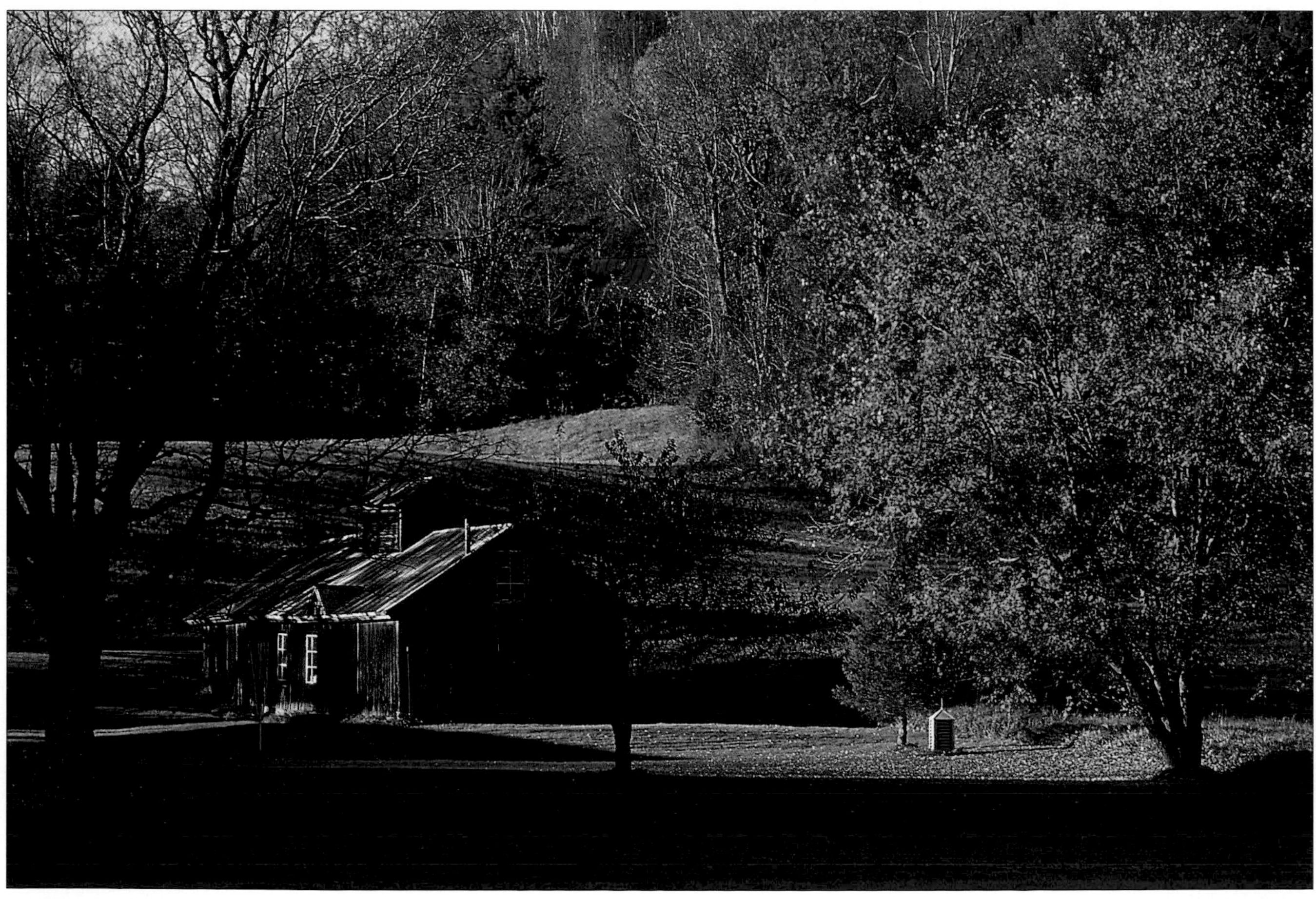

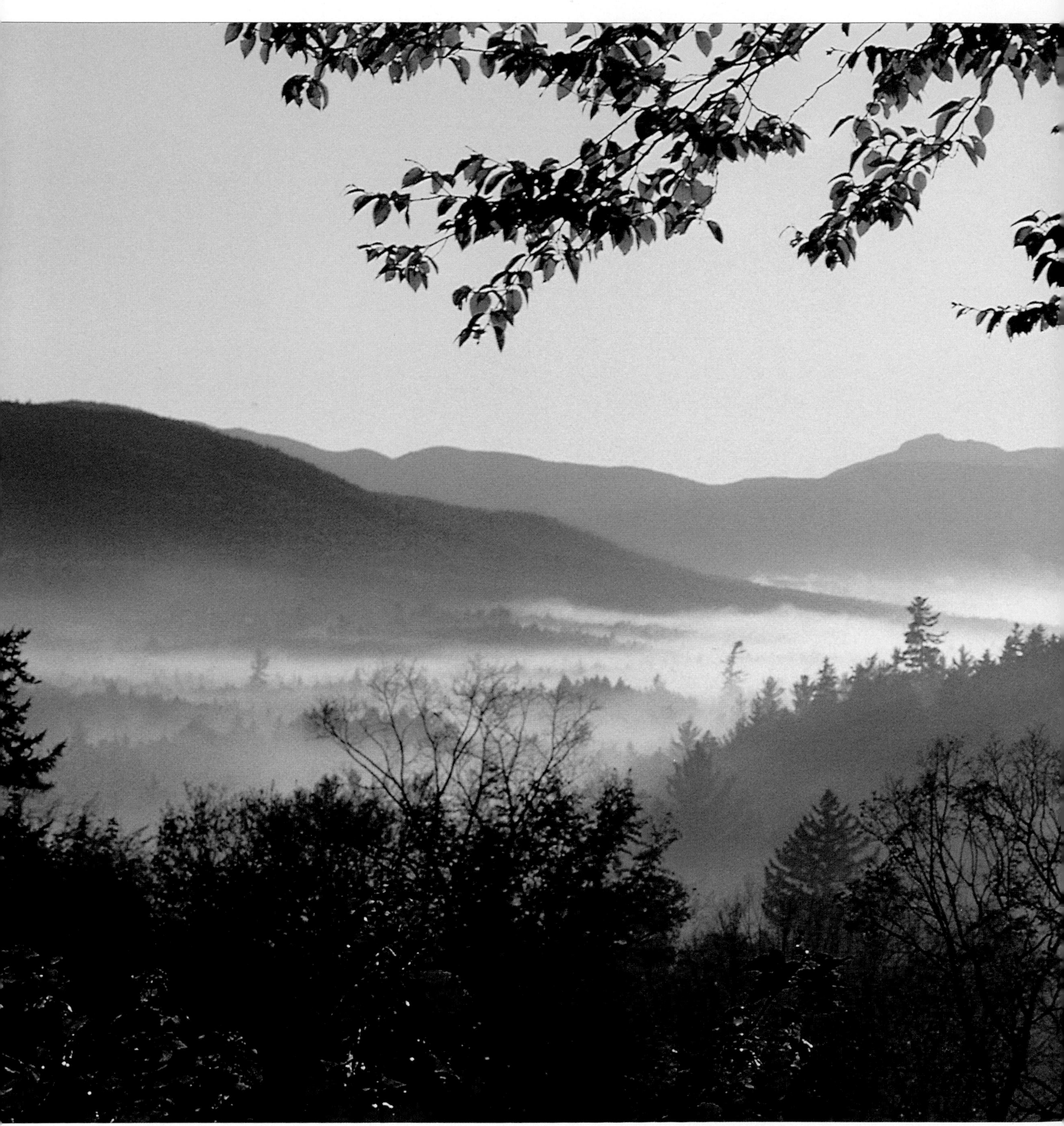

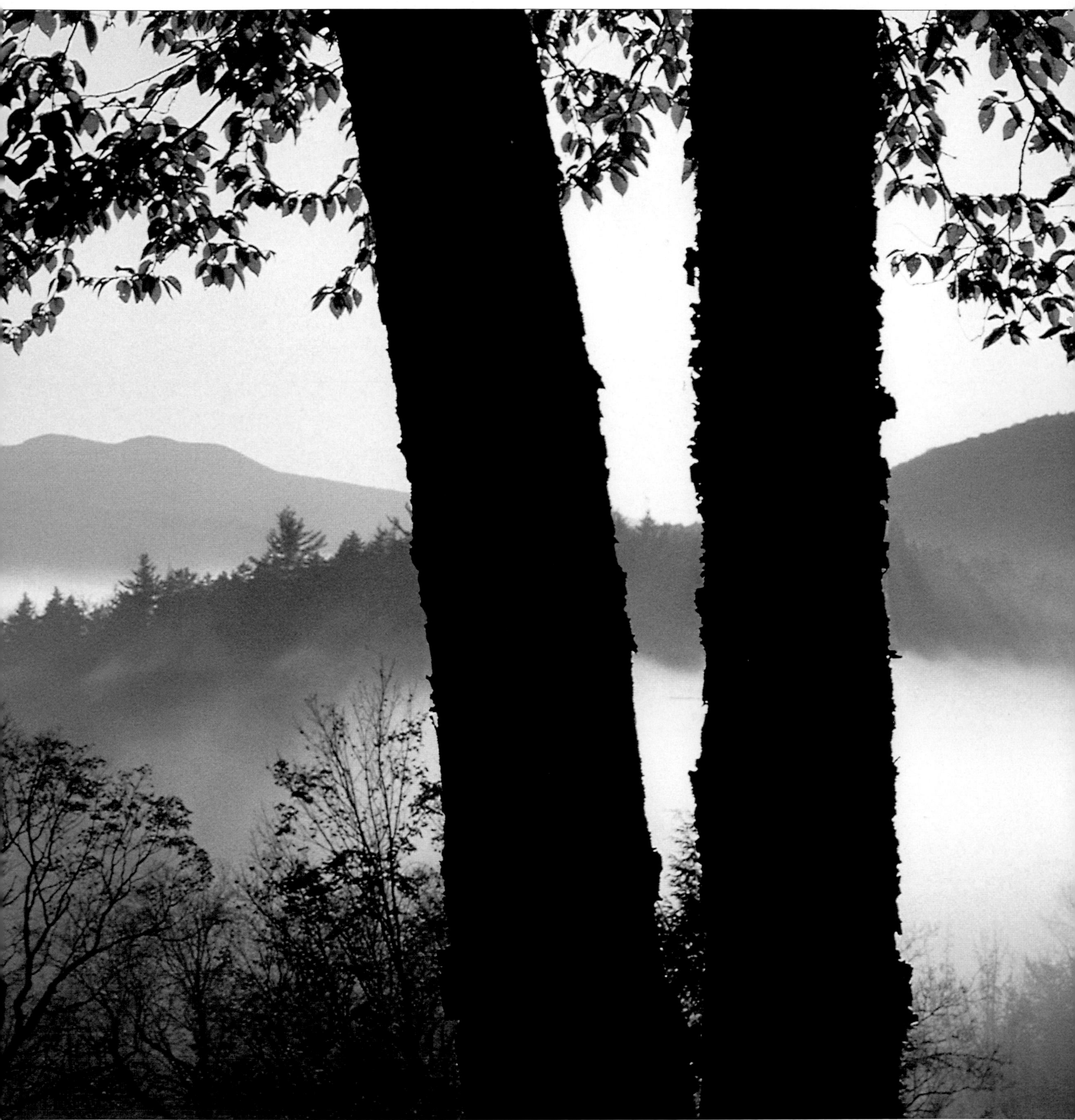

Captain Littlepage

"It was a hard life at sea in those days, I am sure," said I, with redoubled interest. "It was a dog's life," said the poor old gentleman, quite reassured, "but it made men of those who followed it." I see a change for the worse even in our own town here; full of loafers now, small and poor as 'tis, who once would have followed the sea, every lazy soul of 'em. There is no occupation so fit for just that class o' men who never get beyond the fo'cas'le. I view it, in addition, that a community narrows down and grows dreadful ignorant when it is shut up to its own affairs, and gets no knowledge of the outside world except from a cheap, unprincipled newspaper. In the old days, a good part o' the best men here knew a hundred ports and something of the way folks lived in them. They saw the world for themselves, and like's not their wives and children saw it with them. They may not have had the best of knowledge to carry with 'em sight-seein', but they were some acquainted with foreign lands an' their laws, an' could see outside the battle for town clerk here in Dunnet; they got some sense o' proportion. Yes, they lived more dignified, and their houses were better within an' without. Shipping's a terrible loss to this part o' New England from a social point o' view, ma'am."

There was a silence in the schoolhouse, but we could hear the noise of the water on a beach below. It sounded like the strange warning wave that gives notice of the turn of the tide. A late golden robin, with the most joyful and eager of voices, was singing close by in a thicket of wild roses.

From *The Country of the Pointed Firs*
Sarah Orne Jewett, 1896

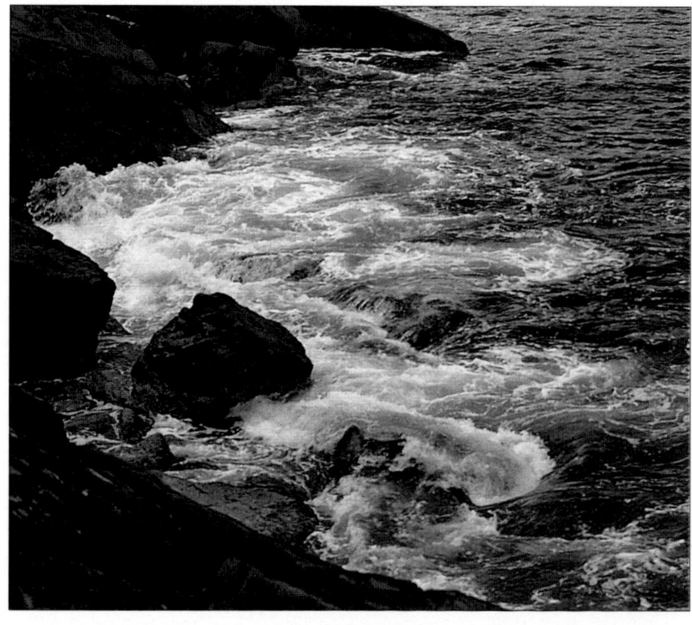

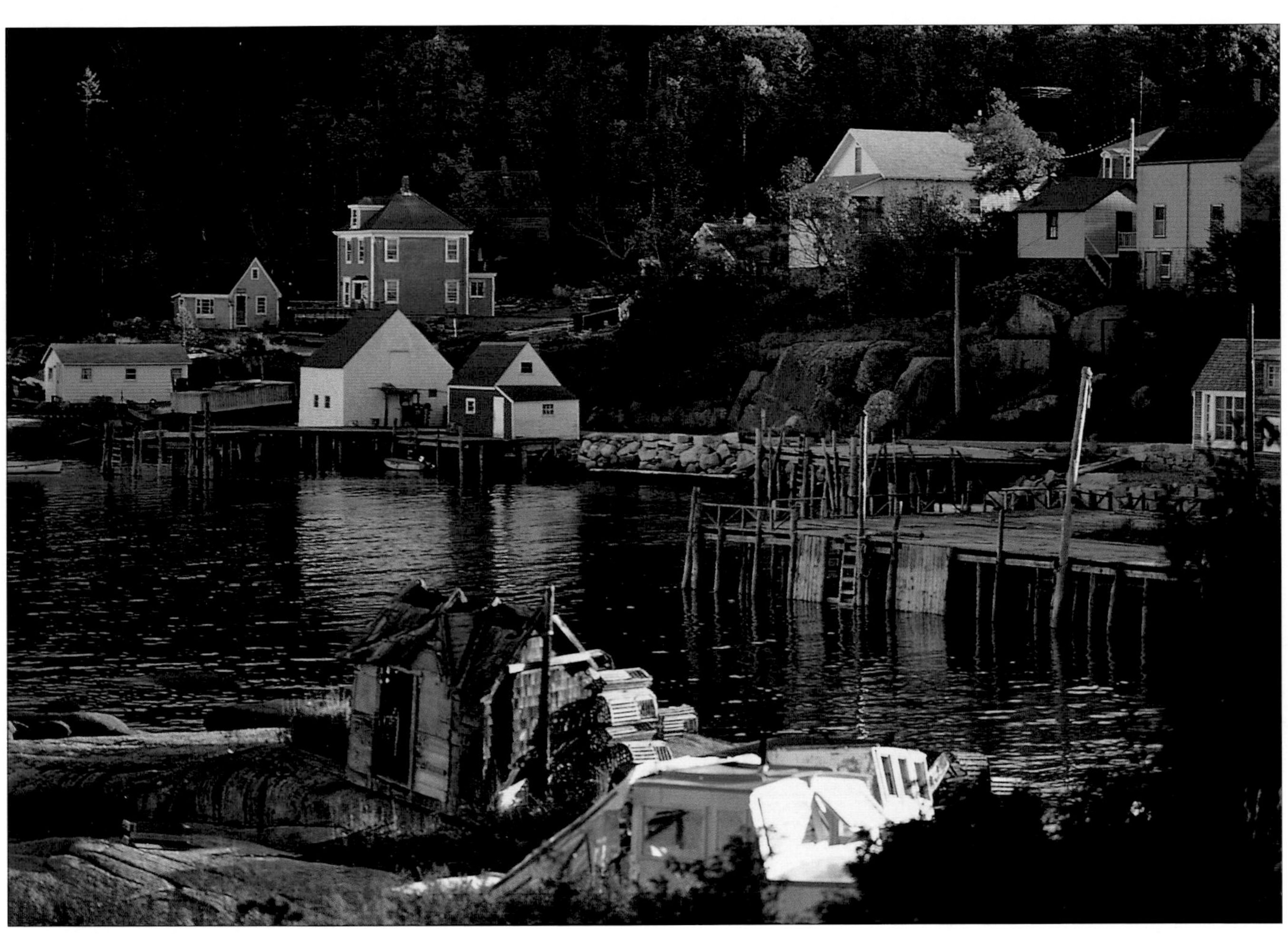

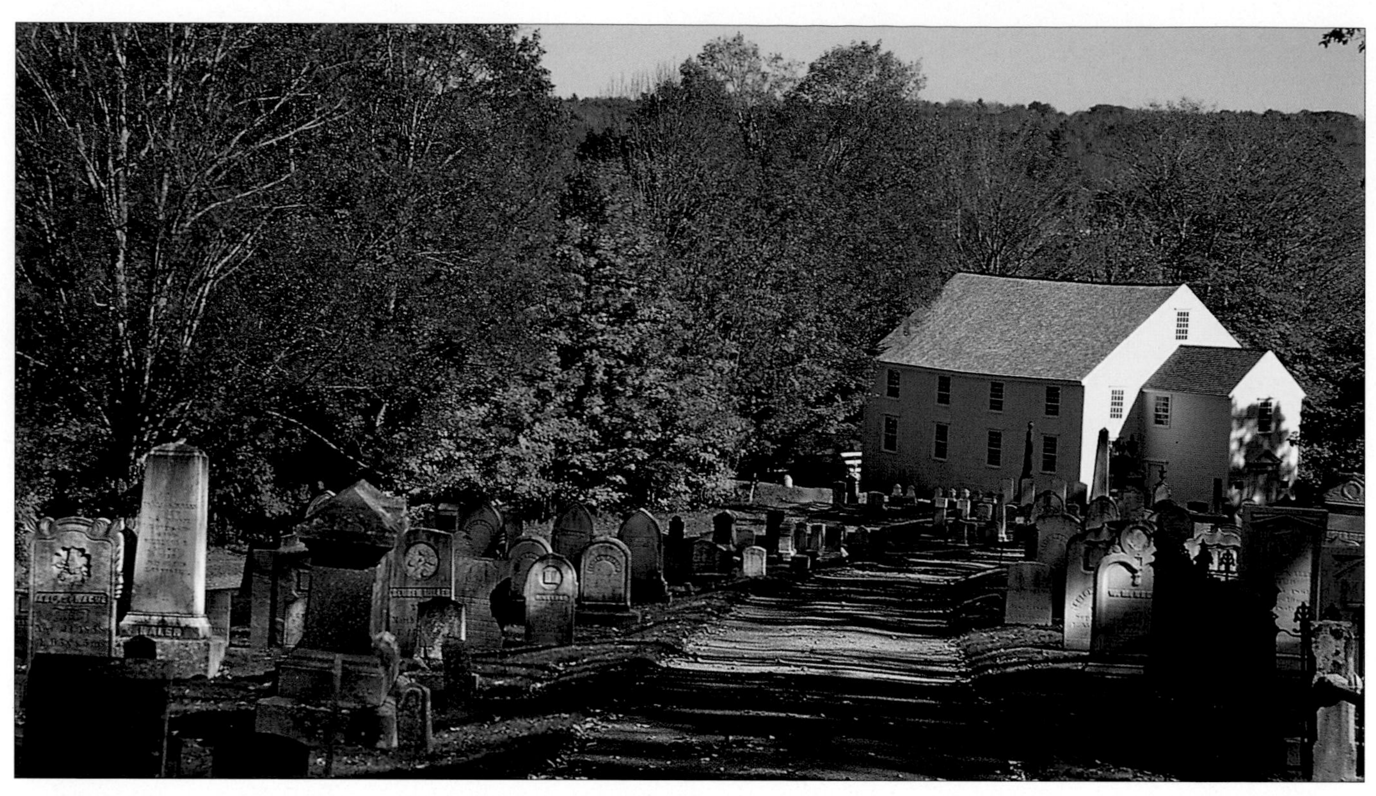

I reason, Earth is short—
And Anguish—absolute—
And many hurt,
But, what of that?

I reason, we could die—
The best Vitality
Cannot excel Decay,
But, what of that?

I reason, that in Heaven—
Somehow, it will be even—
Some new Equation, given—
But, what of that?

Emily Dickinson, 1862

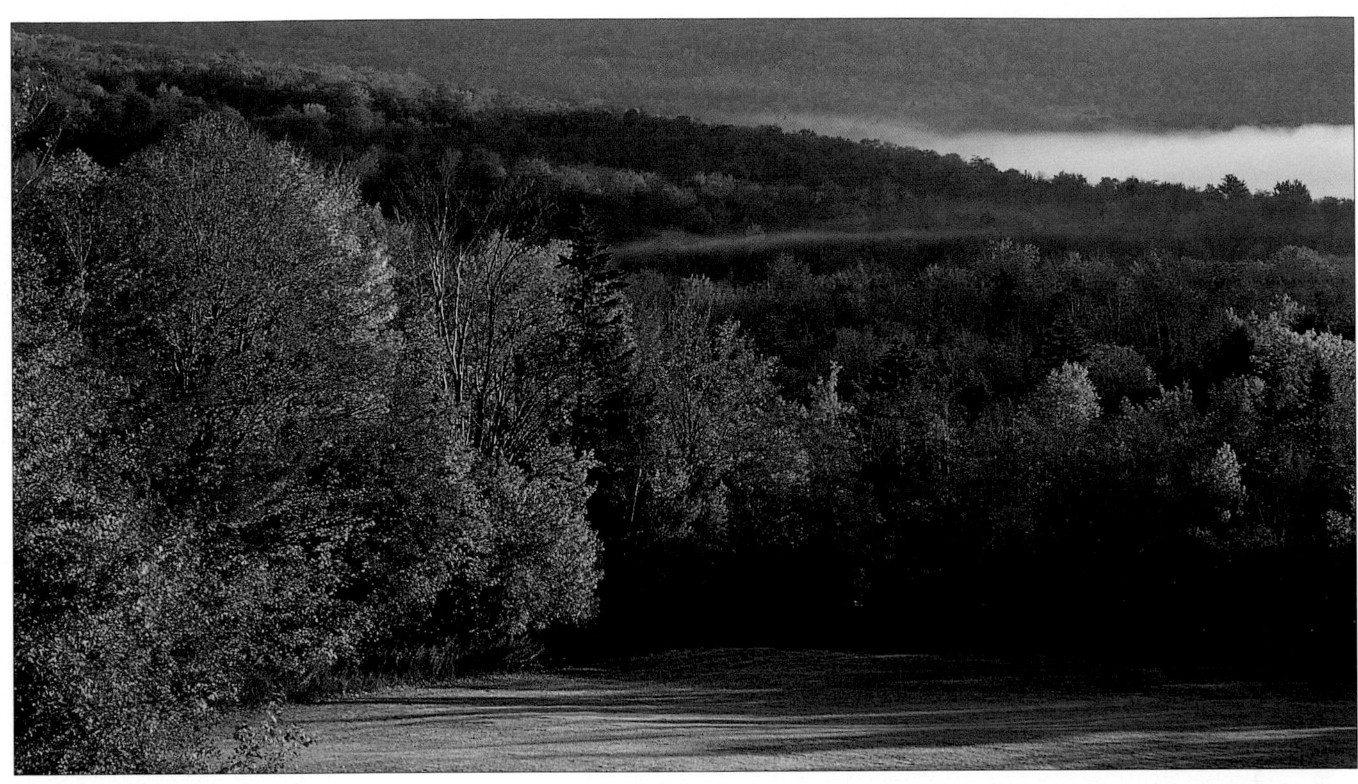

This is my letter to the World
That never wrote to me—
The simple News that Nature told—
With tender Majesty

Her Message is committed
To Hands I cannot see—
For love of Her—Sweet—countrymen—
Judge tenderly—of Me

Emily Dickinson, 1862

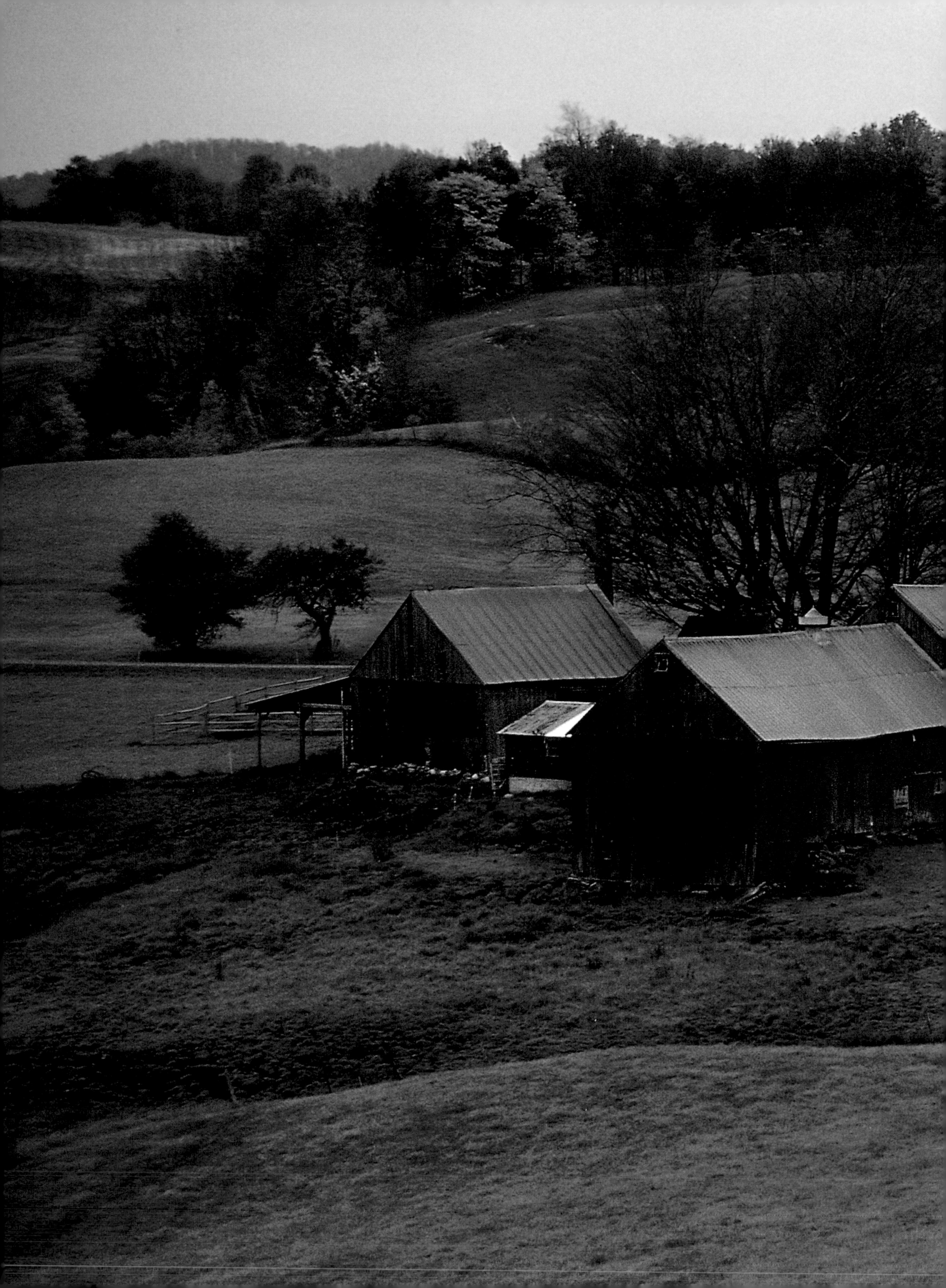

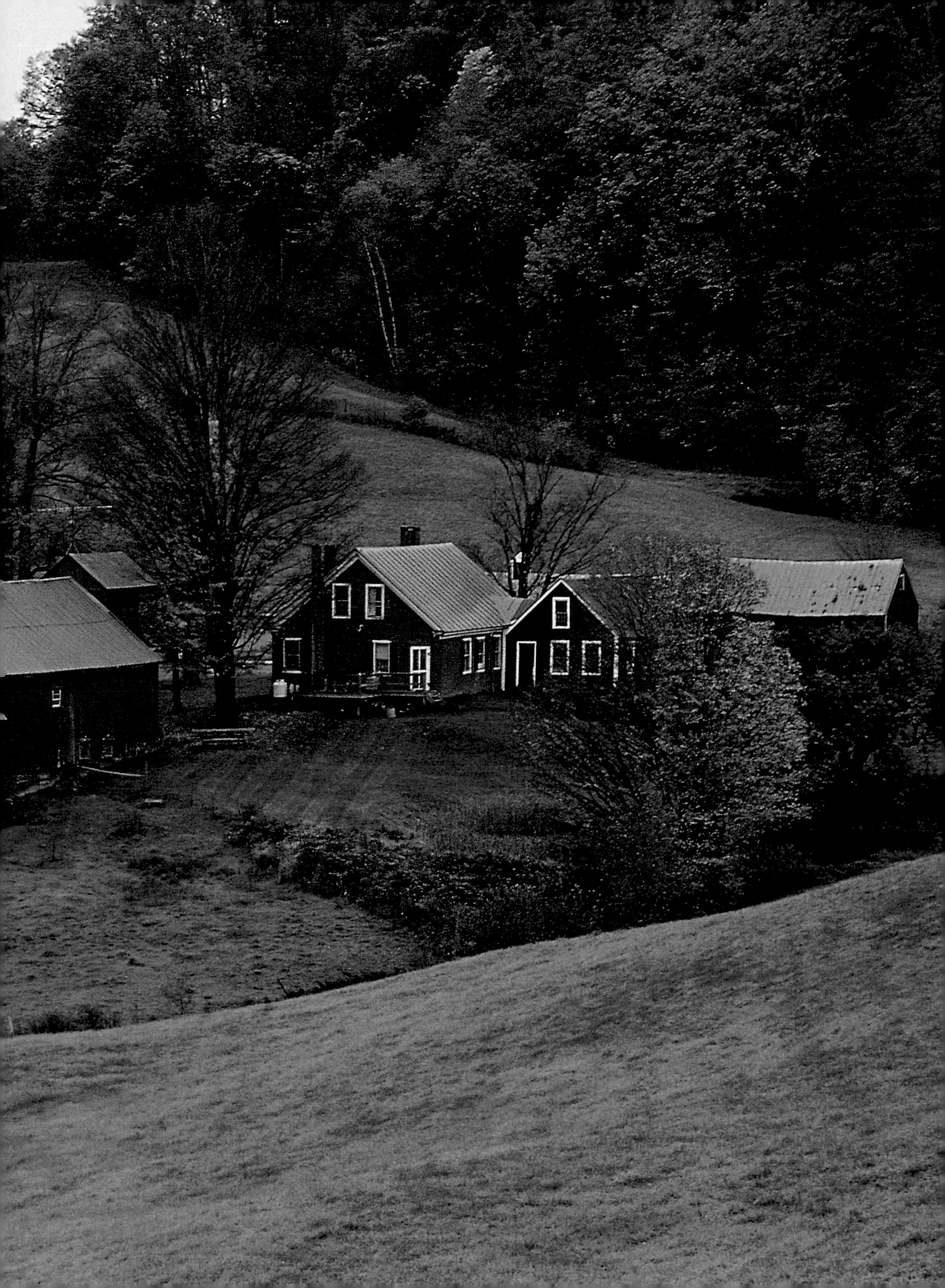

Nothing Gold Can Stay

Nature's first green is gold,
Her hardest hue to hold.
Her early leaf's a flower;
But only so an hour.
Then leaf subsides to leaf.
So Eden sank to grief,
So dawn goes down to day.
Nothing gold can stay.

Robert Frost, 1923

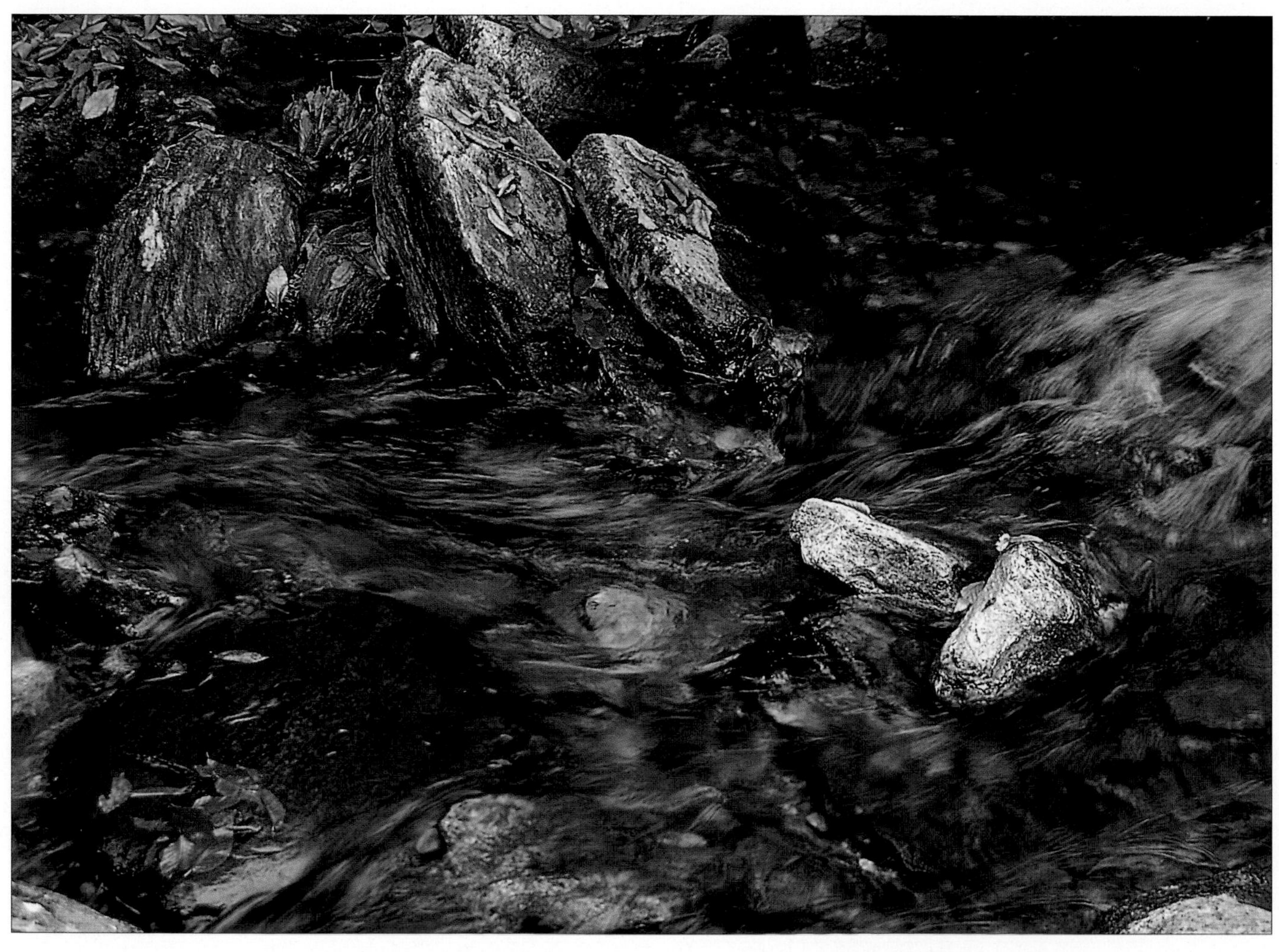

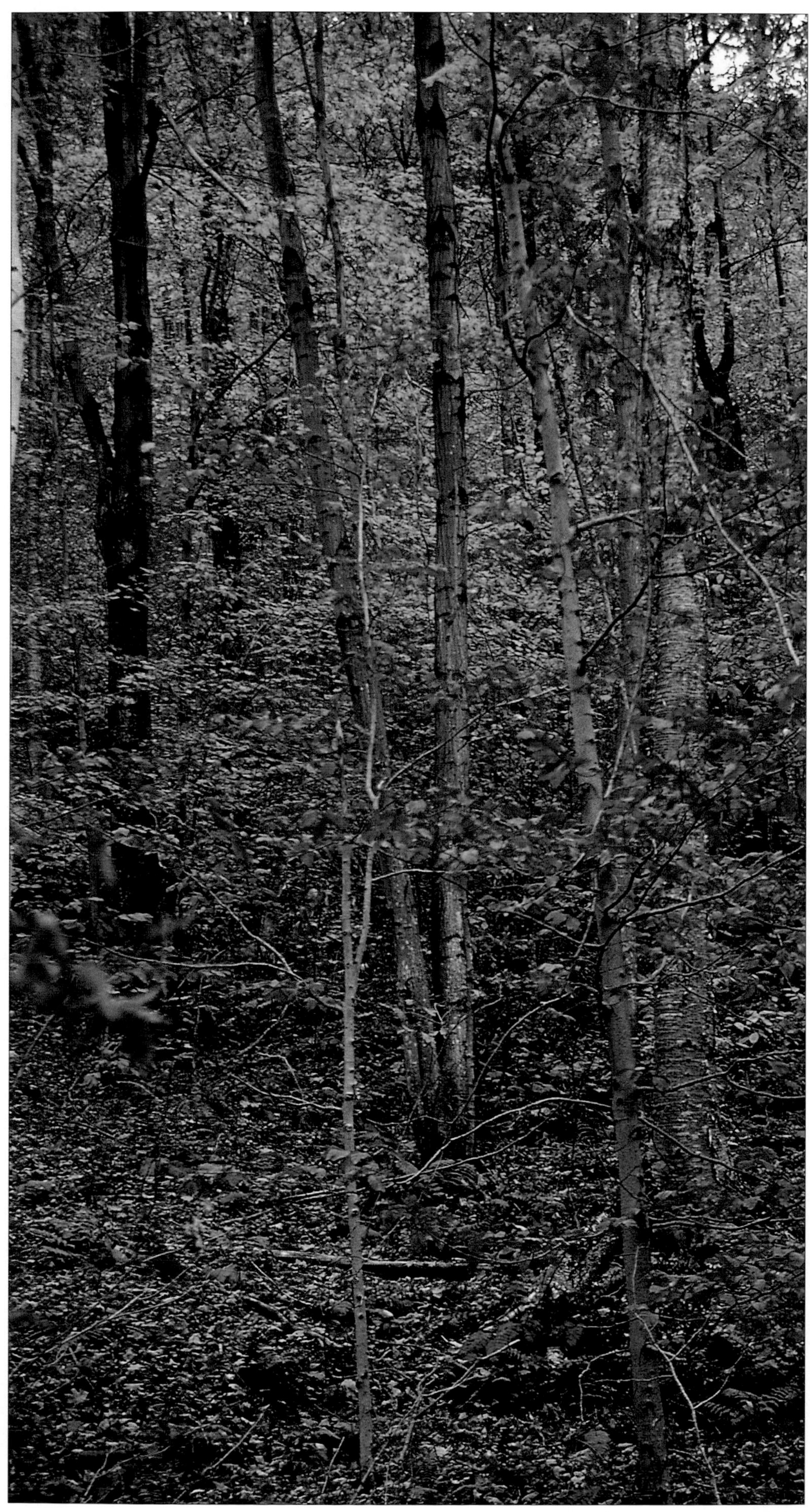

My Lost Youth

Often I think of the beautiful town
That is seated by the sea;
Often in thought go up and down
The pleasant streets of that dear old town,
And my youth comes back to me.
And a verse of a Lapland song
Is haunting my memory still:
"A boy's will is the wind's will,
And the thoughts of youth are long, long thoughts."

I can see the shadowy lines of its trees,
And catch, in sudden gleams,
The sheen of the far-surrounding seas,
And islands that were the Hesperides
Of all my boyish dreams.
And the burden of that old song,
It murmurs and whispers still:
"A boy's will is the wind's will,
And the thoughts of youth are long, long thoughts."

I remember the black wharves and the slips,
And the sea-tides tossing free;
And Spanish sailors with bearded lips,
And the beauty and mystery of the ships,
And the magic of the sea.
And the voice of that wayward song
Is singing and saying still:
"A boy's will is the wind's will,
And the thoughts of youth are long, long thoughts."

Excerpt
Henry Wadsworth Longfellow, 1855

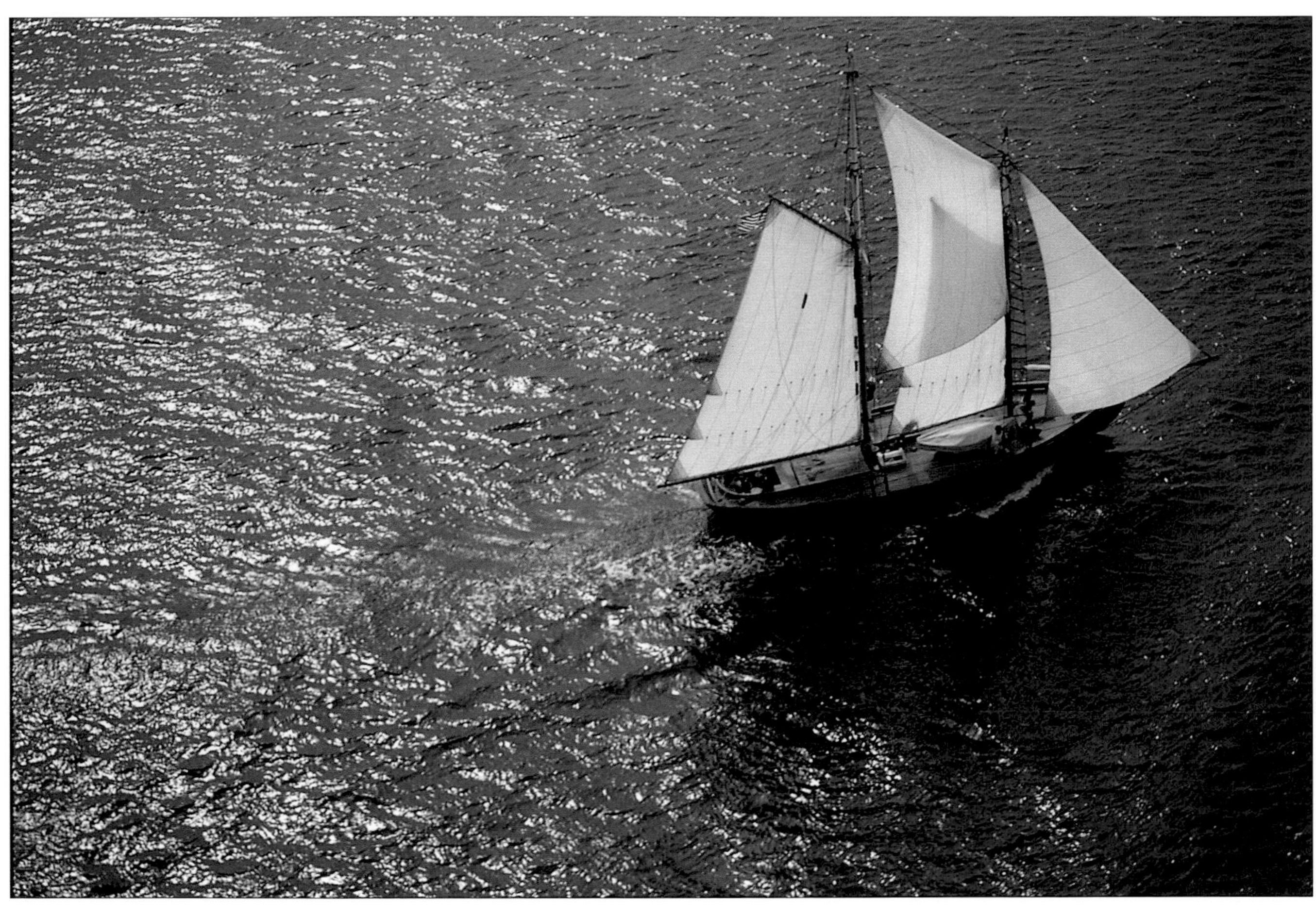

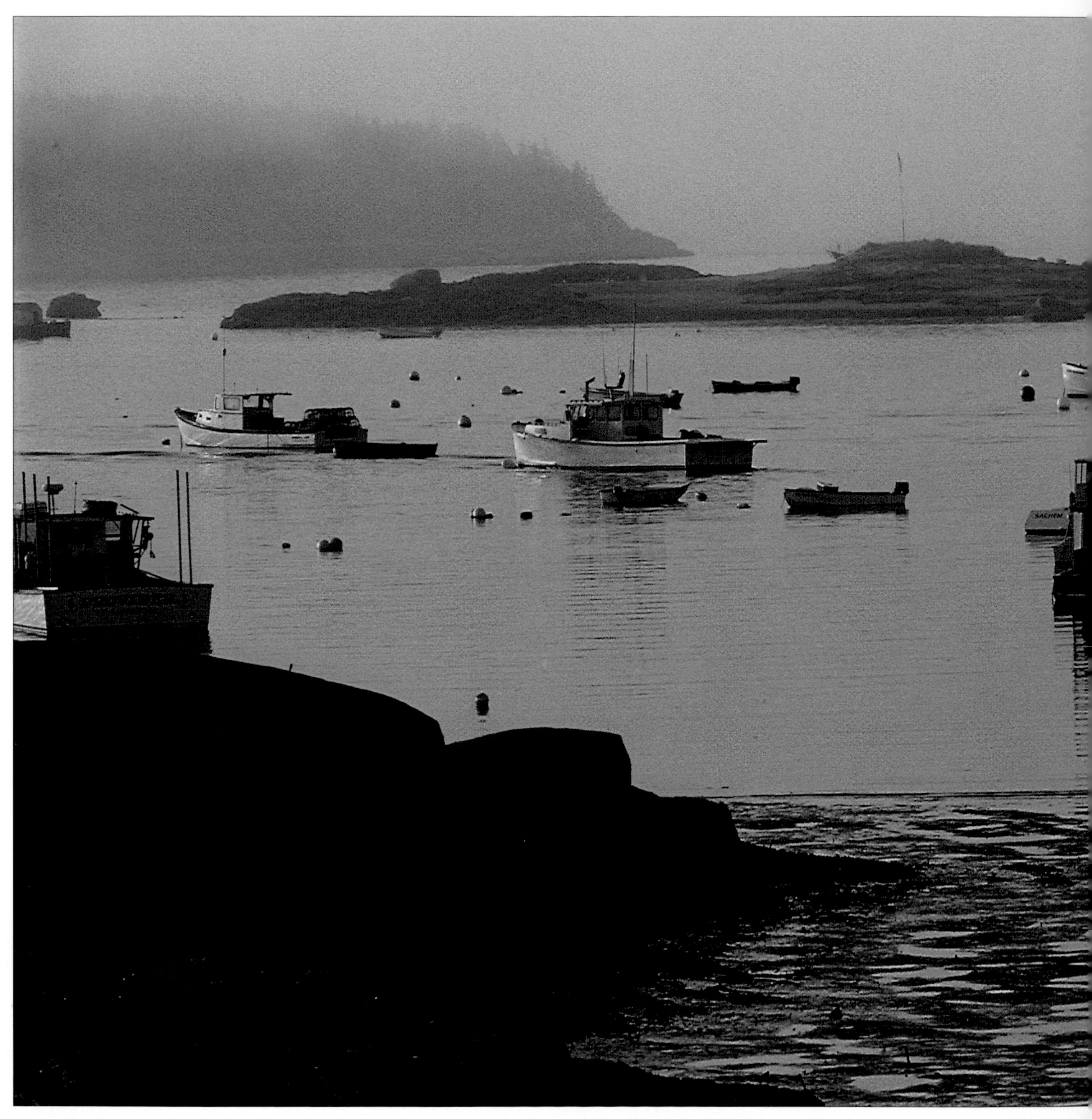
SACHEM

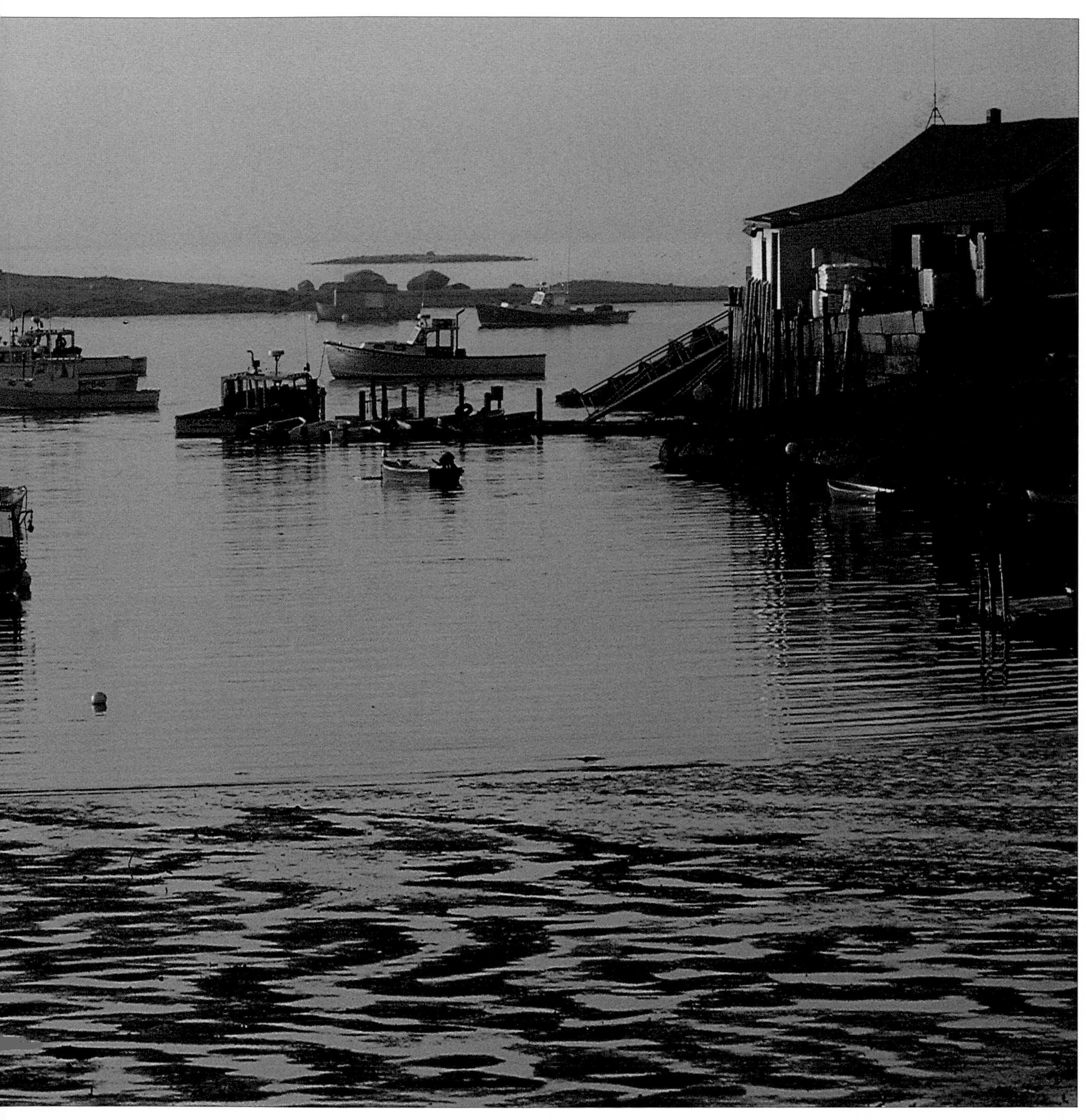

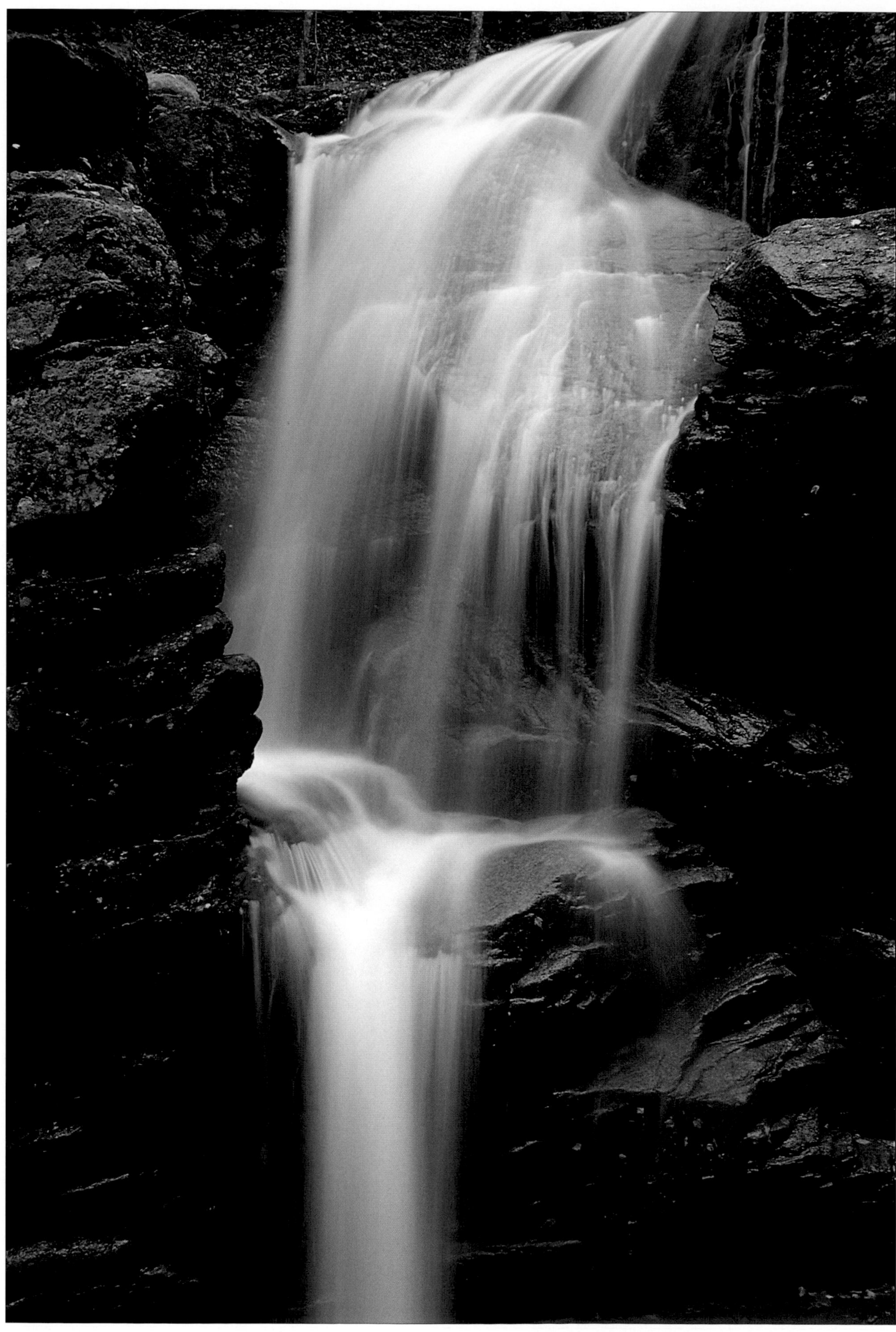

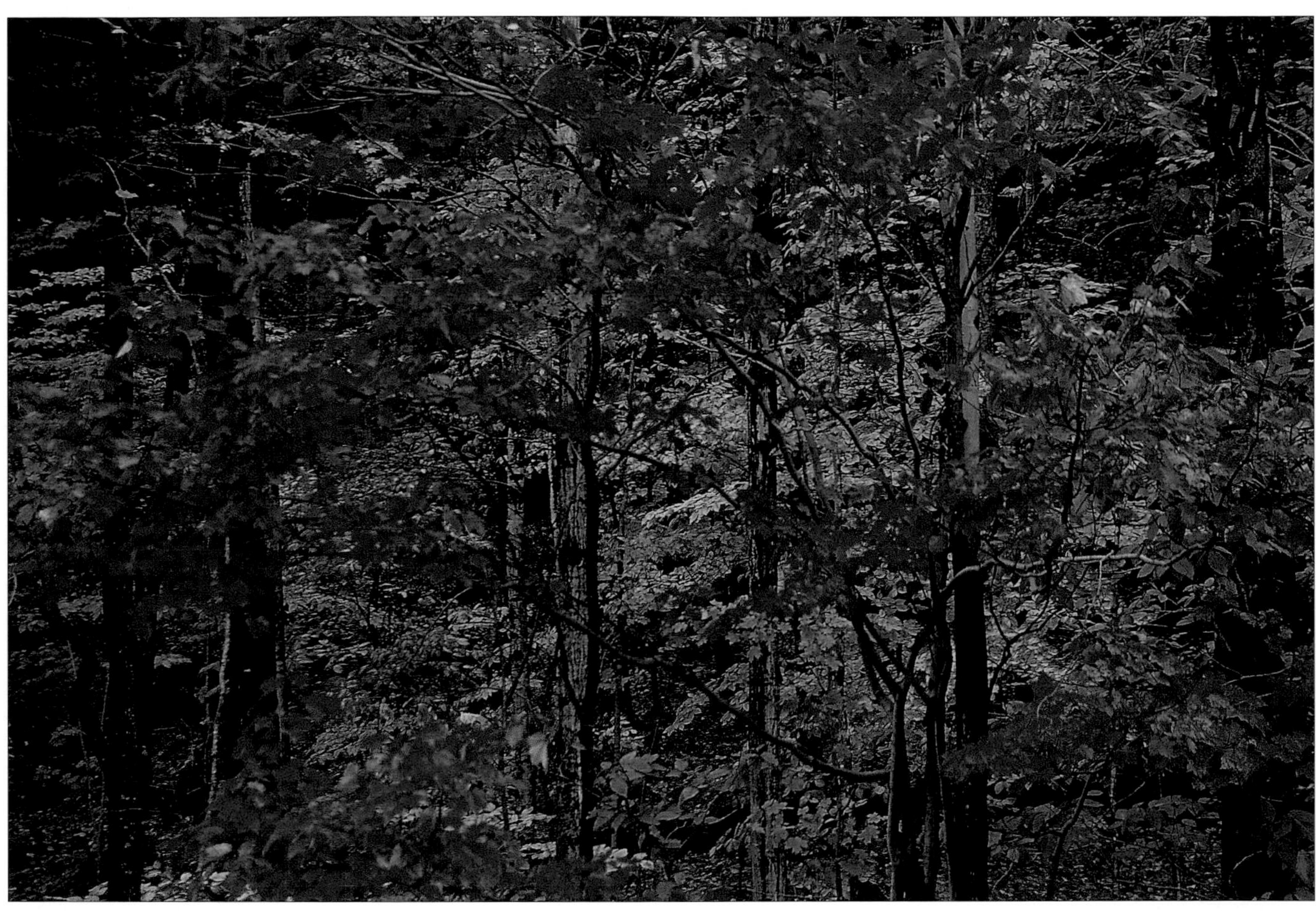

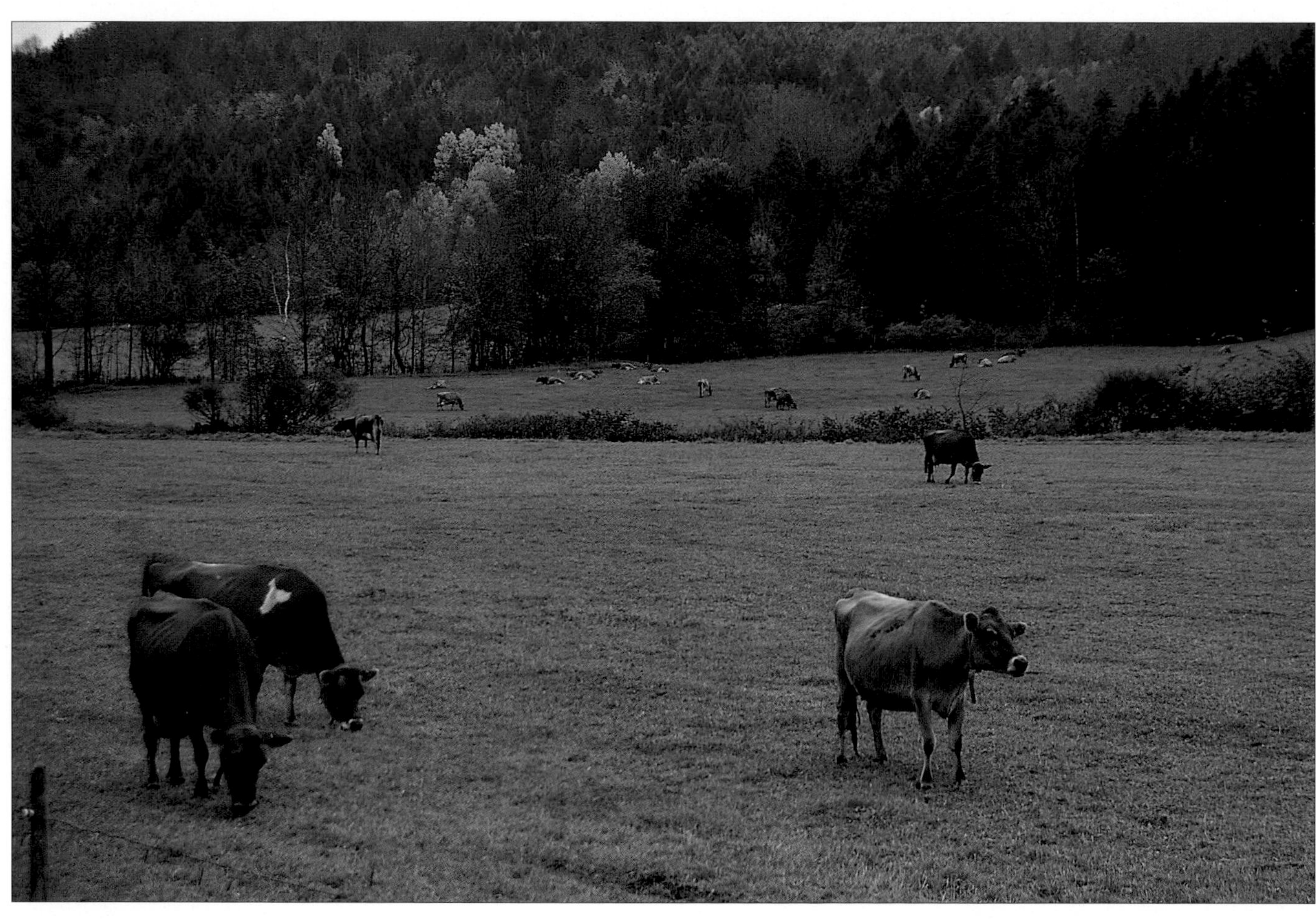

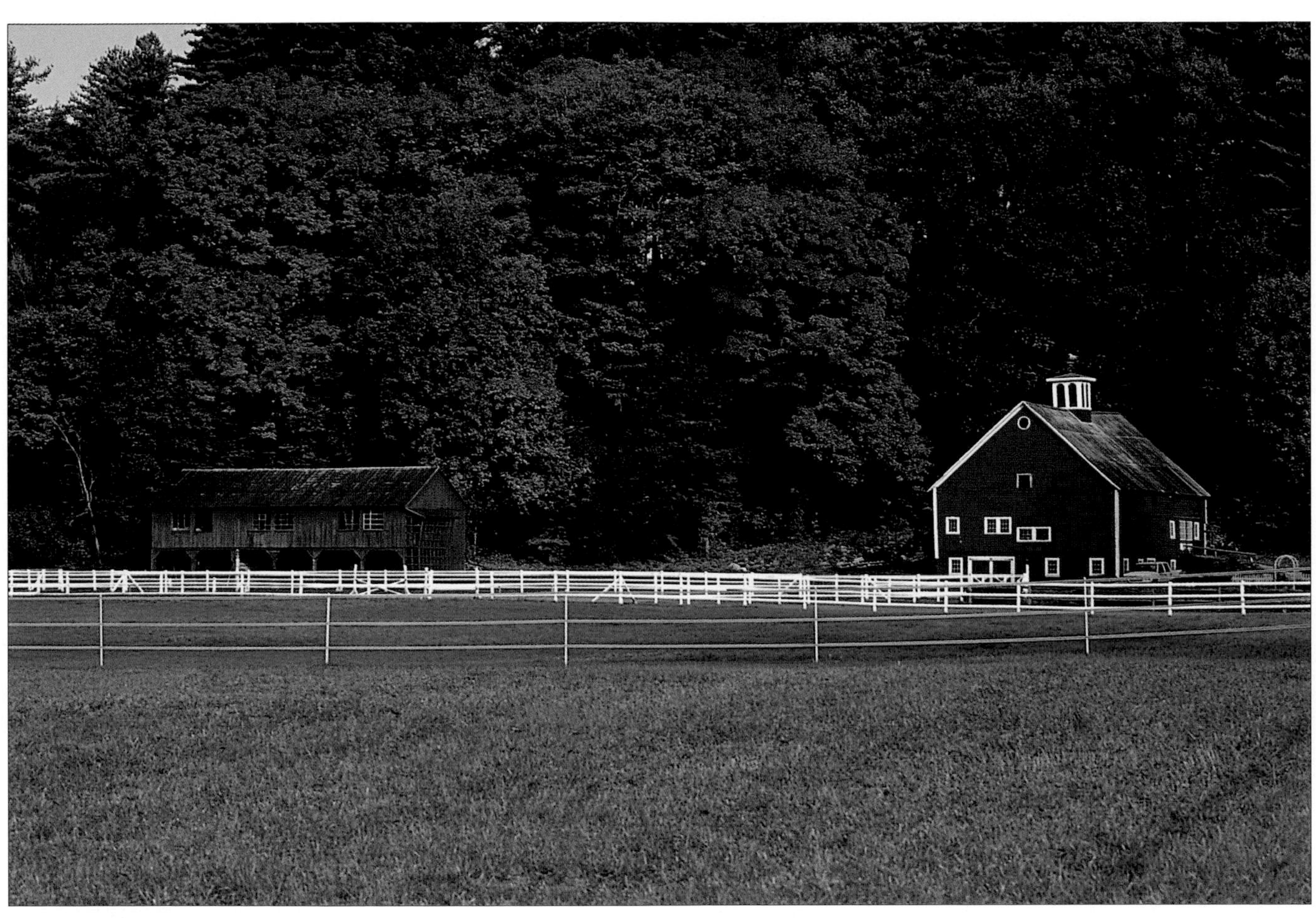

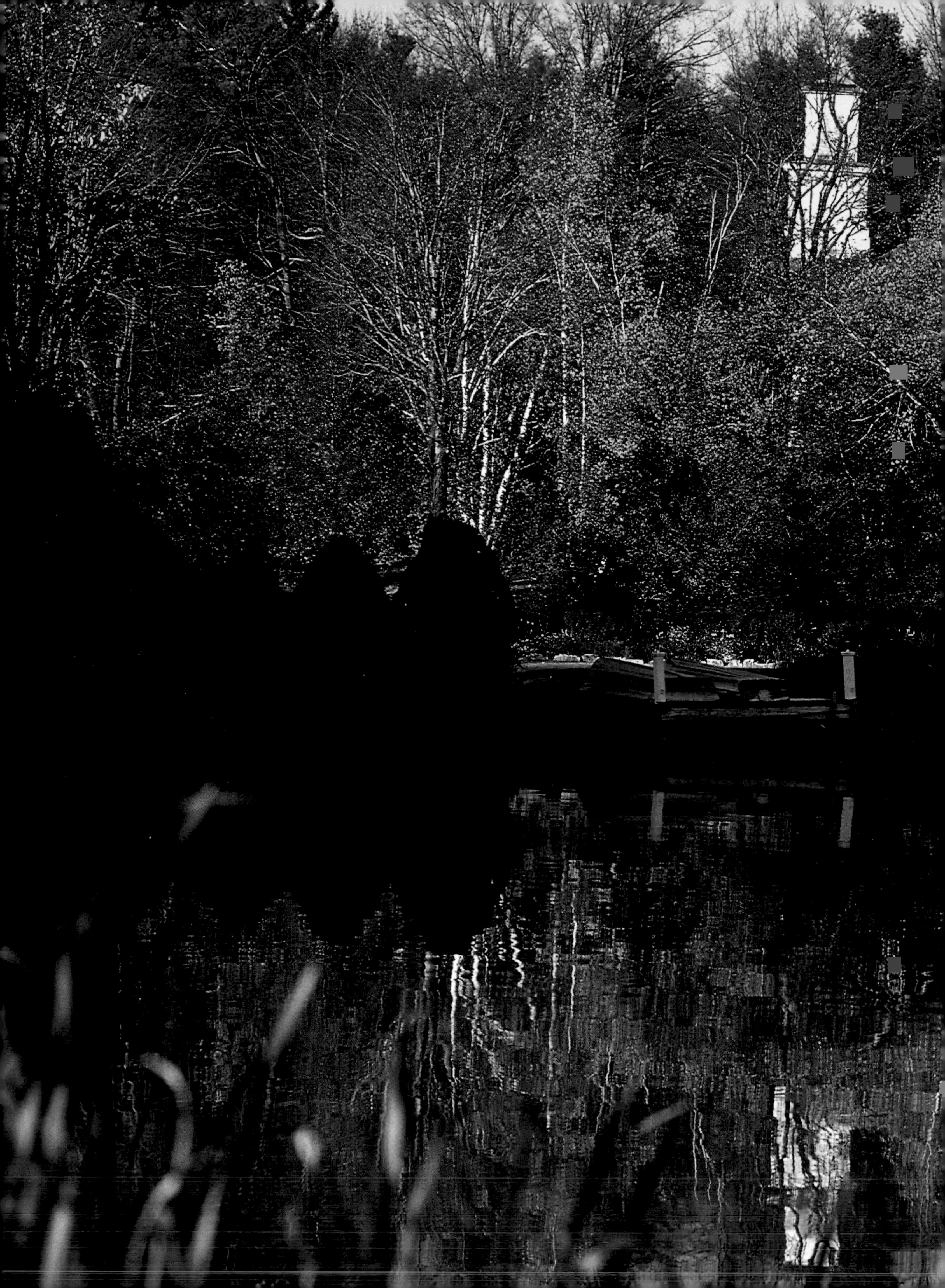

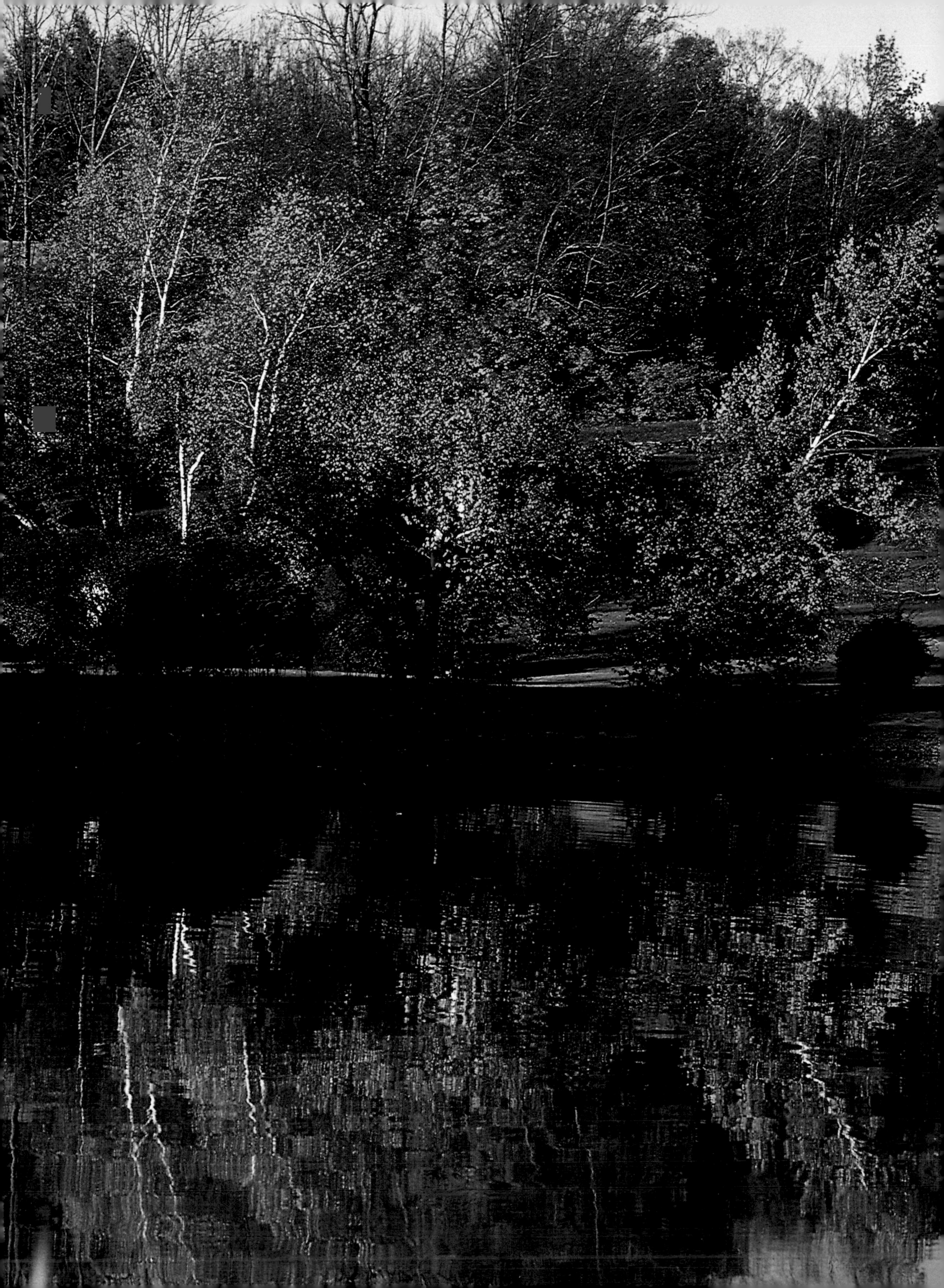

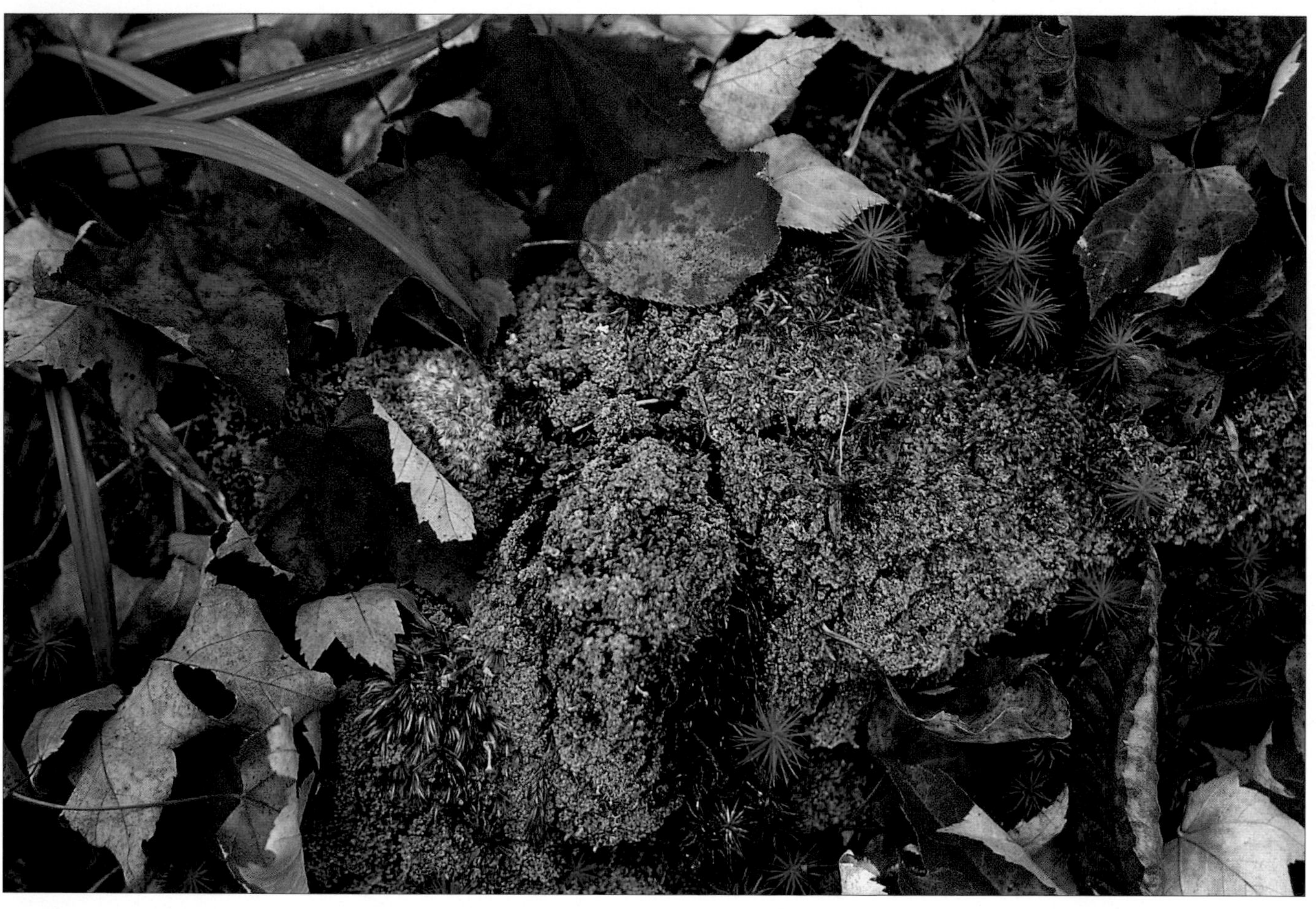

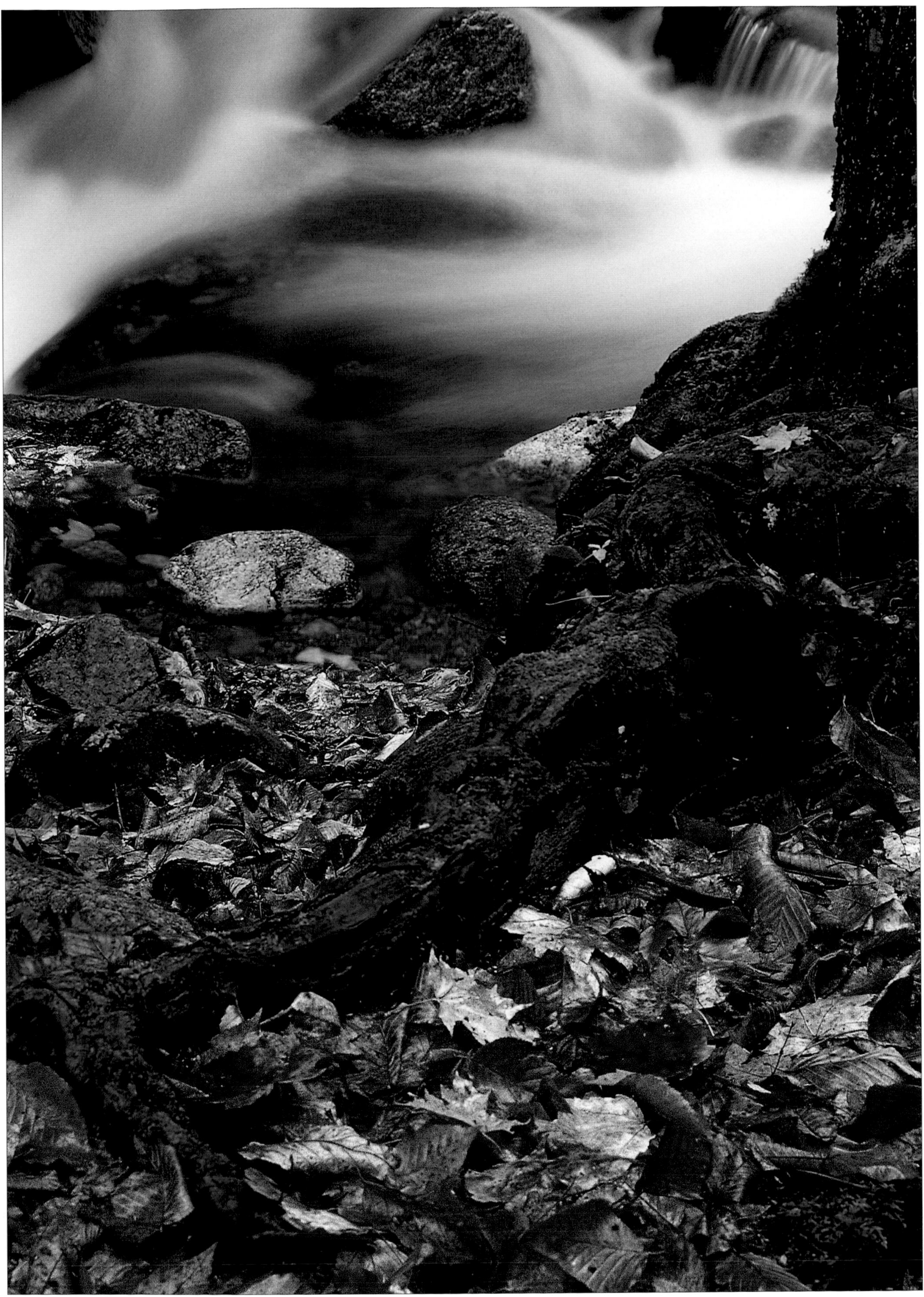

A Mistaken Charity

There were in a green field a little, low, weather-stained cottage, with a foot-path leading to it from the highway several rods distant, and two old women—one with a tin pan and old knife searching for dandelion greens among the short young grass, and the other sitting on the door-step watching her, or, rather, having the appearance of watching her.

"Air there enough for a mess, Harriét?" asked the old woman on the door-step. She accented oddly the last syllable of the Harriet, and there was a curious quality in her feeble, cracked old voice; the quavering notes that she used reached out of themselves, and asked, and groped like fingers in the dark. One would have known by the voice that the old woman was blind.

The old woman on her knees in the grass searching for dandelions did not reply; she evidently had not heard the question. So the old woman on the door-step, after waiting a few minutes with her head turned expectantly, asked again, varying her question slightly, and speaking louder:

"Air there enough for a mess, do ye s'pose, Harriét?"

The old woman in the grass heard this time. She rose slowly and laboriously; the effort of straightening out the rheumatic old muscles was evidently a painful one; then she eyed the greens heaped up in the tin pan, and pressed them down with her hand.

"Wa'al, I don't know, Charlotte," she replied, hoarsely. "There's plenty on 'em here, but I 'ain't got near enough for a mess; they do bile down so when you get 'em in the pot; an' it's all I can do to bend my j'ints enough to dig 'em."

"I'd give consider'ble to help ye, Harriét," said the old woman on the door-step.

But the other did not hear her; she was down on her knees in the grass again, anxiously spying out the dandelions.

So the old woman on the door-step crossed her little shrivelled hands over her calico knees, and sat quite still, with the soft spring wind blowing over her.

The old wooden door-step was sunk low down among the grasses, and the whole house to which it belonged had an air of settling down and mouldering into the grass as into its own grave.

When Harriet Shattuck grew deaf and rheumatic, and had to give up her work as tailoress, and Charlotte Shattuck lost her eyesight, and was unable to do any more sewing for her livelihood, it was a small and trifling charity for the rich man who held a mortgage on the little house in which they had been born and lived all their lives to give them the use of it, rent and interest free. He might as well have taken credit to himself for not charging a squirrel for his tenement in some old decaying tree in his woods.

So ancient was the little habitation, so wavering and mouldering, the hands that had fashioned it had lain still so long in their graves, that it almost seemed to have fallen below its distinctive rank as a house. Rain and snow had filtered through its roof, mosses had grown over it, worms had eaten it, and birds built their nests under its eaves; nature had almost completely overrun and obliterated the work of man, and taken her own to herself again, till the house seemed as much a natural ruin as an old tree-stump.

After Charlotte's eyes failed her, and Harriet had the rheumatic fever, and the little hoard of earnings went to the doctors, times were harder with them, though still it could not be said that they actually suffered. The people about, who were mostly farmers, and good friendly folk, helped them out with their living. One would donate a barrel of apples from his abundant harvest to the two poor old women, one a barrel of potatoes, another a load of wood for the winter fuel, and many a farmer's wife had bustled up the narrow foot-path with a pound of butter, or a dozen fresh eggs, or a nice bit of pork. Besides all this, there was a tiny garden patch behind the house, with a straggling row of currant bushes in it, and one of gooseberries, where Harriet contrived every year to raise a few pumpkins, which were the pride of her life. On the right of the garden were two old apple-trees, a Baldwin and a Porter, both yet in a tolerably good fruit-bearing state.

This morning the two apple-trees were brave with flowers, the currant bushes looked alive, and the pumpkin seeds were in the ground. Harriet cast complacent glances in their direction from time to time, as she painfully dug her dandelion greens. She was a short, stoutly built old woman, with a large face coarsely wrinkled, with a suspicion of a stubble of beard on the square chin.

When her tin pan was filled to her satisfaction with the sprawling, spidery greens, and she was hobbling stiffly towards her sister on the door-step, she saw another woman standing before her with a basket in her hand.

"Good-morning, Harriet," she said, in a loud, strident voice, as she drew near. "I've been frying some doughnuts, and I brought you over some warm."

"I've been tellin' her it was real good in her," piped Charlotte from the door-step, with an anxious turn of her sightless face towards the sound of her sister's footstep.

Harriet said nothing but a hoarse "Good-mornin', Mis' Simonds." Then she took the basket in her hand, lifted the towel off the top, selected a doughnut, and deliberately tasted it.

"Tough," said she. "I s'posed so. If there is anything I 'spise on this airth it's a tough doughnut."

"Oh, Harriét!" said Charlotte, with a frightened look.

"They air tough," said Harriet, with hoarse defiance, "and if there is anything I 'spise on this airth it's a tough doughnut."

The woman whose benevolence and cookery were being thus ungratefully received only laughed. She was quite fleshy, and had a round, rosy, determined face.

"Well, Harriet," said she, "I am sorry they are tough, but perhaps you had better take them out on a plate, and give me my basket. You may be able to eat two or three of them if they are tough."

"They air tough—turrible tough," said Harriet, stubbornly; but she took the basket into the house and emptied it of its contents nevertheless.

"I suppose your roof leaked as bad as ever in that heavy rain day before yesterday?" said the visitor to Harriet, with an inquiring squint towards the mossy shingles, as she was about to leave with her empty basket.

"It was turrible," replied Harriet, with crusty acquiescence—"turrible. We had to set pails an' pans everywheres, an' move the bed out."

"Mr. Upton ought to fix it."

"There ain't any fix to it; the old ruff ain't fit to nail new shingles on to; the hammerin' would bring the whole thing down on our heads," said Harriet, grimly.

"Well, I don't know as it can be fixed, it's so old. I suppose the wind comes in bad around the windows and doors too?"

"It's like livin' with a piece of paper, or mebbe a sieve, 'twixt you an' the wind an' the rain," quoth Harriet, with a jerk of her head.

"You ought to have a more comfortable home in your old age," said the visitor, thoughtfully.

"Oh, it's well enough," cried Harriet, in quick alarm, and with a complete change of tone; the woman's remark had brought an old dread over her. "The old house 'll last as long as Charlotte an' me do. The rain ain't so bad, nuther is the wind; there's room enough for us in the dry places, an' out of the way of the doors an' windows. It's enough sight better than goin' on the town." Her square, defiant old face actually looked pale as she uttered the last words and stared apprehensively at the woman.

"Oh, I did not think of your doing that," she said, hastily and kindly. "We all know how you feel about that, Harriet, and not one of us neighbors will see you and Charlotte go to the poorhouse while we've got a crust of bread to share with you."

Harriet's face brightened. "Thank ye, Mis' Simonds," she said, with reluctant courtesy. "I'm much obleeged to you an' the neighbors. I think mebbe we'll be able to eat some of them doughnuts if they air tough," she added, mollifyingly, as her caller turned down the foot-path.

"My, Harriét," said Charlotte, lifting up a weakly, wondering, peaked old face, "what did you tell her them doughnuts was tough fur?"

"Charlotte, do you want everybody to look down on us, an' think we ain't no account at all, just like any beggars, 'cause they bring us in vittles?" said Harriet, with a grim glance at her sister's meek, unconscious face.

"No, Harriét," she whispered.

"Do you want to go to the poor-house?"

"No, Harriét." The poor little old woman on the door-step fairly cowered before her aggressive old sister.

"Then don't hender me agin when I tell folks their doughnuts is tough an' their pertaters is poor. If I don't kinder keep up an' show some sperrit, I sha'n't think nothing of myself, an' other folks won't nuther, and fust thing we know they'll kerry us to the poorhouse. You'd 'a been there before now if it hadn't been for me, Charlotte."

Charlotte looked meekly convinced, and her sister sat down on a chair in the doorway to scrape her dandelions.

"Did you git a good mess, Harriét?" asked Charlotte, in a humble tone.

"Toler'ble."

Excerpt, (Edited)
Mary E. Wilkins Freeman, 1887

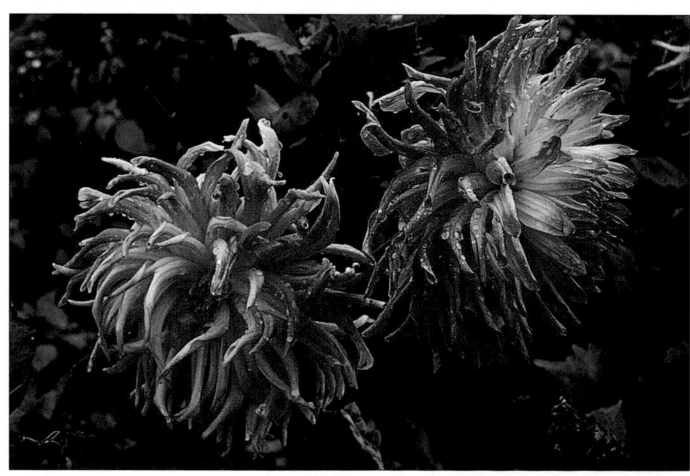

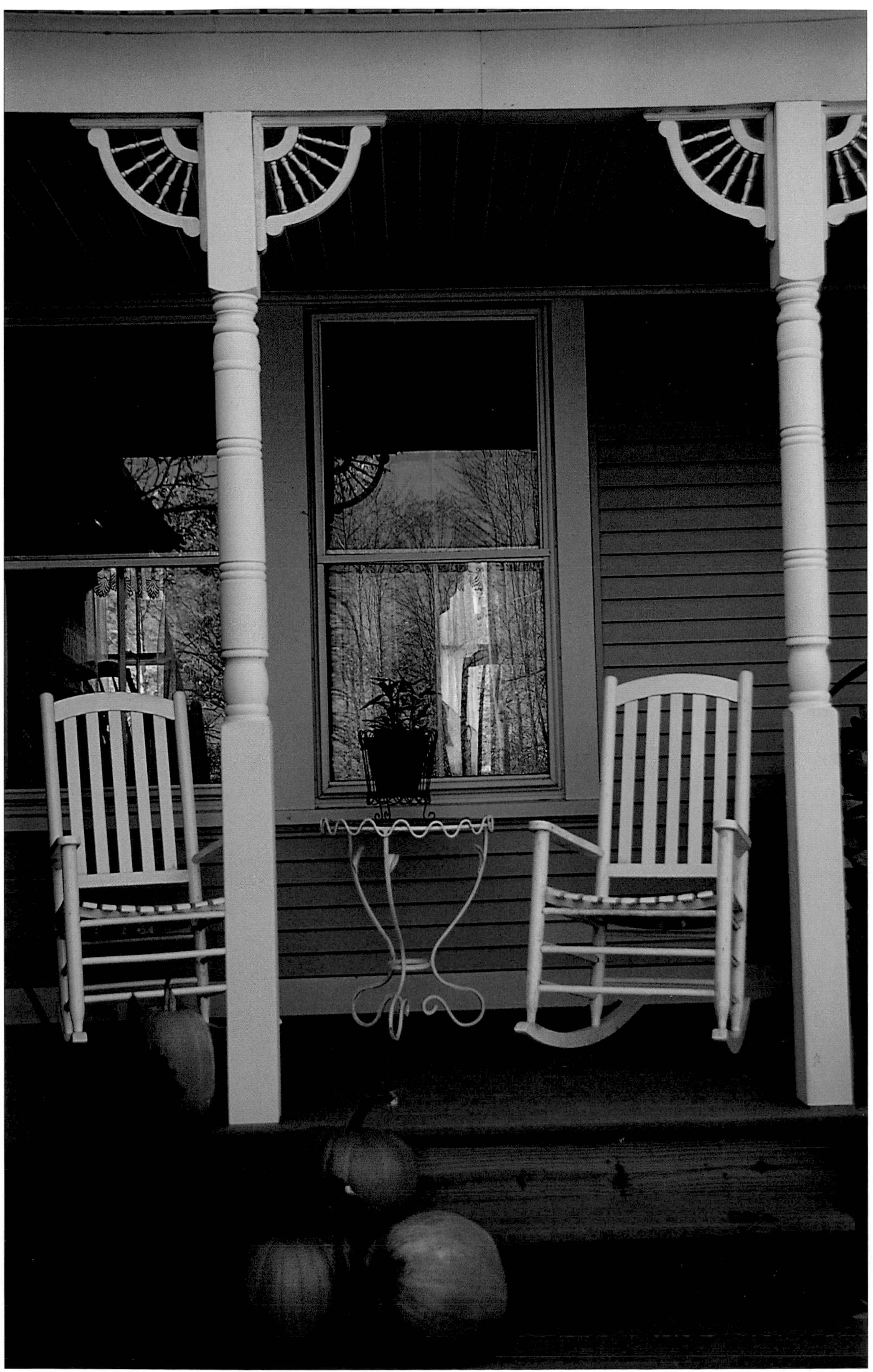

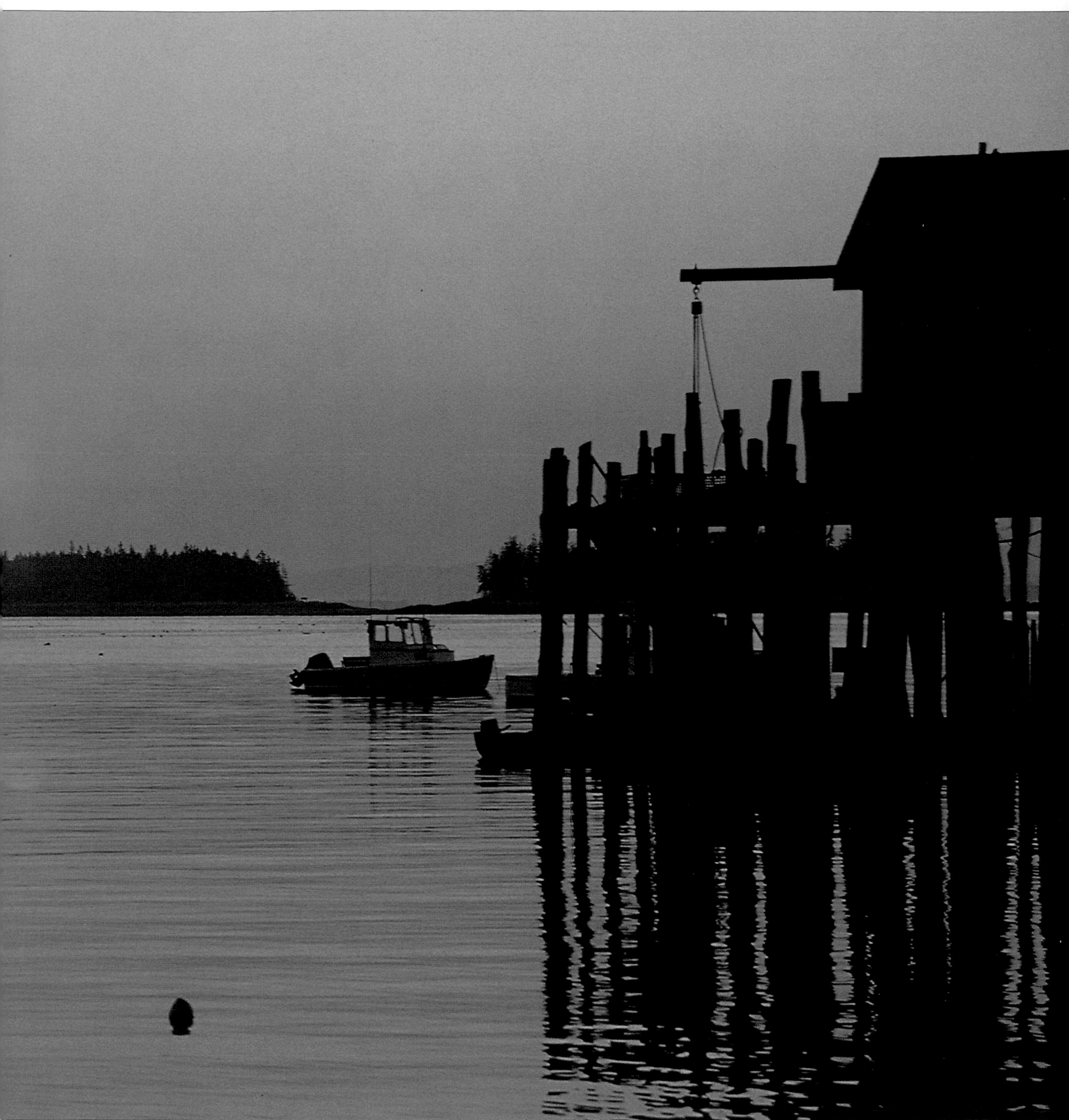

To make a prairie it takes a clover and one bee,
One clover, and a bee,
And revery.
The revery alone will do,
If bees are few.

Emily Dickinson, 1896

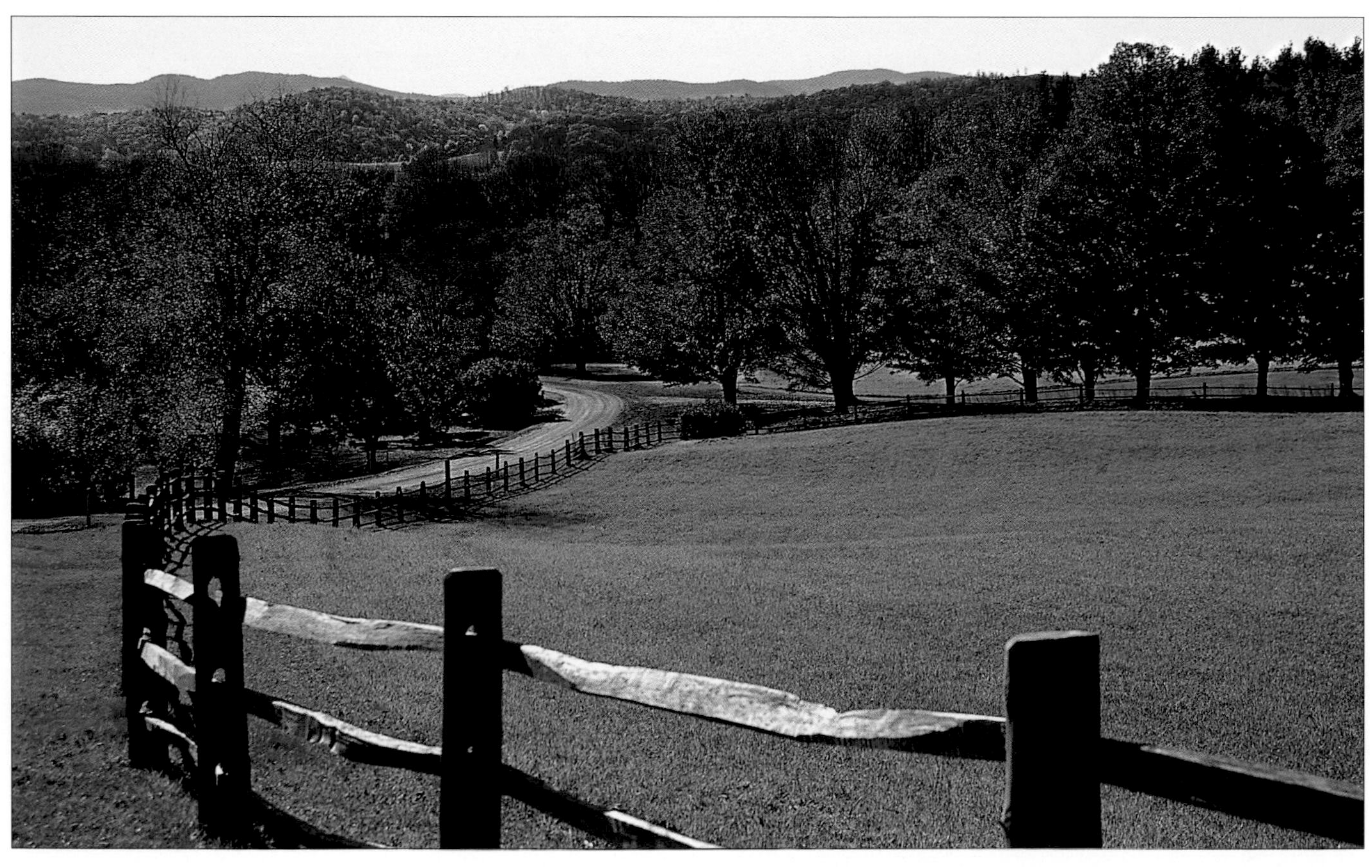

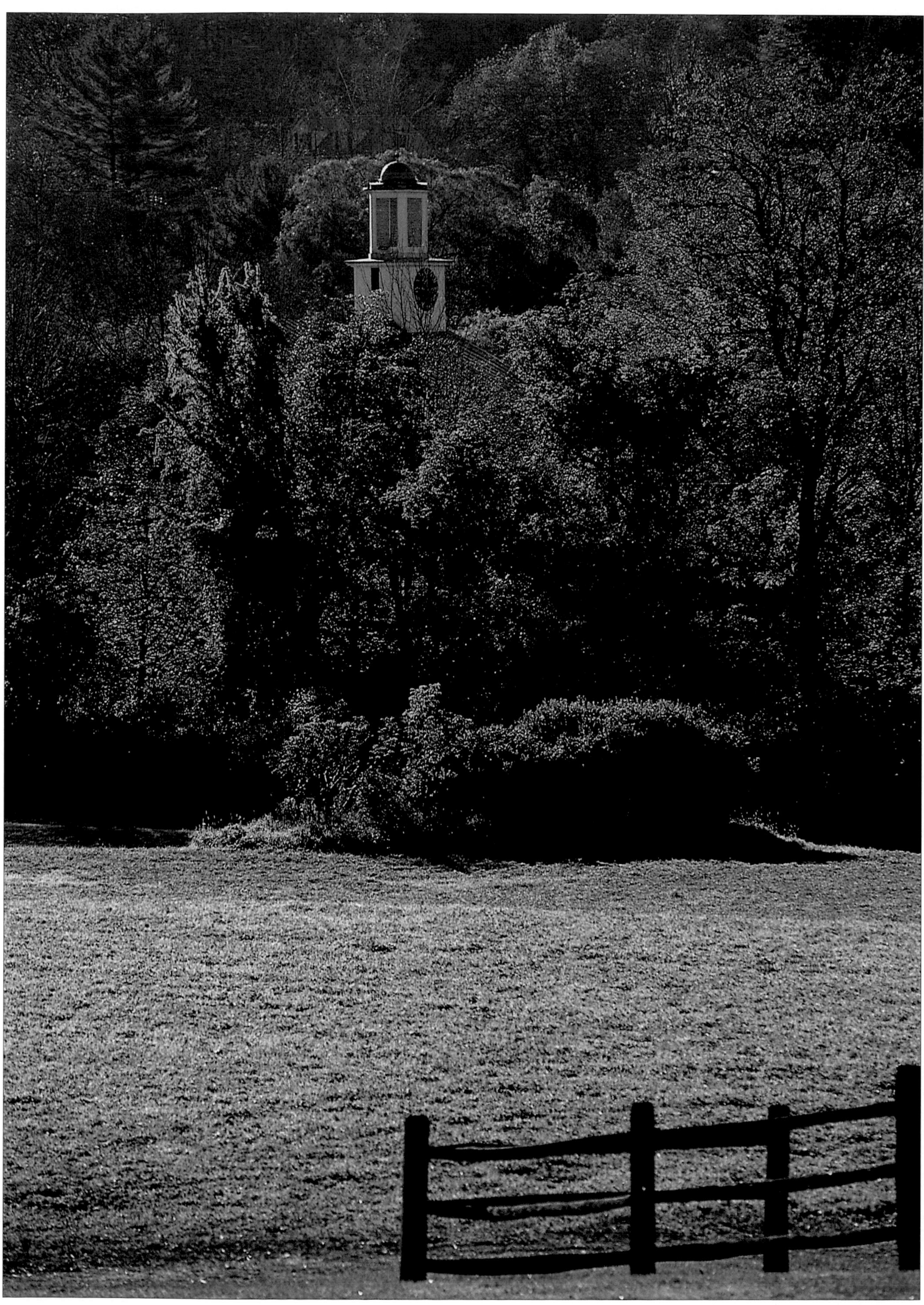

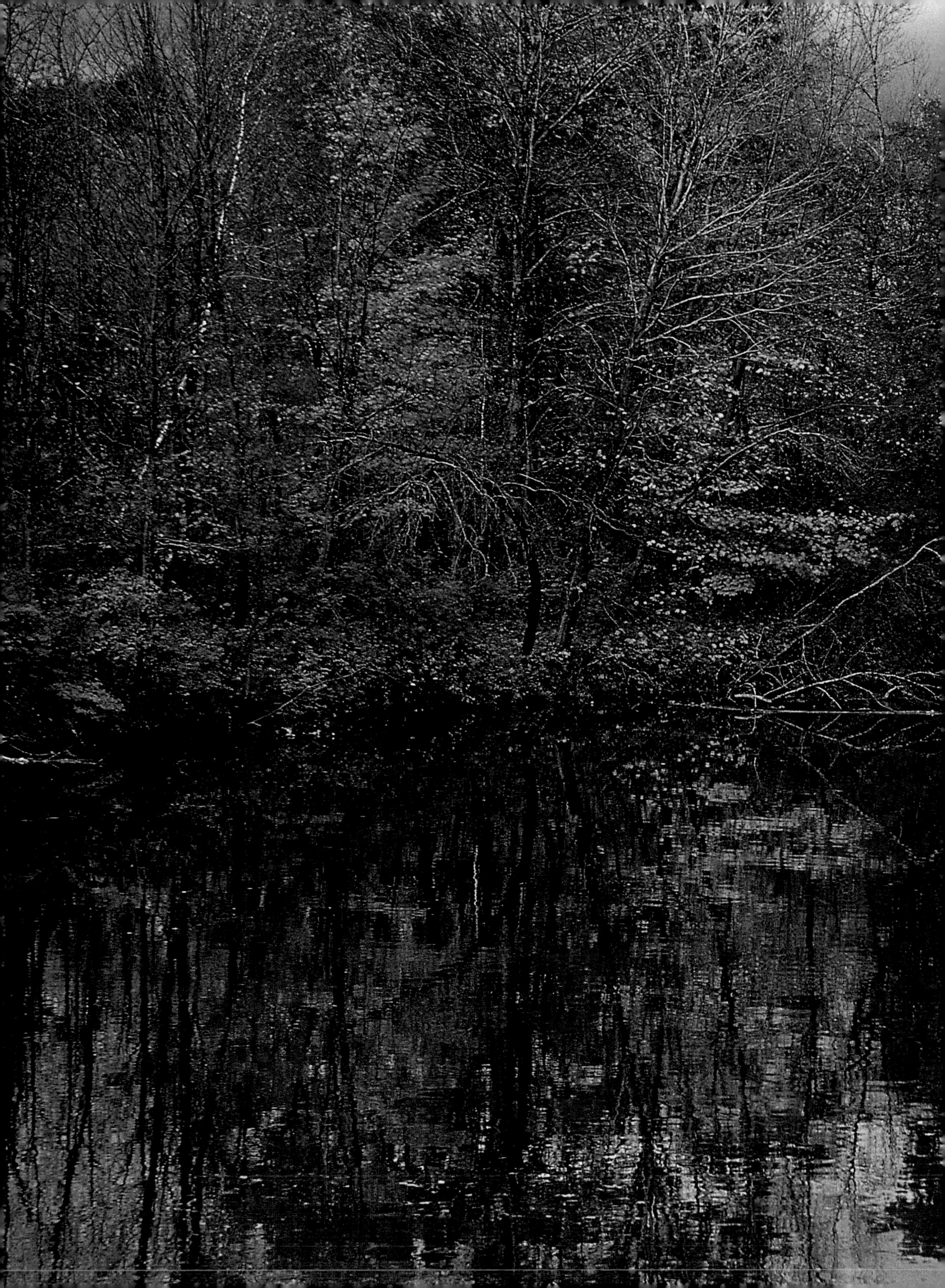

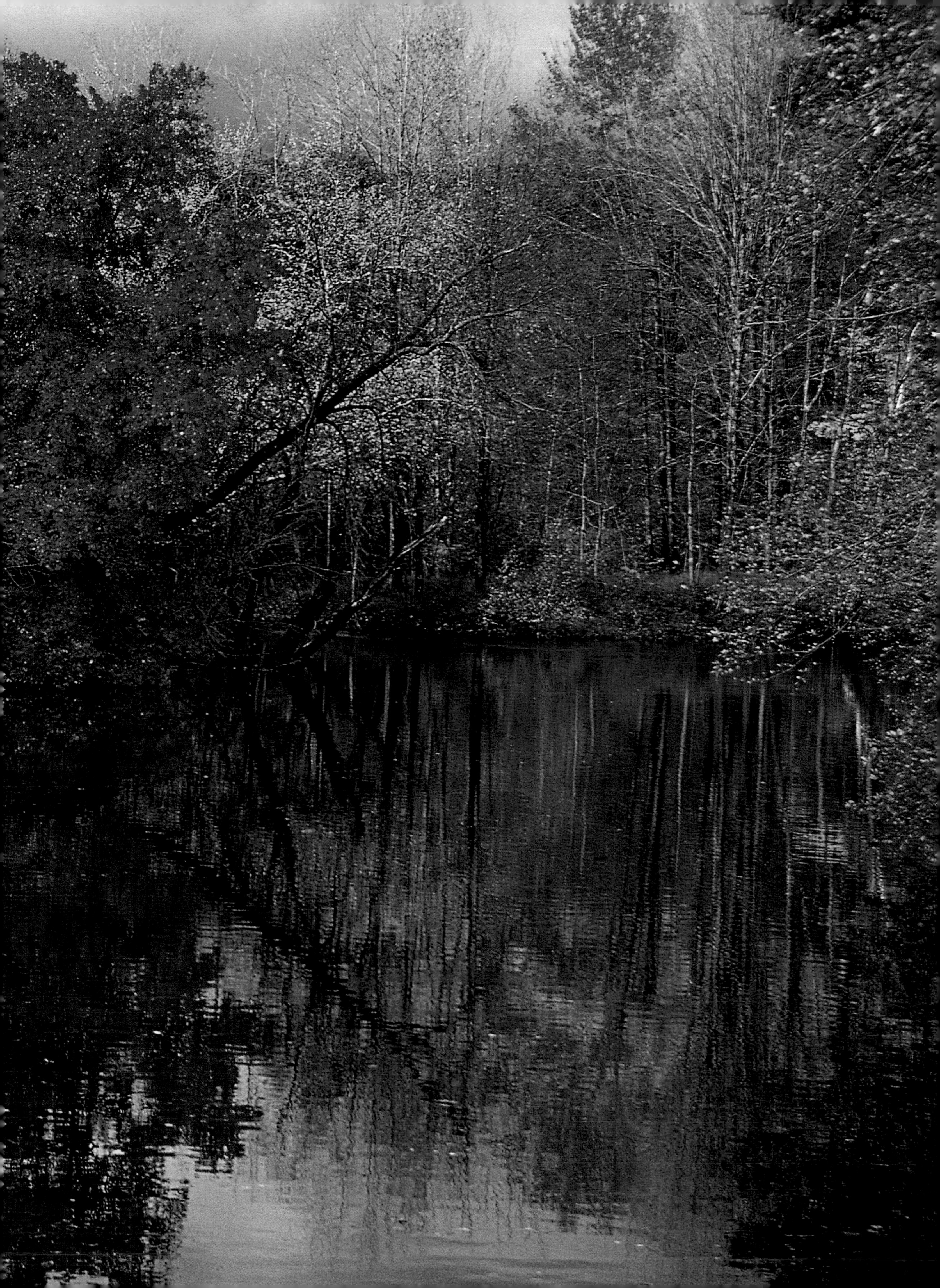

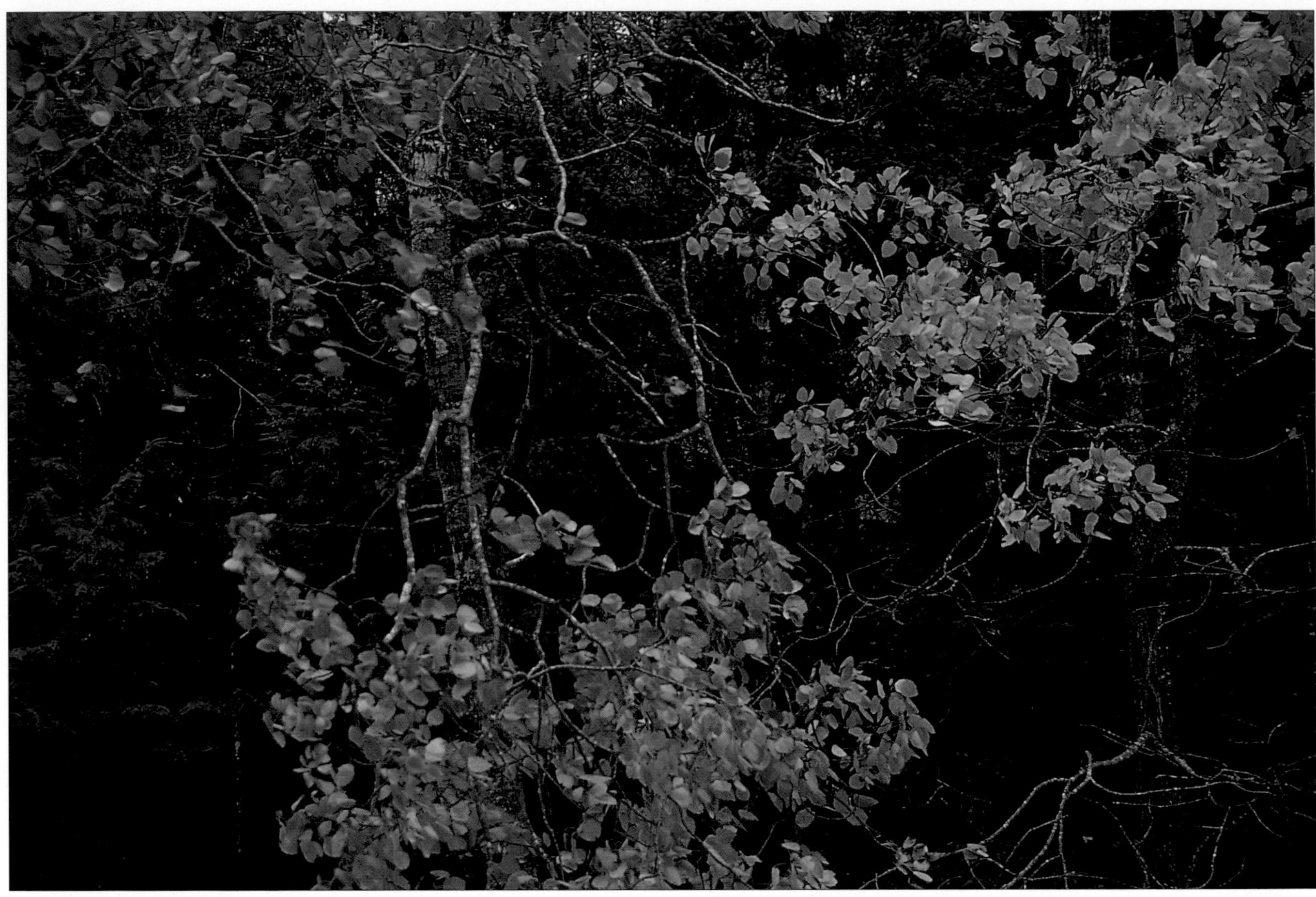

Nature

To speak truly, few adult persons can see nature. Most persons do not see the sun. At least they have a very superficial seeing. The sun illuminates only the eye of the man, but shines into the eye and the heart of the child. The lover of nature is he whose inward and outward senses are still truly adjusted to each other; who has retained the spirit of infancy even into the era of manhood.

In the woods is perpetual youth. Within these plantations of God, a decorum and sanctity reign, a perennial festival is dressed, and the guest sees not how he should tire of them in a thousand years. In the woods, we return to reason and faith. There I feel that nothing can befall me in life,—no disgrace, no calamity (leaving me my eyes), which nature cannot repair. Standing on the bare ground,—my head bathed by the blithe air and uplifted into infinite space,—all mean egotism vanishes. I become a transparent eyeball; I am nothing; I see all; the currents of the Universal being circulate through me; I am part of particle of God. The name of the nearest friend sounds then foreign and accidental: to be brothers, to be acquaintances, master or servant, is then a trifle and a disturbance. To the attentive eye, each moment of the year has its own beauty, and in the same field, it beholds, every hour, a picture which was never seen before, and which shall never be seen again.

Ralph Waldo Emerson, 1833-1836

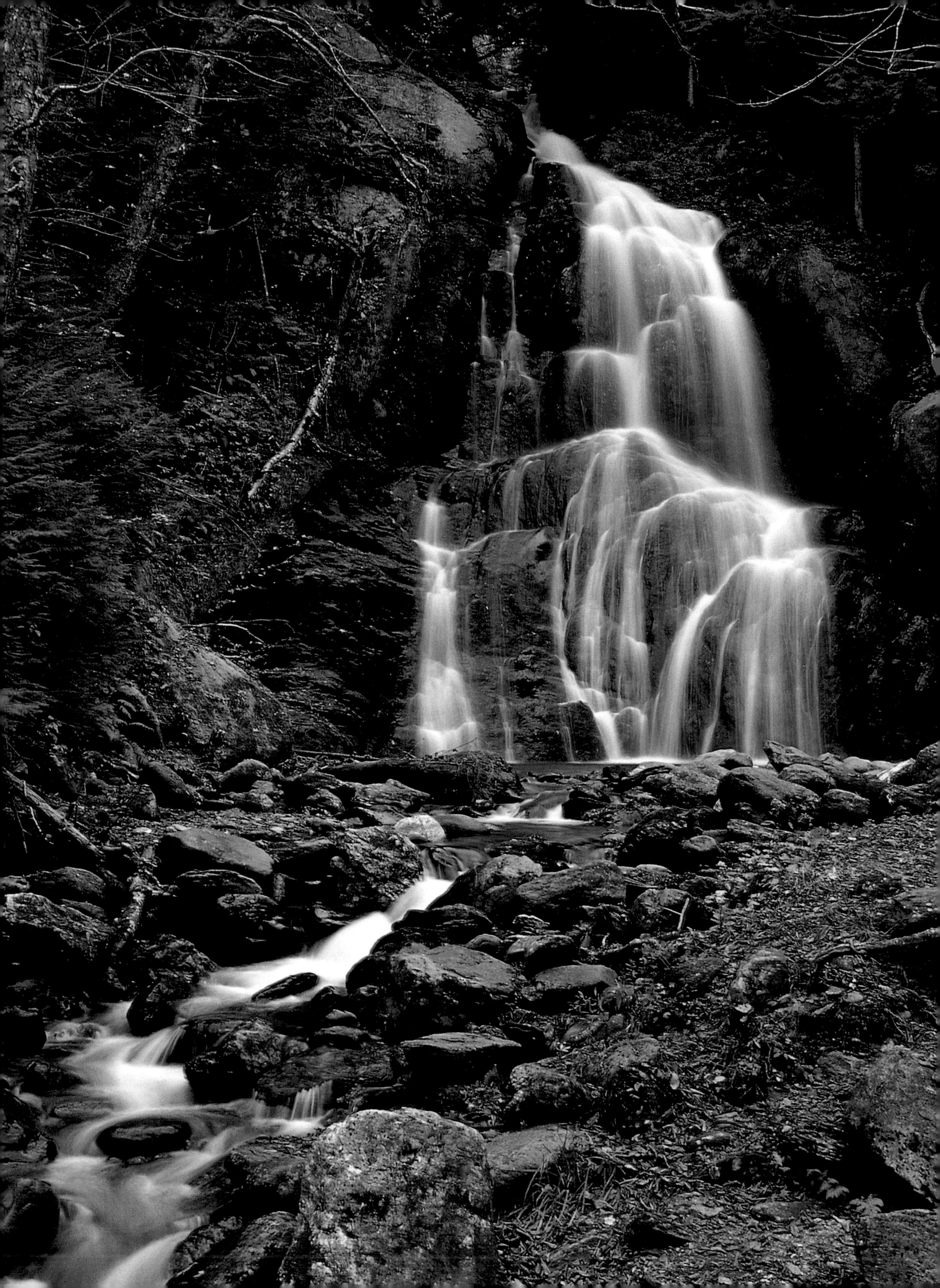

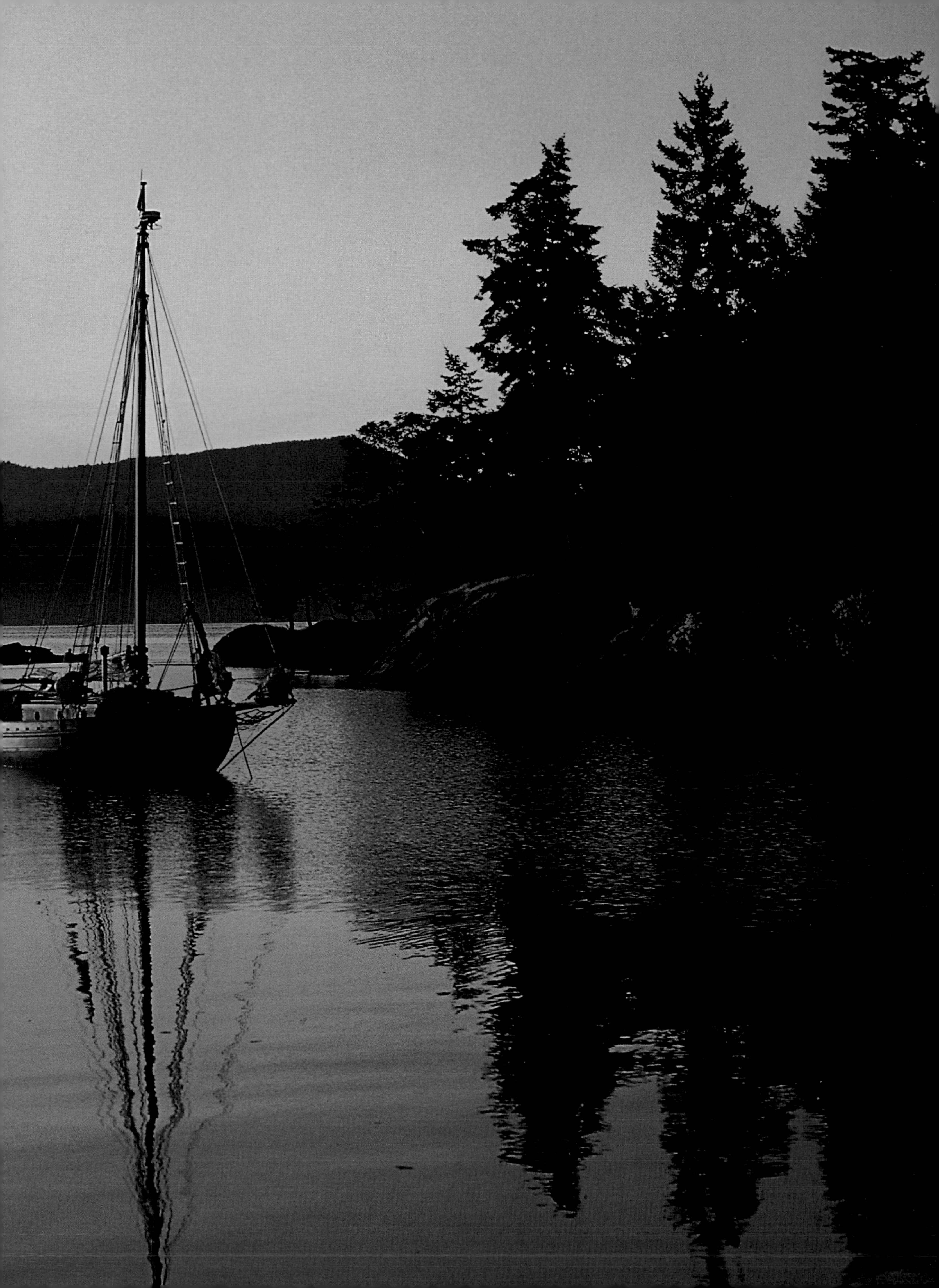

Mending Wall

Something there is that doesn't love a wall,
That sends the frozen-ground-swell under it,
And spills the upper boulders in the sun;
And makes gaps even two can pass abreast.
The work of hunters is another thing:
I have come after them and made repair
Where they have left not one stone on a stone,
But they would have the rabbit out of hiding,
To please the yelping dogs. The gaps I mean,
No one has seen them made or heard them made,
But at spring mending-time we find them there.
I let my neighbor know beyond the hill;
And on a day we meet to walk the line
And set the wall between us once again.
We keep the wall between us as we go.
To each the boulders that have fallen to each.
And some are loaves and some so nearly balls
We have to use a spell to make them balance:
'Stay where you are until our backs are turned!'
We wear our fingers rough with handling them.
Oh, just another kind of out-door game.
One on a side. It comes to little more:
There where it is we do not need the wall:
He is all pine and I am apple orchard.
My apple trees will never get across
And eat the cones under his pines, I tell him.
He only says, 'Good fences make good neighbors'.
Spring is the mischief in me, and I wonder
If I could put a notion in his head:
'Why do they make good neighbors? Isn't it
Where there are cows? But here there are no cows.
Before I built a wall I'd ask to know
What I was walling in or walling out,
And to whom I was like to give offense.
Something there is that doesn't love a wall,
That wants it down.' I could say 'Elves' to him,
But it's not elves exactly, and I'd rather
He said it for himself. I see him there
Bringing a stone grasped firmly by the top
In each hand, like an old-stone savage armed.
He moves in darkness as it seems to me,
Not of woods only and the shade of trees.
He will not go behind his father's saying,
And he likes having thought of it so well
He says again, "Good fences make good neighbors."

Robert Frost, 1914

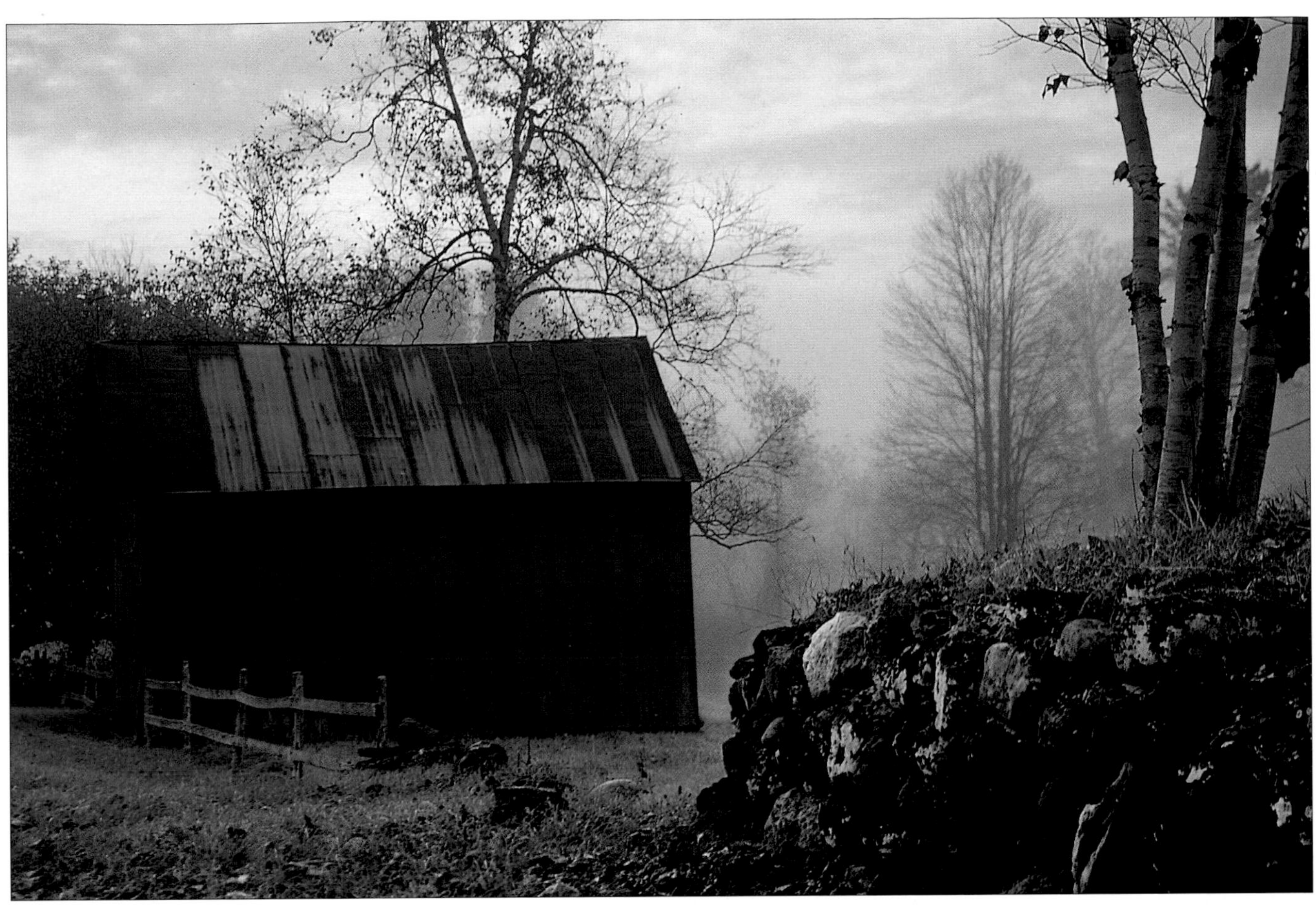

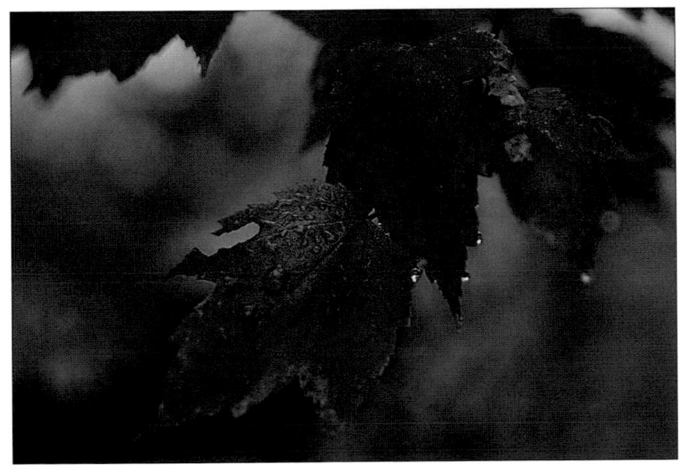

After Apple-Picking

My long two-pointed ladder's sticking through a tree
Toward heaven still,
And there's a barrel that I didn't fill
Beside it, and there may be two or three
Apples I didn't pick upon some bough.
But I am done with apple-picking now.
Essence of winter sleep is on the night,
The scent of apples: I am drowsing off.
I cannot rub the strangeness from my sight
I got from looking through a pane of glass
I skimmed this morning from the drinking trough
And held against the world of hoary grass.
It melted, and I let it fall and break.
But I was well
Upon my way to sleep before it fell,
And I could tell
What form my dreaming was about to take.
Magnified apples appear and disappear,
Stem end and blossom end,
And every fleck of russet showing clear.
My instep arch not only keeps the ache,
It keeps the pressure of a ladder-round.
I feel the ladder sway as the boughs bend.
And I keep hearing from the cellar bin
The rumbling sound
Of load on load of apples coming in.
For I have had too much
Of apple-picking: I am overtired
Of the great harvest I myself desired.
There were ten thousand thousand fruit to touch,
Cherish in hand, lift down, and not let fall.
For all
That struck the earth,
No matter if not bruised or spiked with stubble,
Went surely to the cider-apple heap
As of no worth.
One can see what will trouble
This sleep of mine, whatever sleep it is.
Were he not gone,
The woodchuck could say whether it's like his
Long sleep, as I describe its coming on,
Or just some human sleep.

Robert Frost, 1914

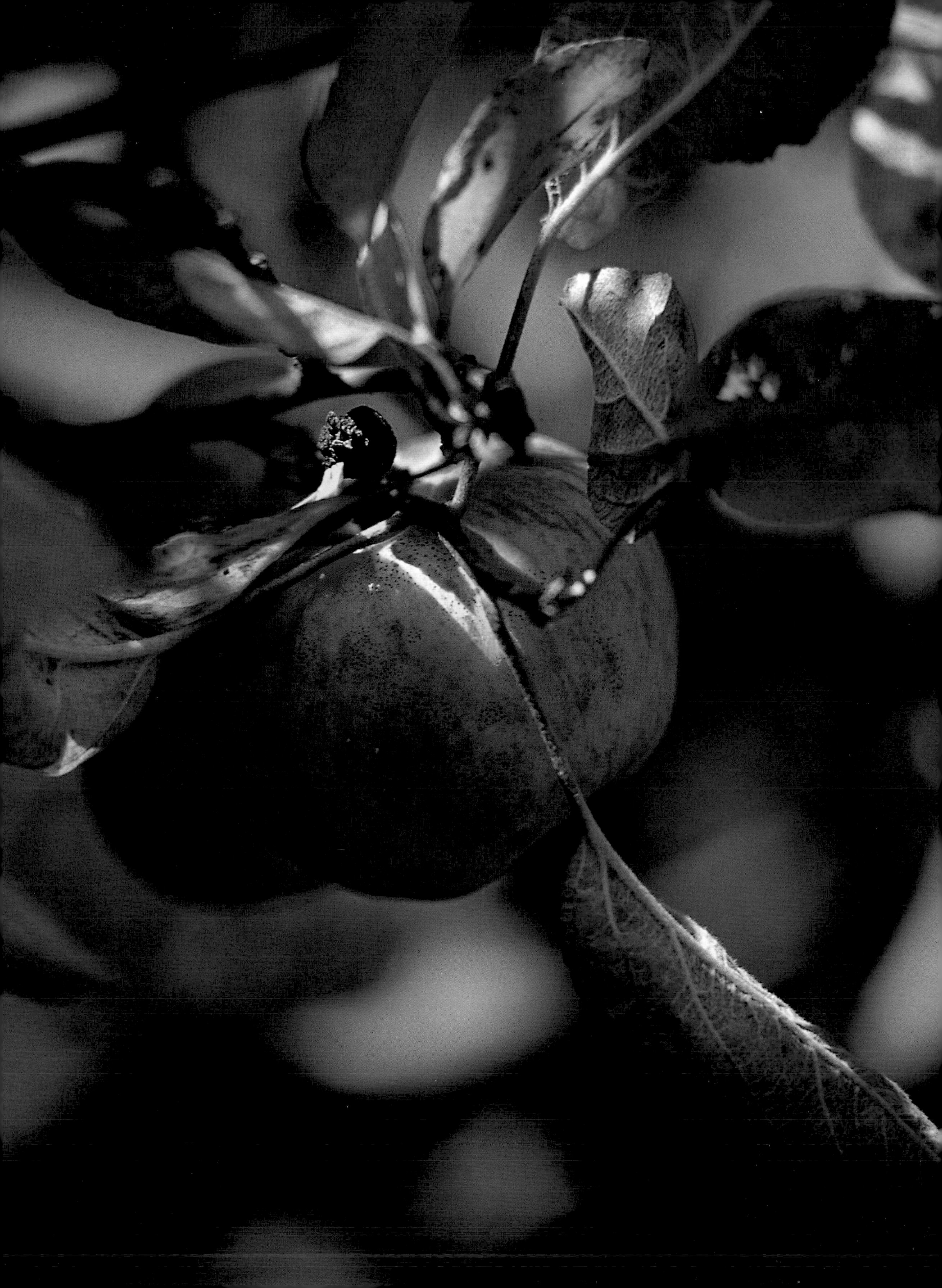

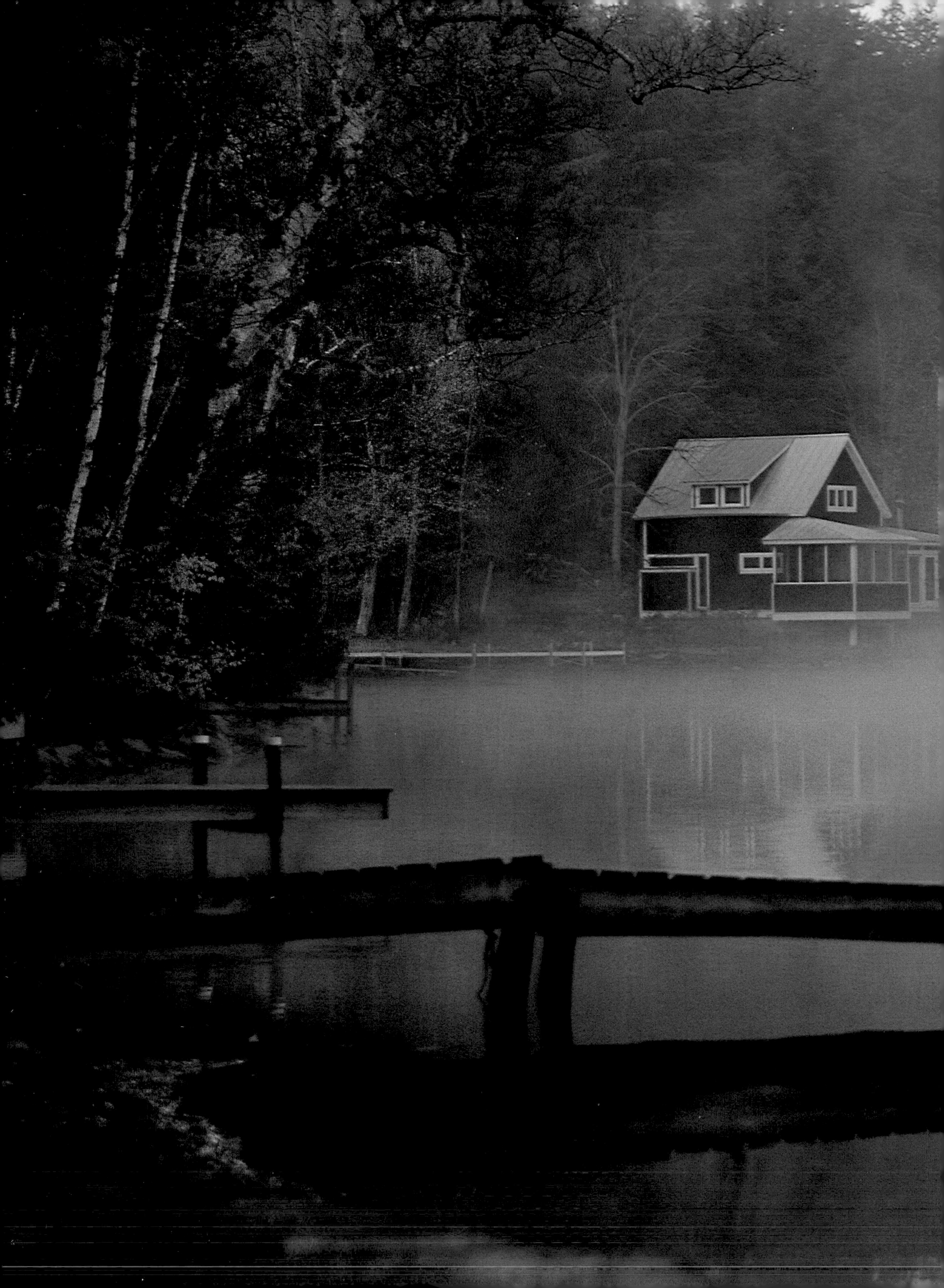

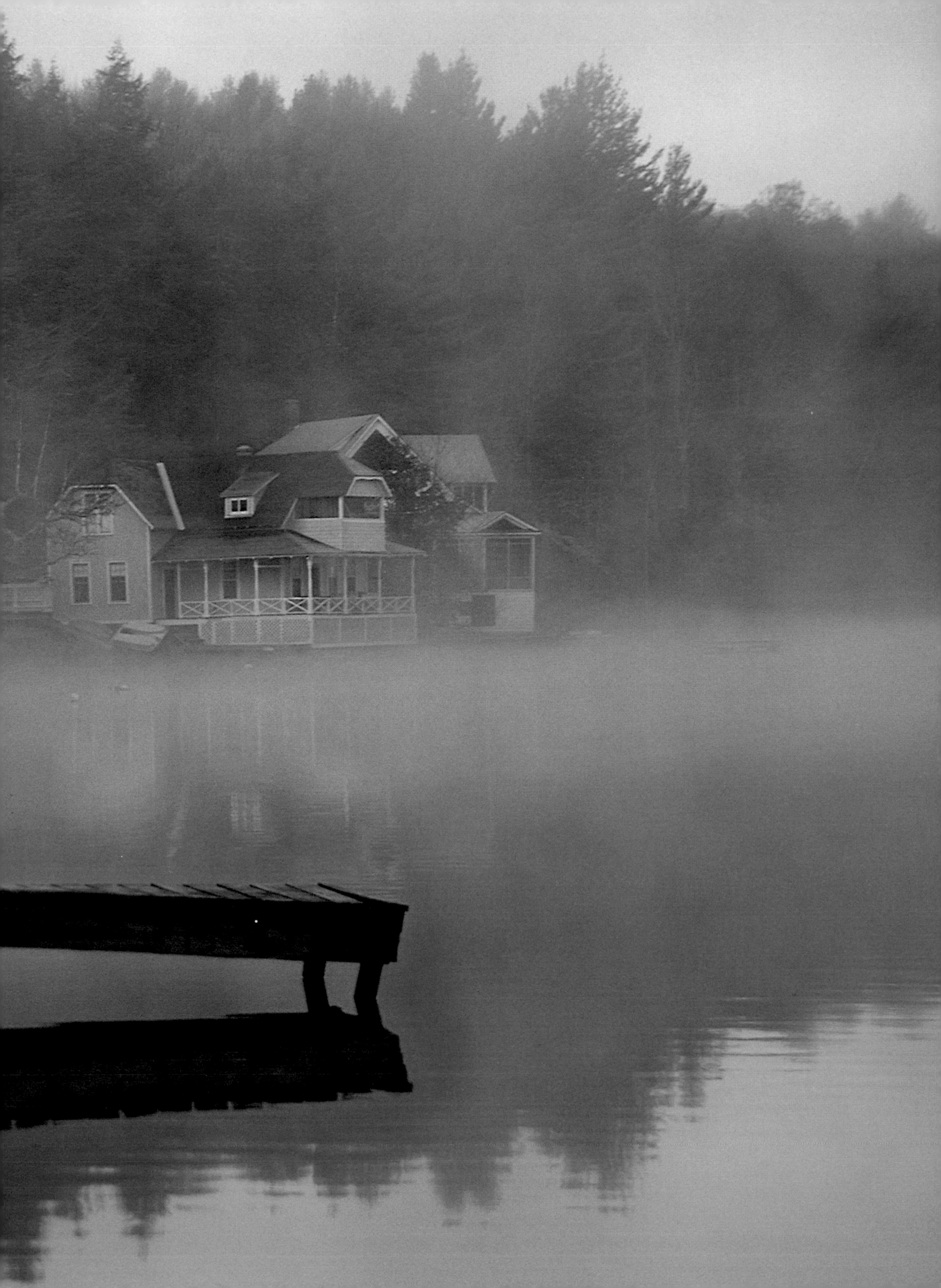

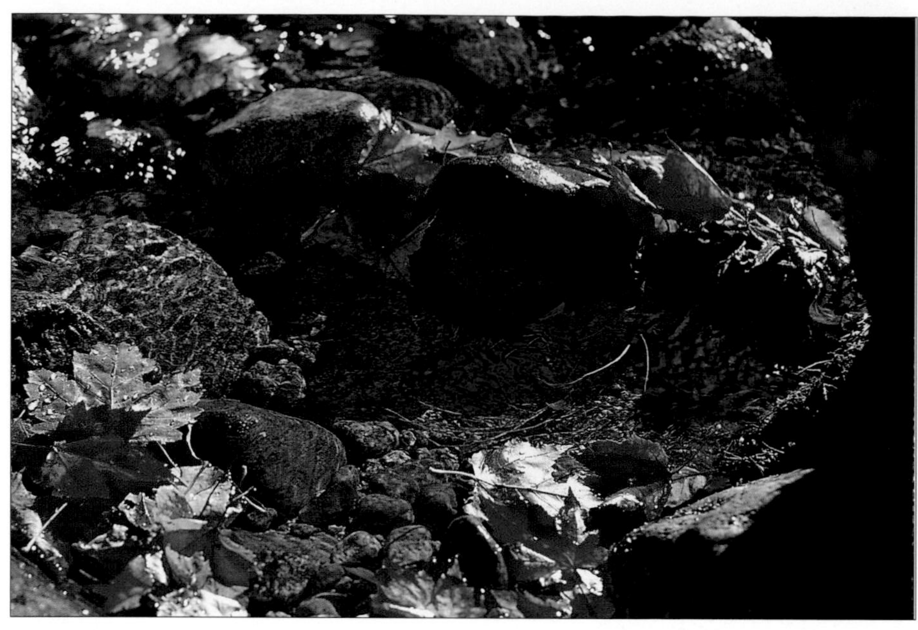

WORDS

Axes
After whose stroke the wood rings,
And the echoes!
Echoes traveling
Off from the centre like horses.

The sap
Wells like tears, like the
Water striving
To re-establish its mirror
Over the rock

That drops and turns,
A white skull,
Eaten by weedy greens.
Years later I
Encounter them on the road—

Words dry and riderless,
The indefatigable hoof-taps.
While
From the bottom of the pool, fixed stars
Govern a life.

Sylvia Plath, 1963

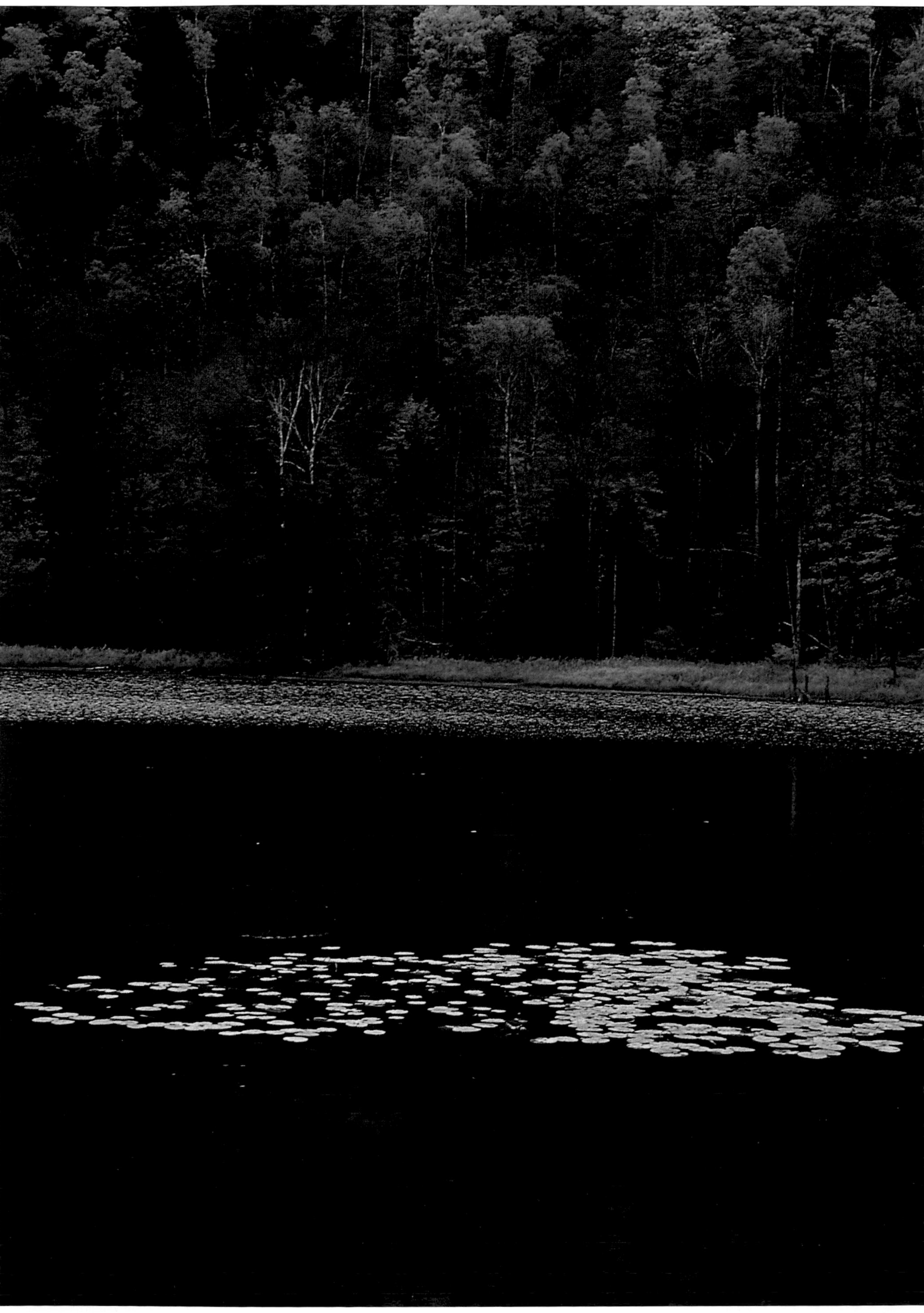

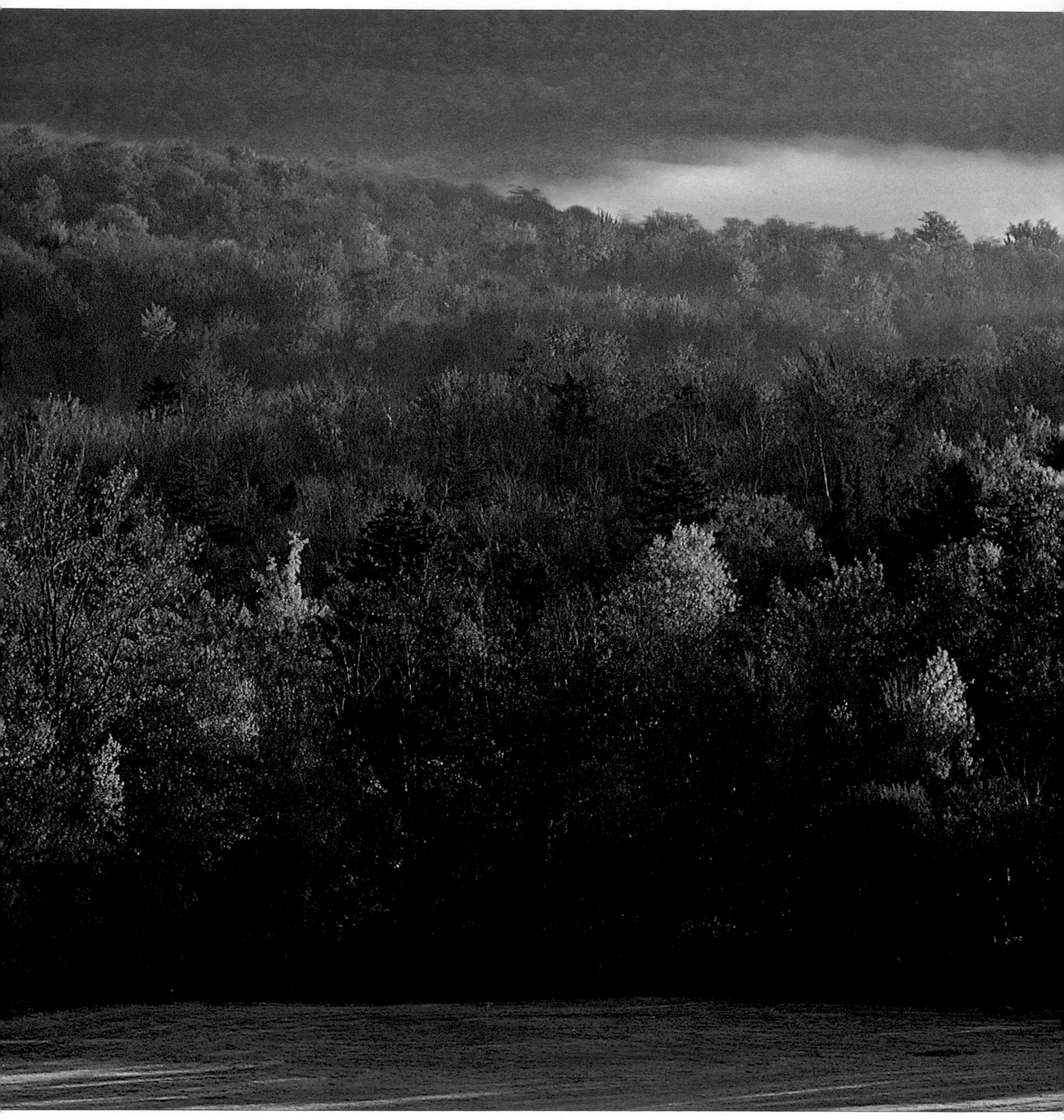

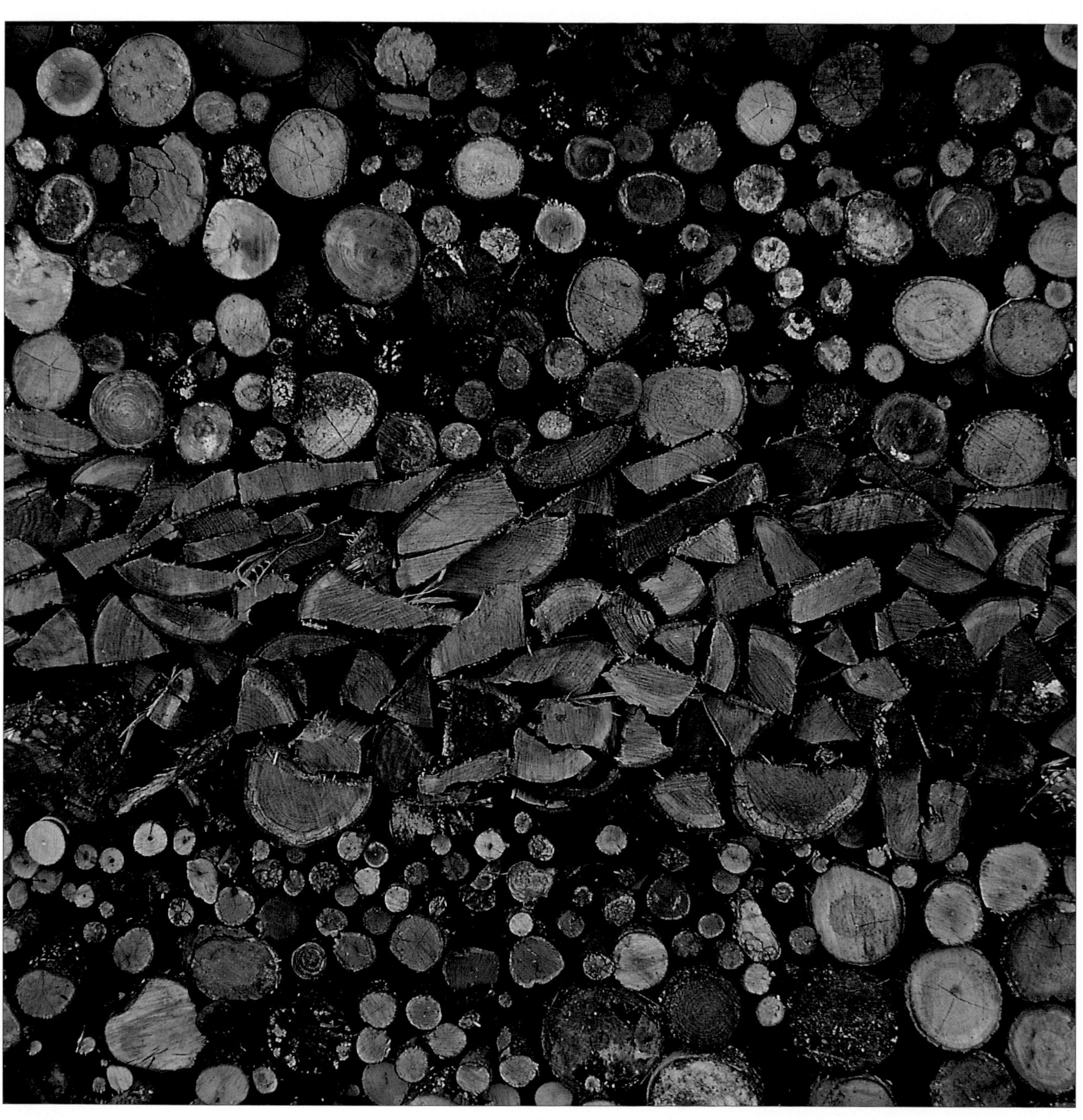

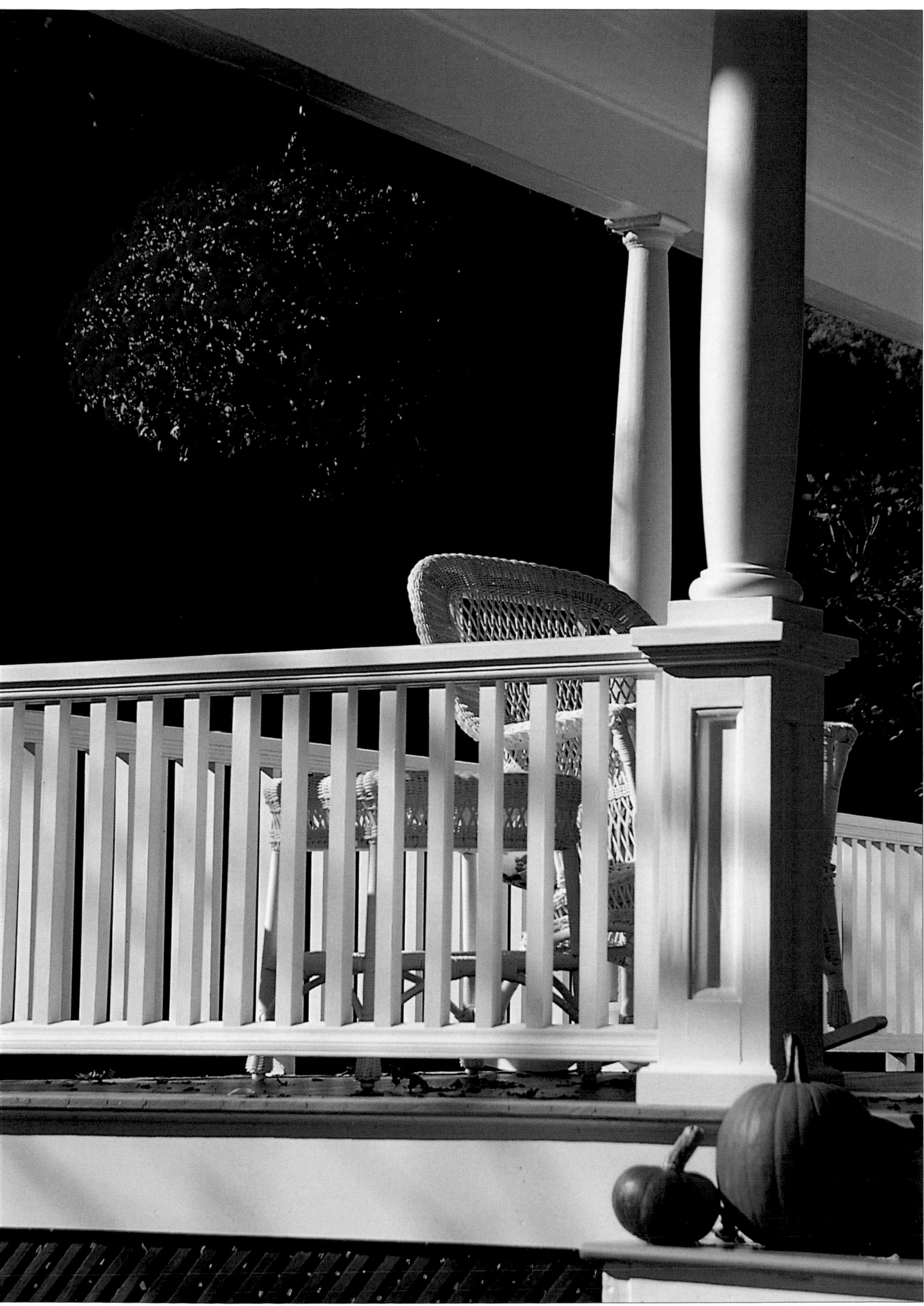

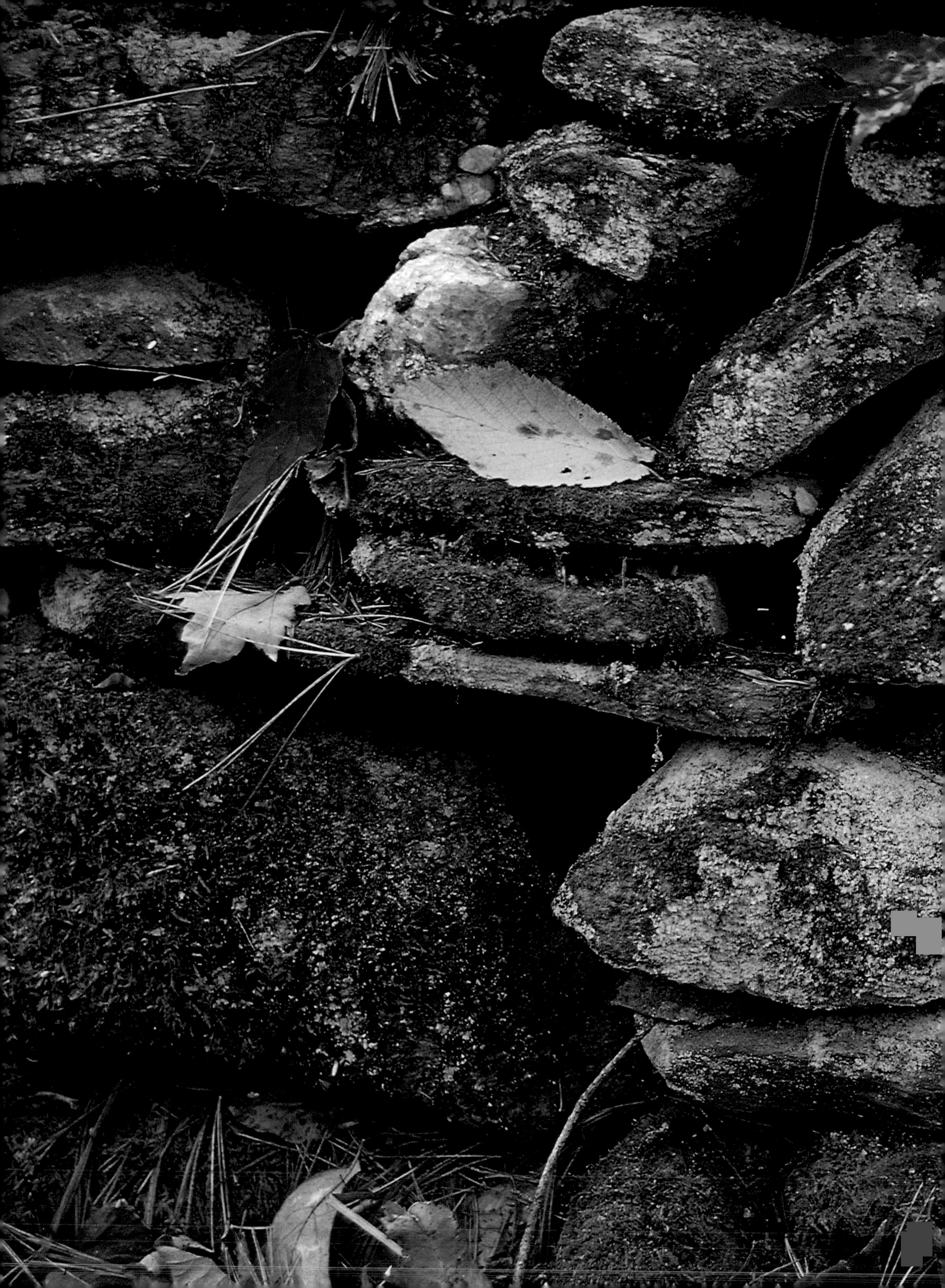

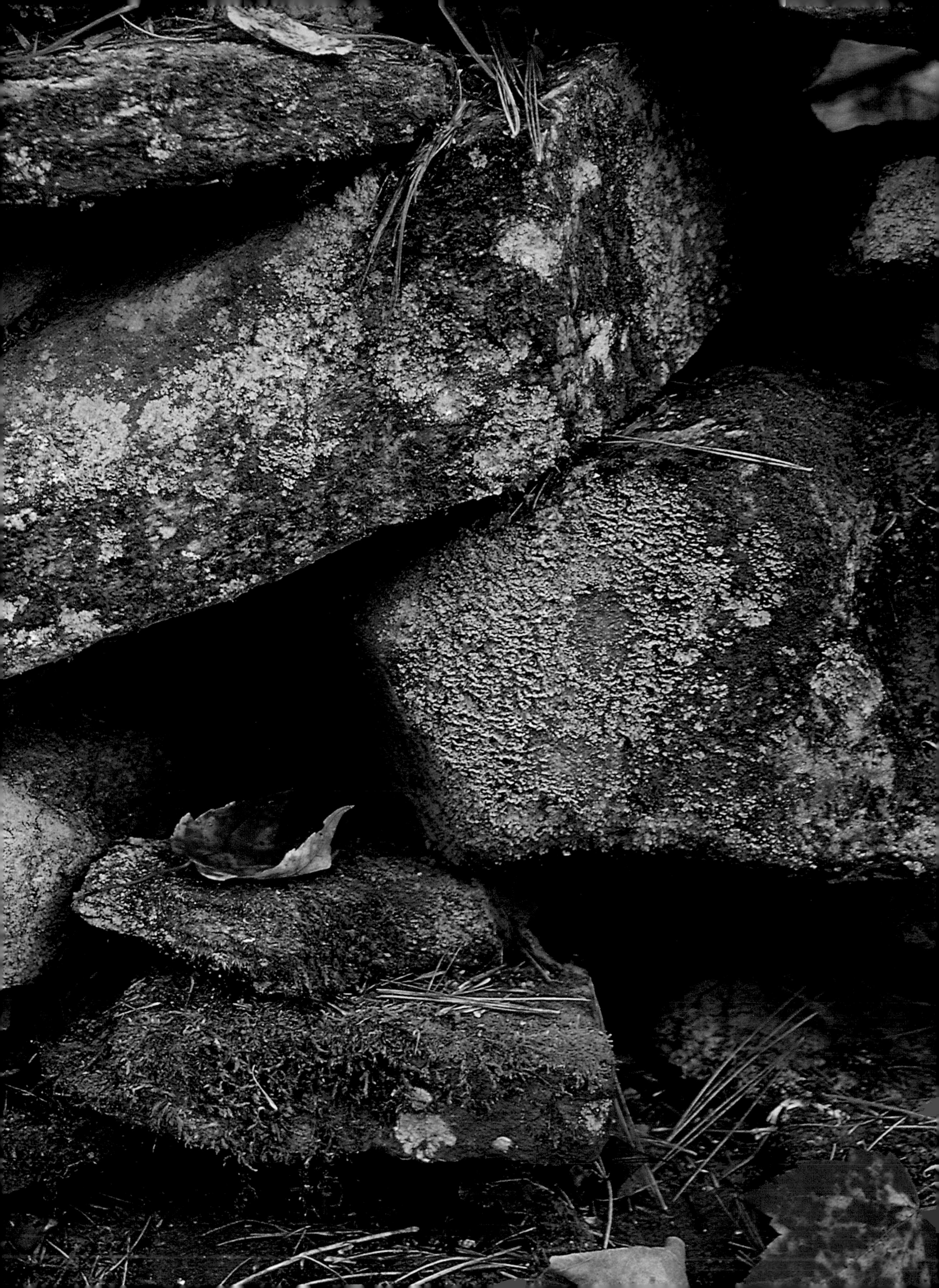

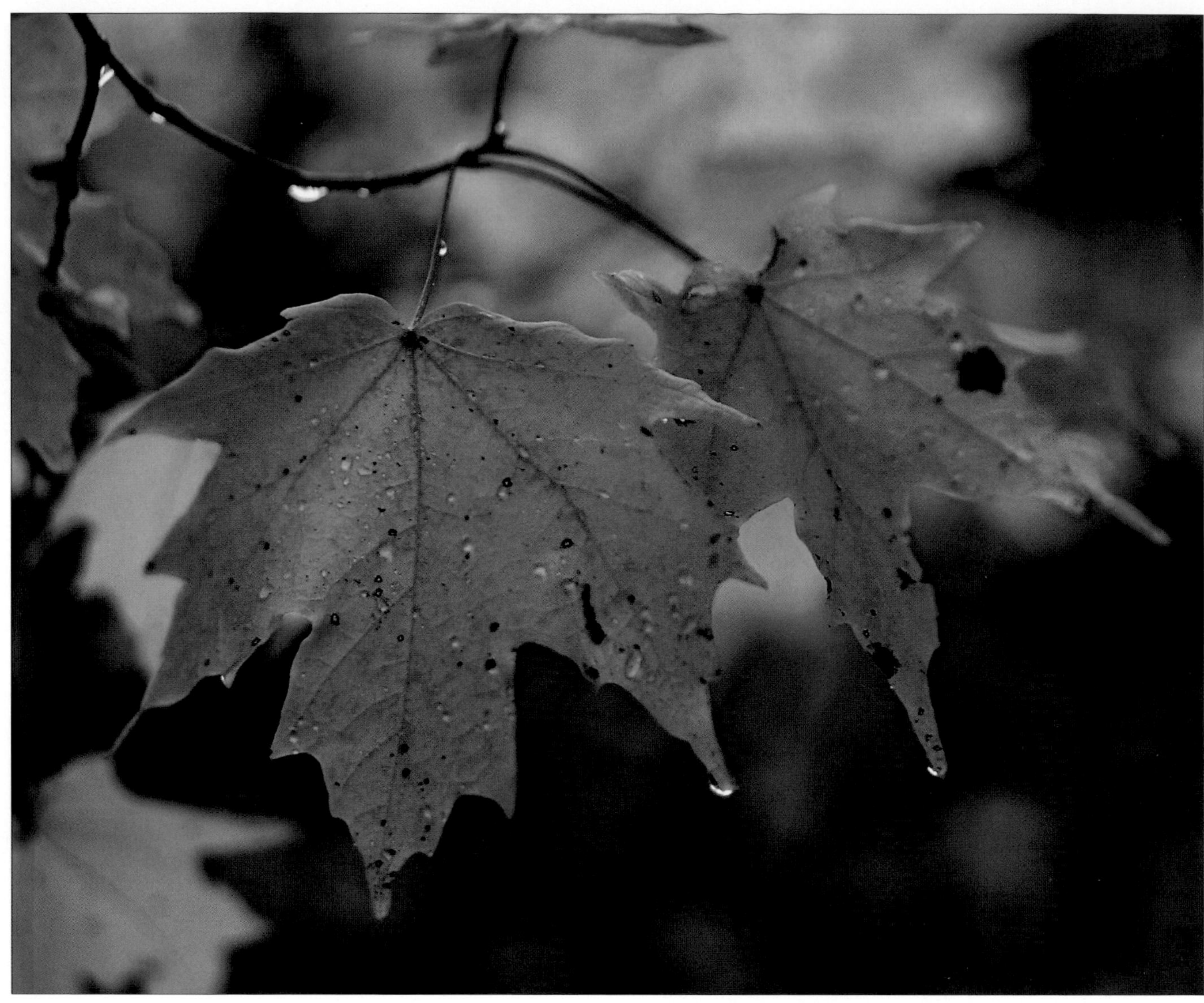

The indescribable innocence and beneficence of Nature—of sun and wind and rain, of summer and winter—such health, such cheer, they afford forever! And such sympathy have they ever with our race, that all Nature would be affected, and the sun's brightness fade, and the winds would sigh humanely, and the clouds rain tears, and the woods shed their leaves and put on mourning in midsummer, if any man should ever for a just cause grieve. Shall I not have intelligence with the earth? Am I not partly leaves and vegetable mould myself?

From *Walden*
Henry David Thoreau, 1854

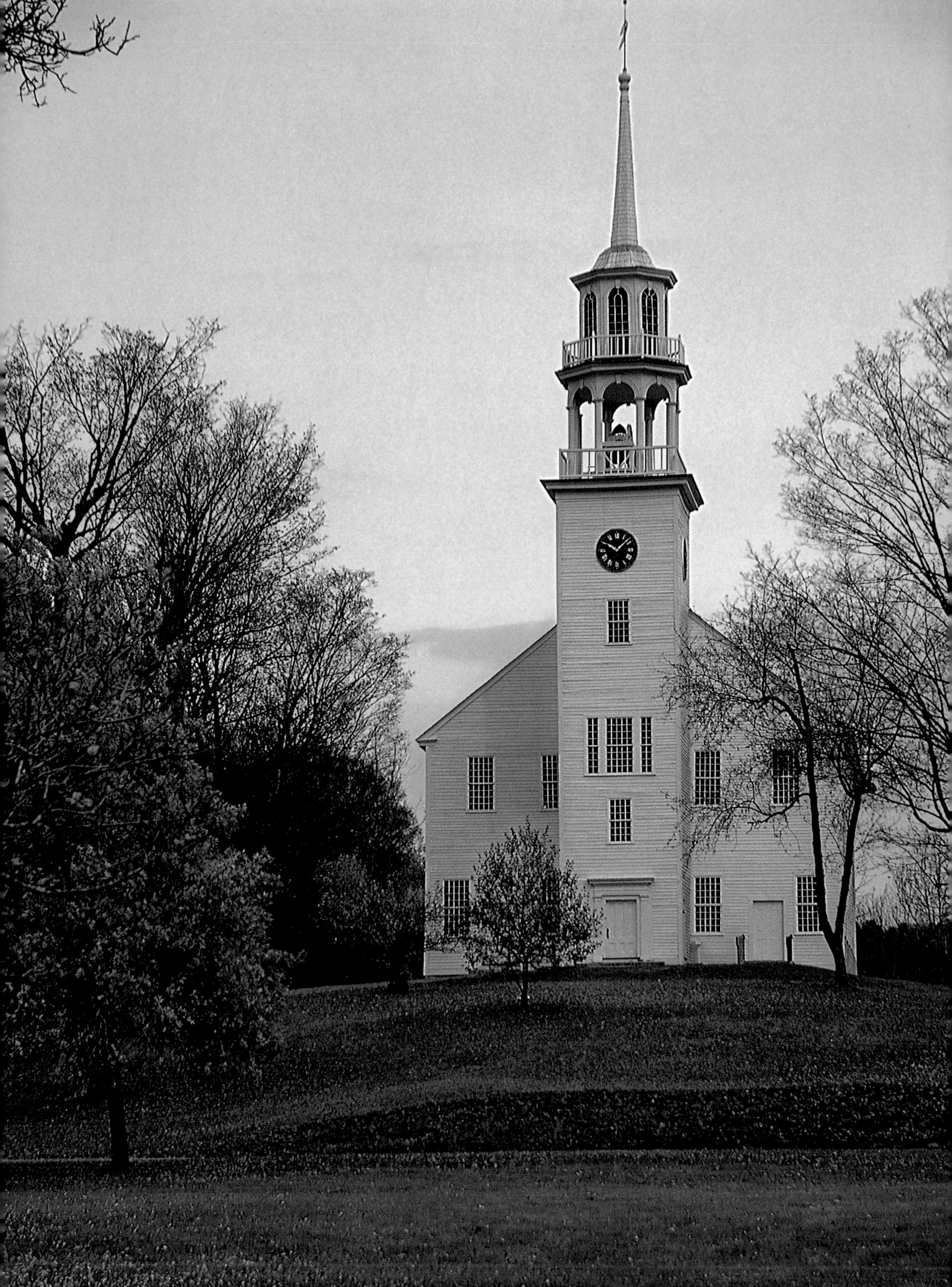

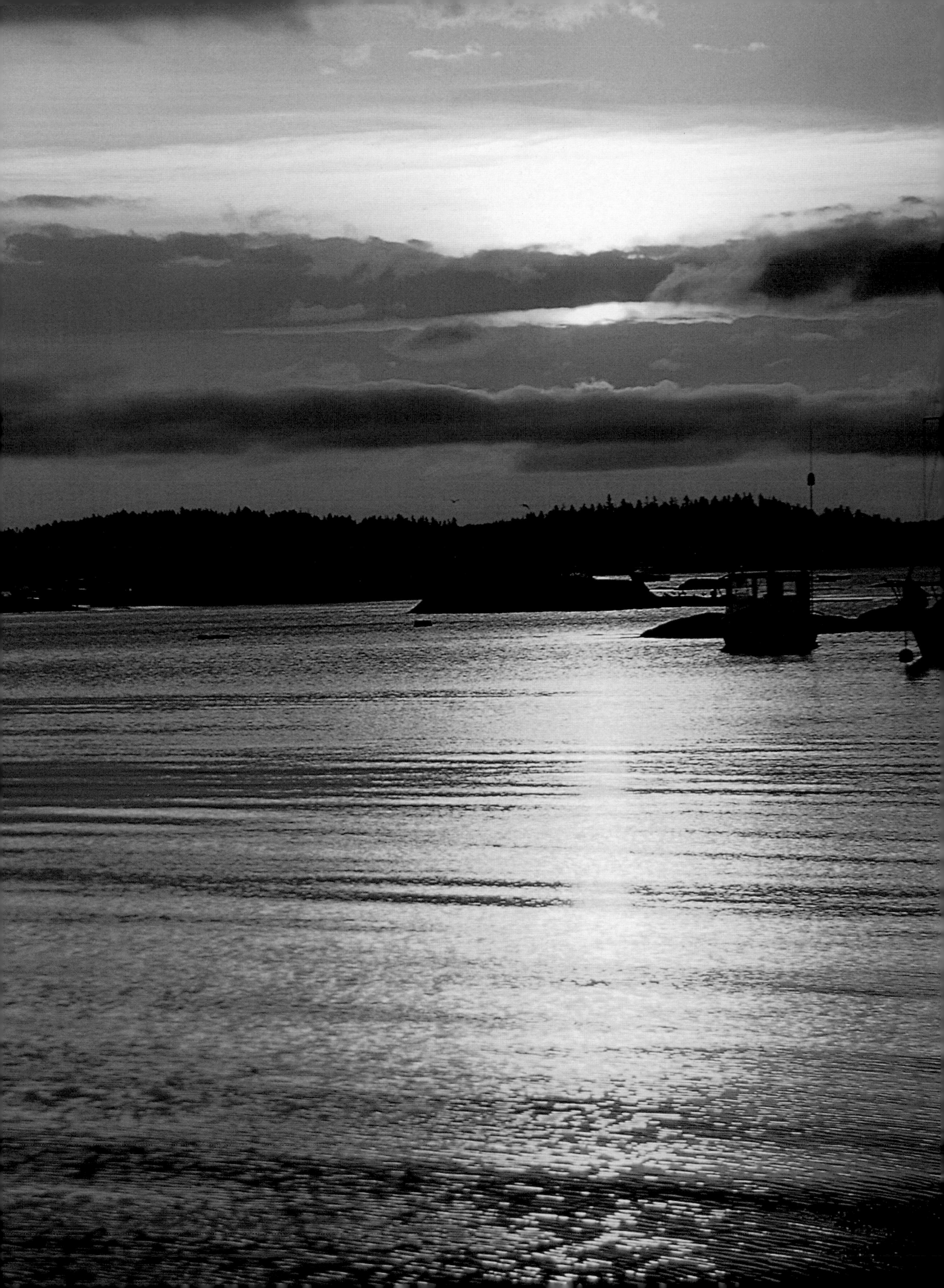

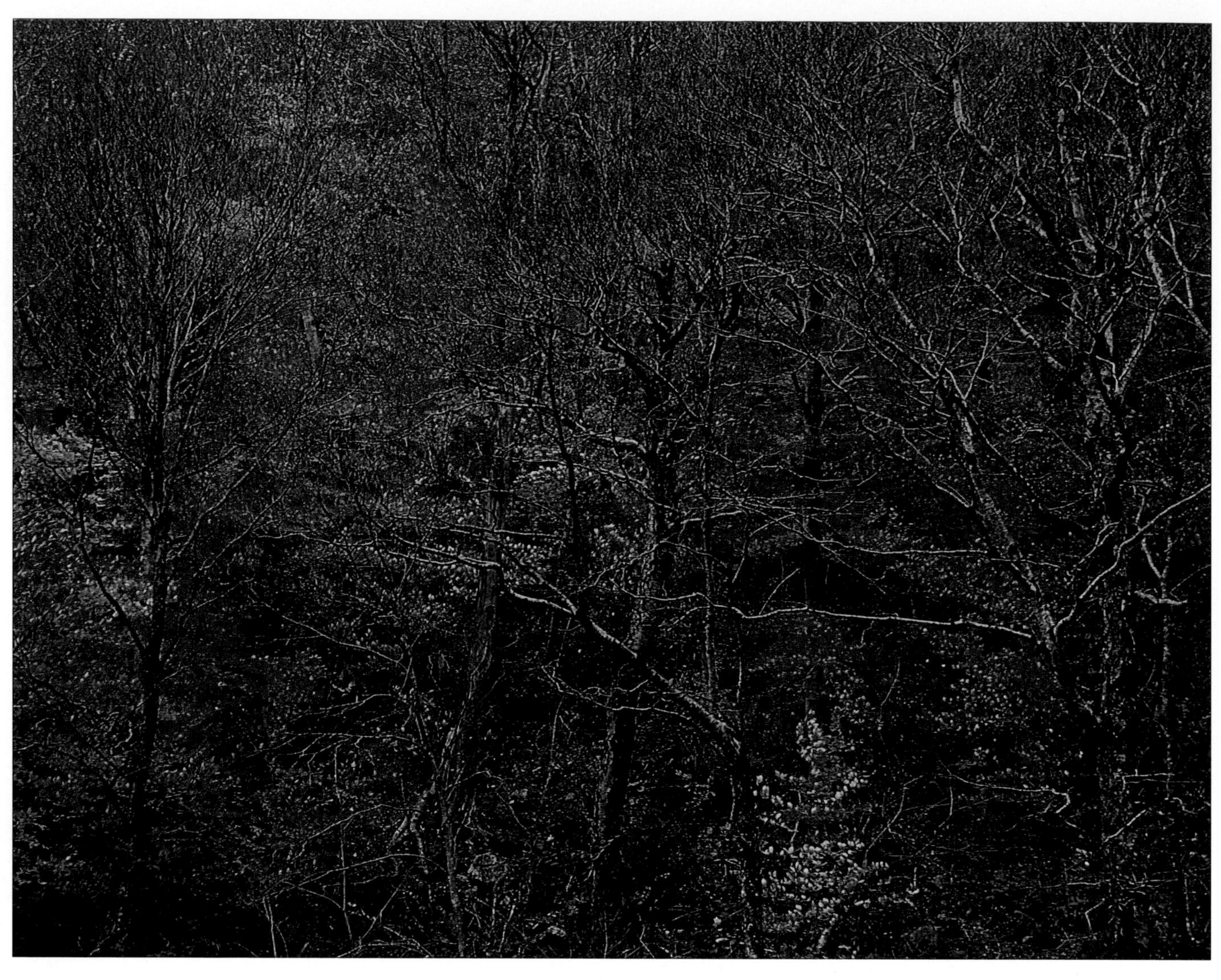

Ulalume—a Ballad

The skies were ashen and sober;
    The leaves they were crisped and sere—
  The leaves they were withering and sere;
It was night, in the lonesome October
  Of my most immemorial year:
It was hard by the dim lake of Auber,
In the misty mid region of Weir:—
It was down by the dank tarn of Auber,
In the ghoul-haunted woodland of Weir.

Excerpt
Edgar Allen Poe, 1847

A Dream Within a Dream

Take this kiss upon the brow!
And, in parting from you now,
Thus much let me avow—
You are not wrong, who deem
That my days have been a dream;
Yet if hope has flown away
In a night, or in a day,
In a vision, or in none,
Is it therefore the less *gone*?
All that we see or seem
Is but a dream within a dream.

I stand amid the roar
Of a surf-tormented shore,
And I hold within my hand
Grains of the golden sand—
How few! yet how they creep

Through my fingers to the deep,
While I weep—while I weep!
O God! can I not grasp
Them with a tighter clasp?
O God! can I not save
One from the pitiless wave?
Is *all* that we see or seem
But a dream within a dream?

Edgar Allen Poe, 1849

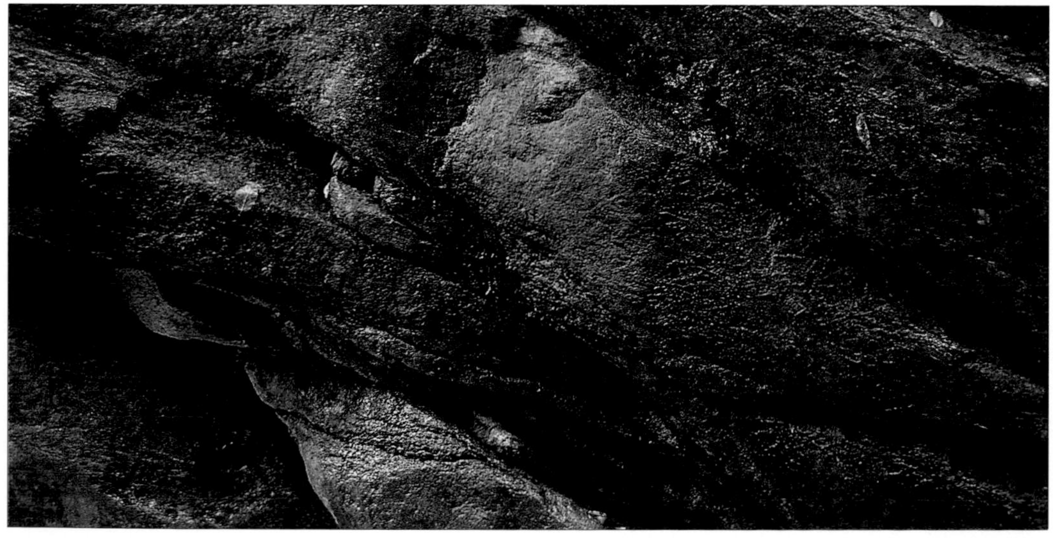

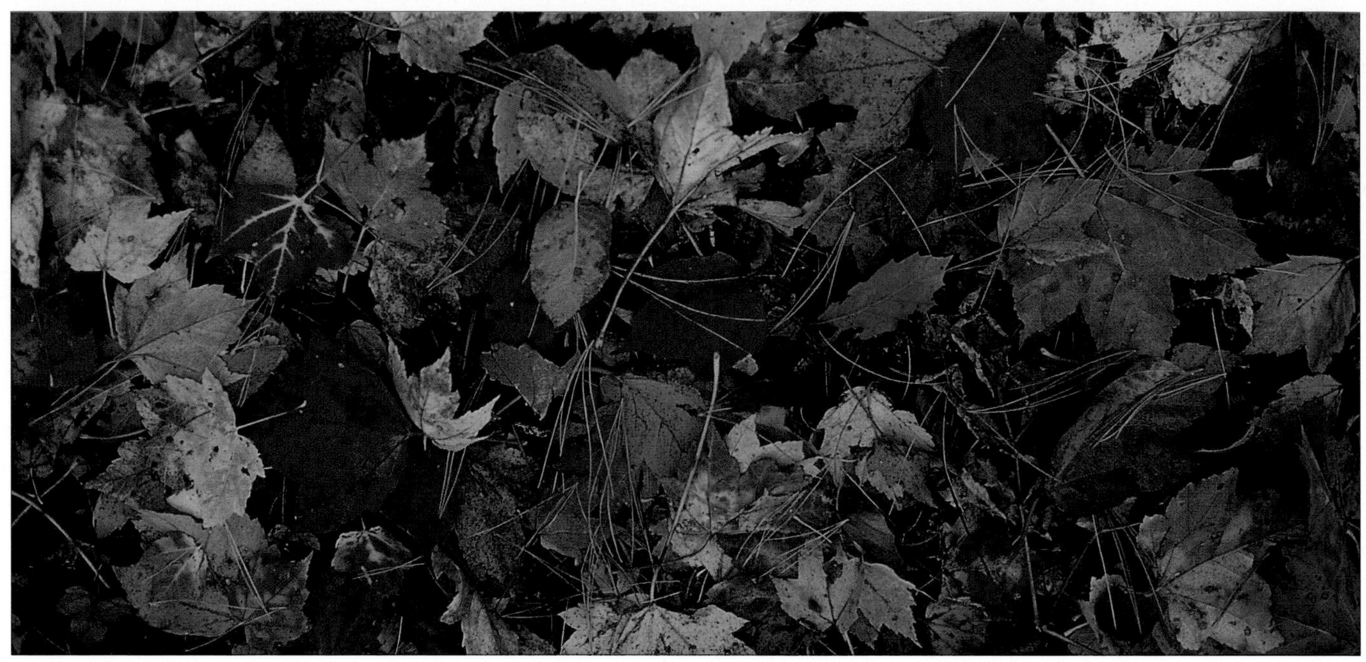

*F*lint's Pond! Such is the poverty of our nomenclature. What right had the unclean and stupid farmer, whose farm abutted on this sky water, whose shores he has ruthlessly laid bare, to give his name to it? Some skin-flint, who loved better the reflecting surface of a dollar, or a bright cent, in which he could see his own brazen face; who regarded even the wild ducks which settled in it as trespassers; his fingers grown into crooked and horny talons from the long habit of grasping harpy-like;—so it is not named for me. I go not there to see him nor to hear of him; who never *saw* it, who never bathed in it, who never loved it, who never protected it, who never spoke a good word for it, nor thanked God that he had made it. Rather let it be named from the fishes that swim in it, the wild fowl or quadrupeds which frequent it, the wild flowers which grow by its shores, or some wild man or child the thread of whose history is interwoven with its own; not from him who could show no title to it but the deed which a like-minded neighbor or legislature gave him,—him who thought only of its money value; whose presence perchance cursed all the shore; who exhausted the land around it, and would fain have exhausted the waters within it; who regretted only that it was not English hay or cranberry meadow,—there was nothing to redeem it, forsooth, in his eyes,—and would have drained and sold it for mud at its bottom. It did not turn his mill, and it was no *privilege* to him to behold it. I respect not his labors, his farm where every thing has its price; who would carry the landscape, who would carry his God, to market, if he could get any thing for him; who goes to market *for* his god as it is; on whose farm nothing grows free, whose fields bear no crops, whose meadows no flowers, whose trees no fruit, but dollars; who loves not the beauty of his fruits, whose fruits are not ripe for him till they are turned to dollars. Give me the poverty that enjoys true wealth.

From *Walden*
Henry David Thoreau

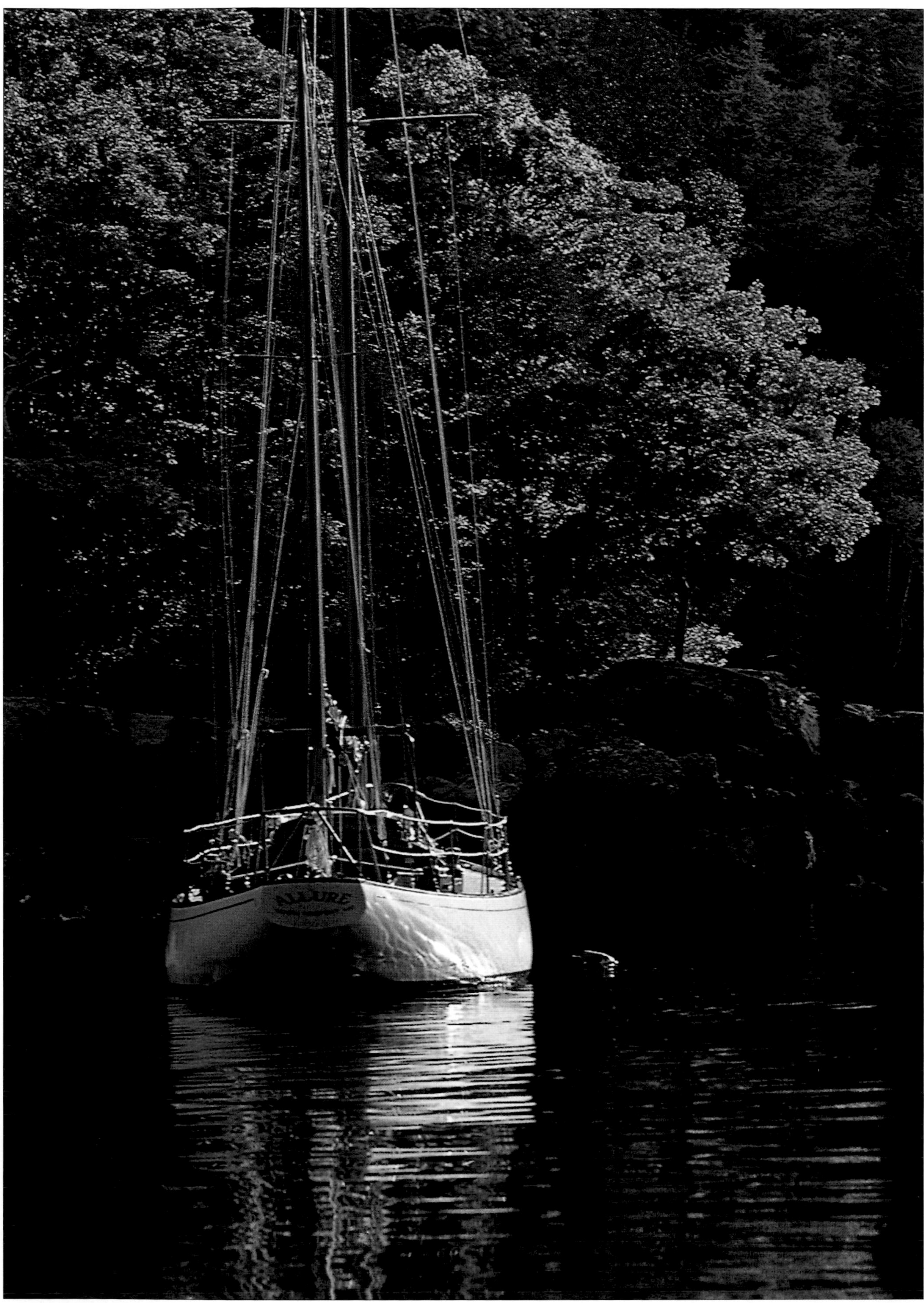
ALLURE

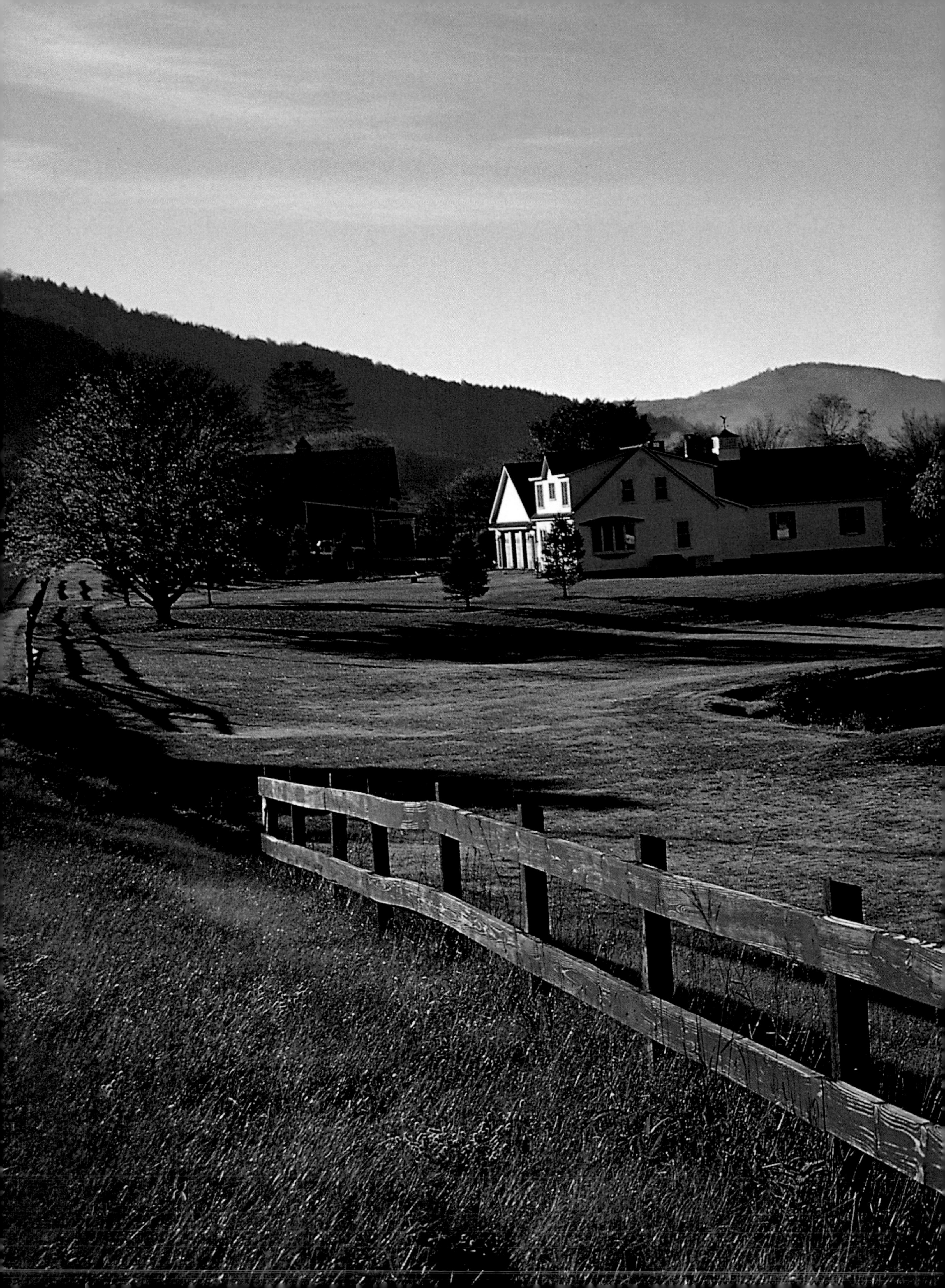

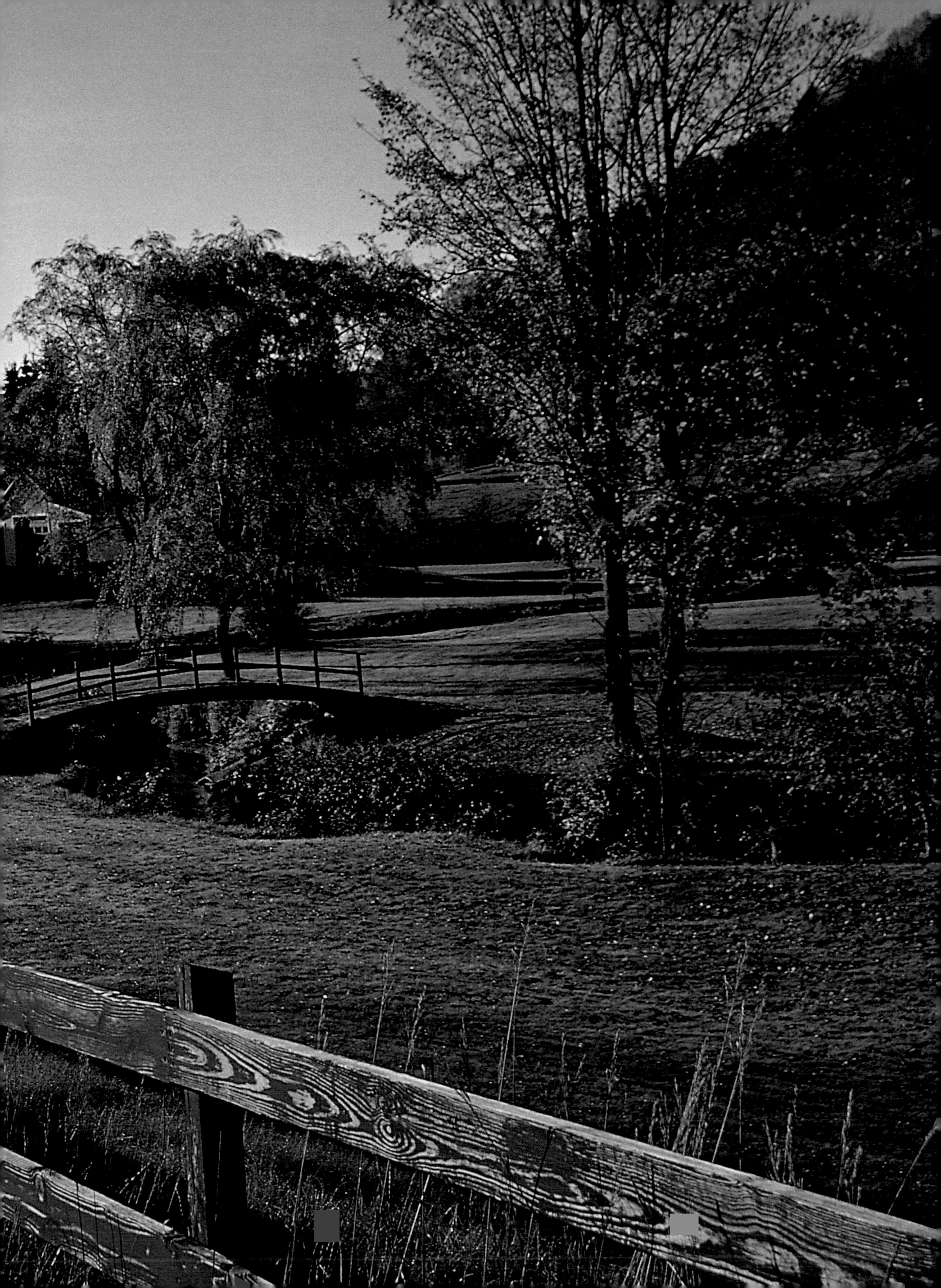

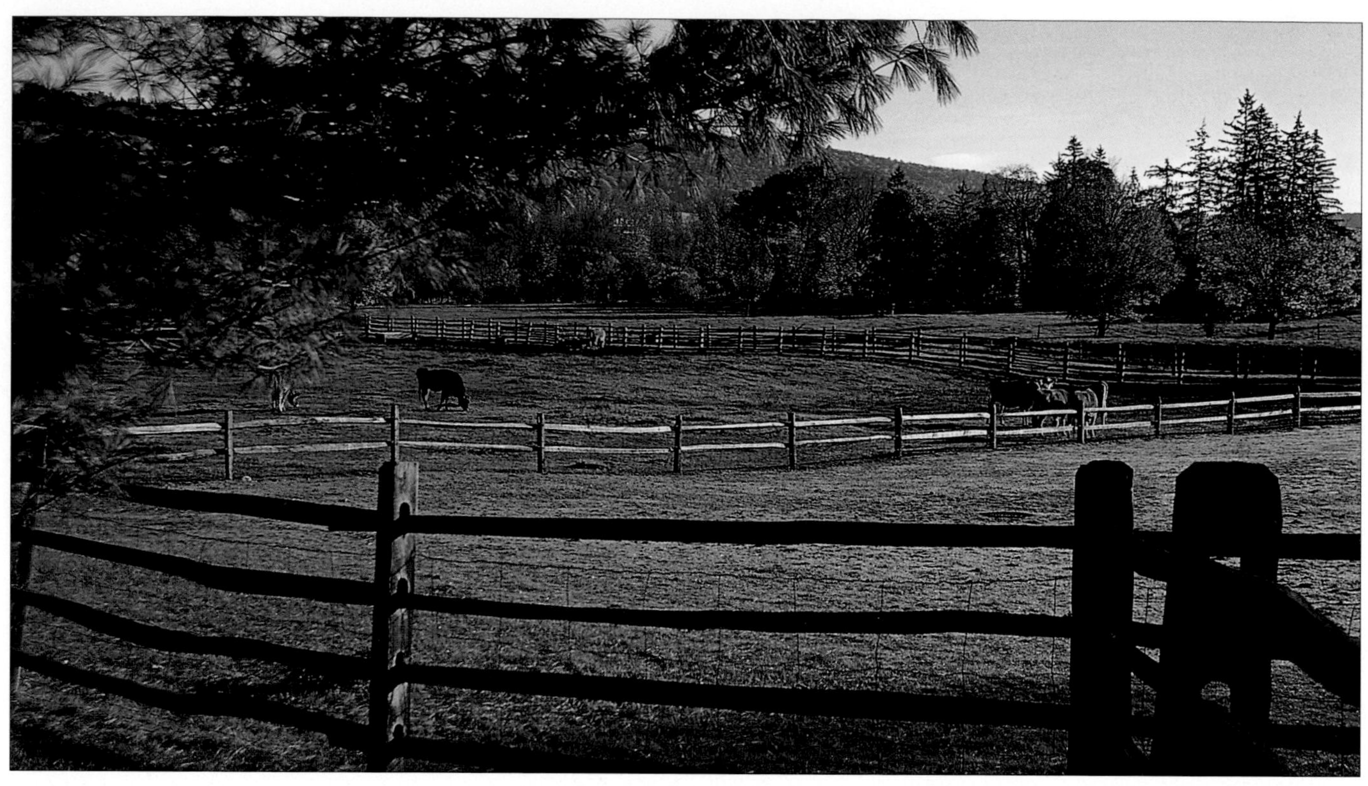

NOBODY LOSES ALL THE TIME

Nobody loses all the time
i had an uncle named
Sol who was a born failure and
nearly everybody said he should have gone
into vaudeville perhaps because my Uncle Sol could
sing McCann He Was A Diver on Xmas Eve like Hell
   Itself which
may or may not account for the fact that my Uncle

Sol indulged in that possibly most inexcusable
of all to use a highfalootin phrase
luxuries that is or to
wit farming and be
it needlessly
added

my Uncle Sol's farm
failed because the chickens
ate the vegetables so
my Uncle Sol had a
chicken farm till the
skunks ate the chickens when

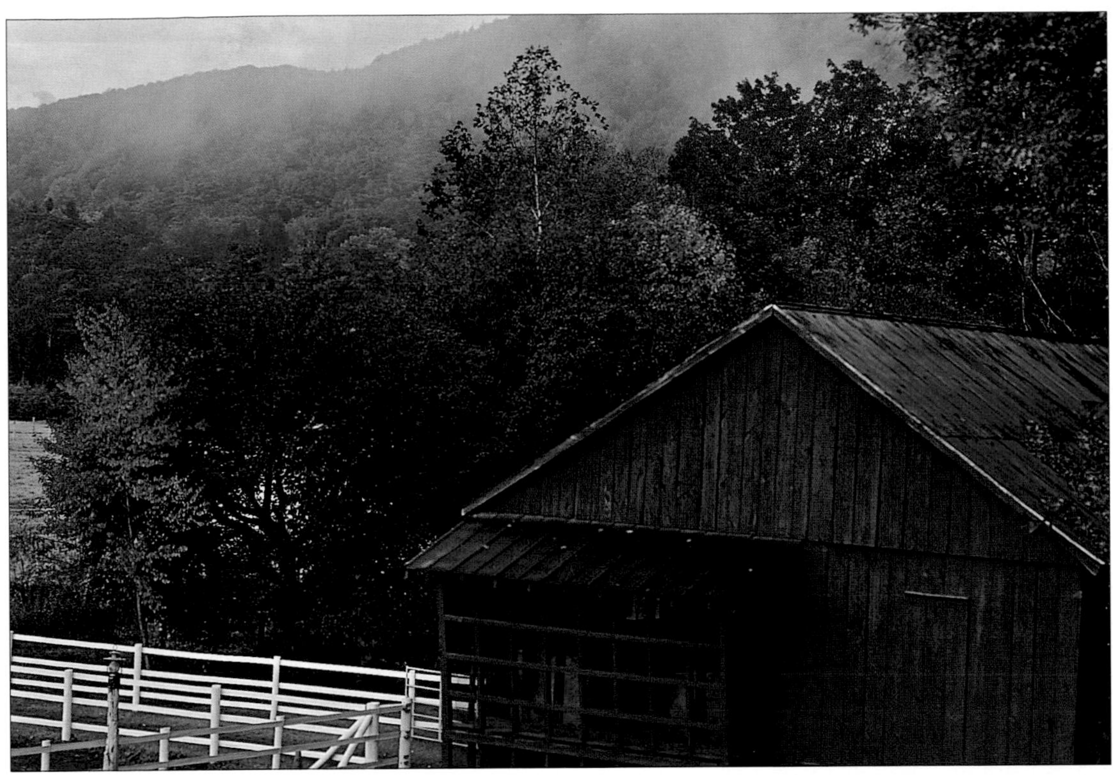

my Uncle Sol
had a skunk farm but
the skunks caught cold and
died and so
my Uncle Sol imitated the
skunks in a subtle manner

or by drowning himself in the watertank
but somebody who'd given my Uncle Sol a Victor
Victrola and records while he lived presented to
him upon the auspicious occasion of his decease a
scruptious not to mention splendiferous funeral with
tall boys in black gloves and flowers and everything and

i remember we all cried like the Missouri
when my Uncle Sol's coffin lurched because
somebody pressed a button
(and down went
my Uncle
Sol

and started a worm farm)

E. E. Cummings, 1926

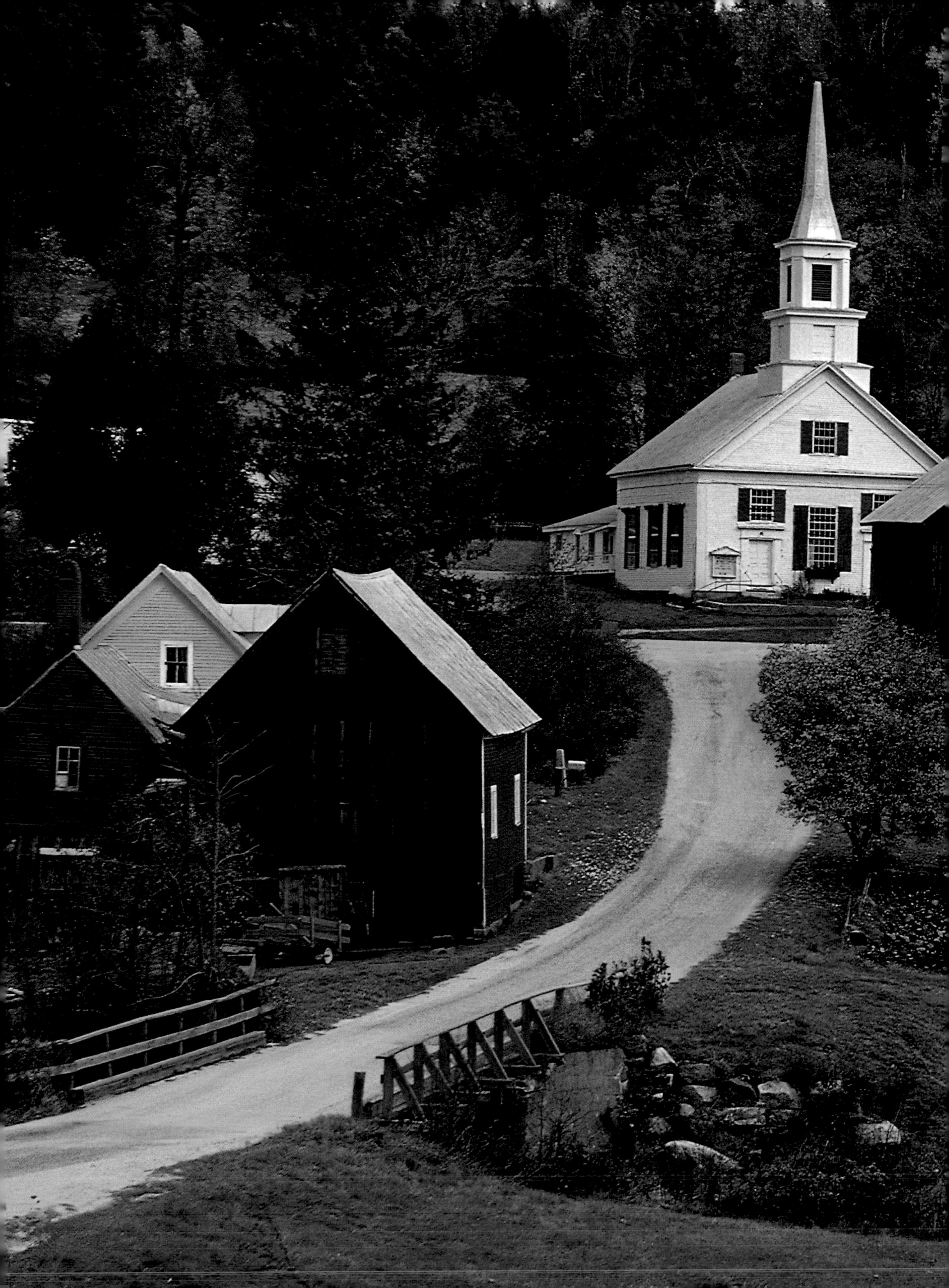

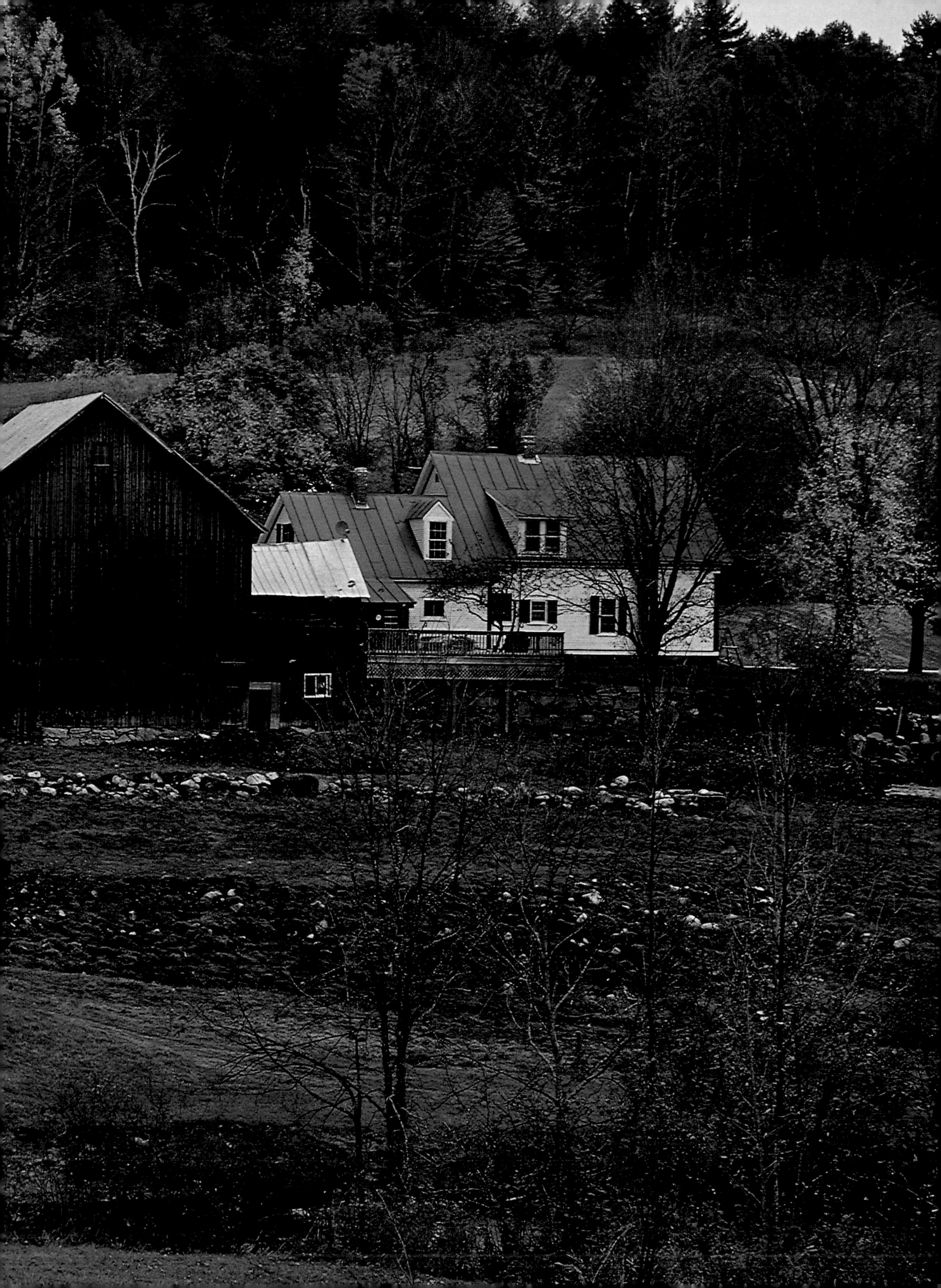

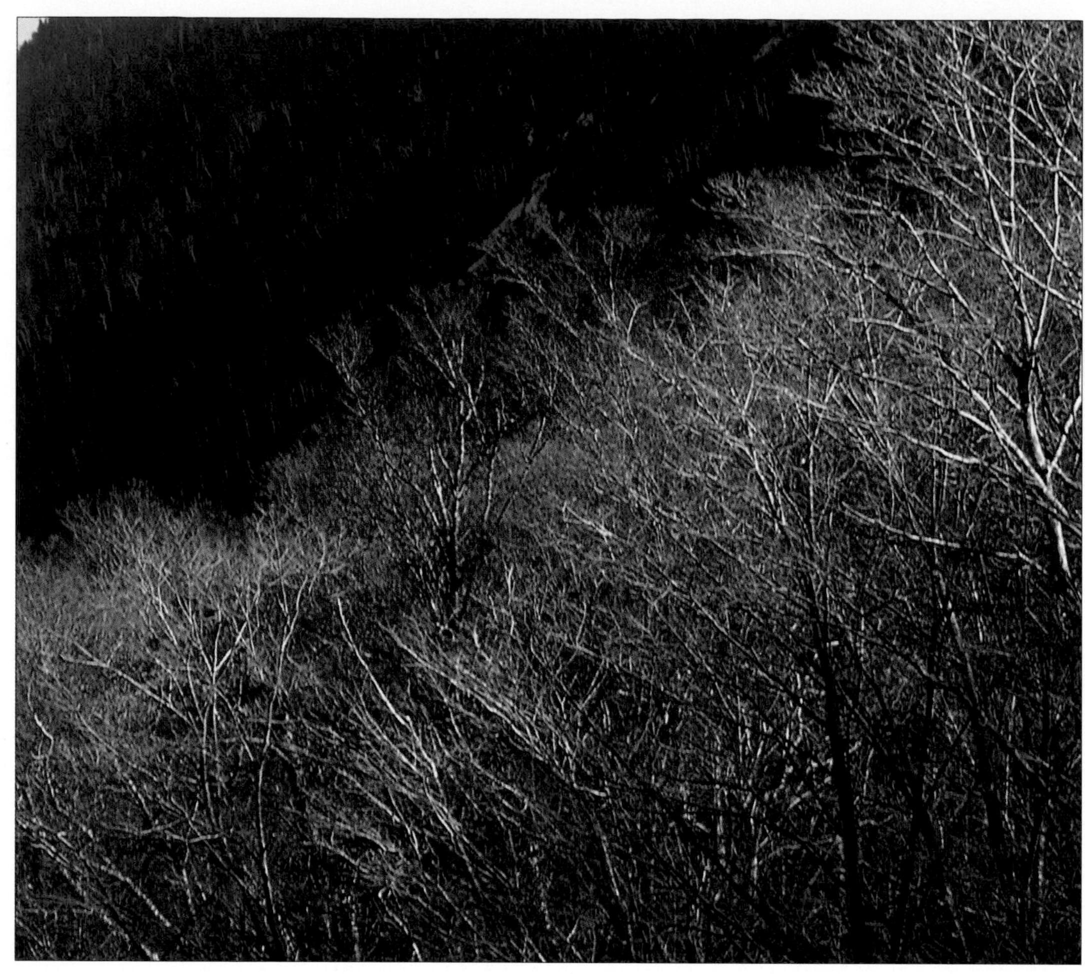

Nature—sometimes sears a Sapling—
Sometimes—scalps a Tree—
Her Green People recollect it
When they do not die—

Fainter Leaves—to Further Seasons—
Dumbly testify—
We—who have the Souls—
Die oftener—Not so vitally—

Emily Dickinson

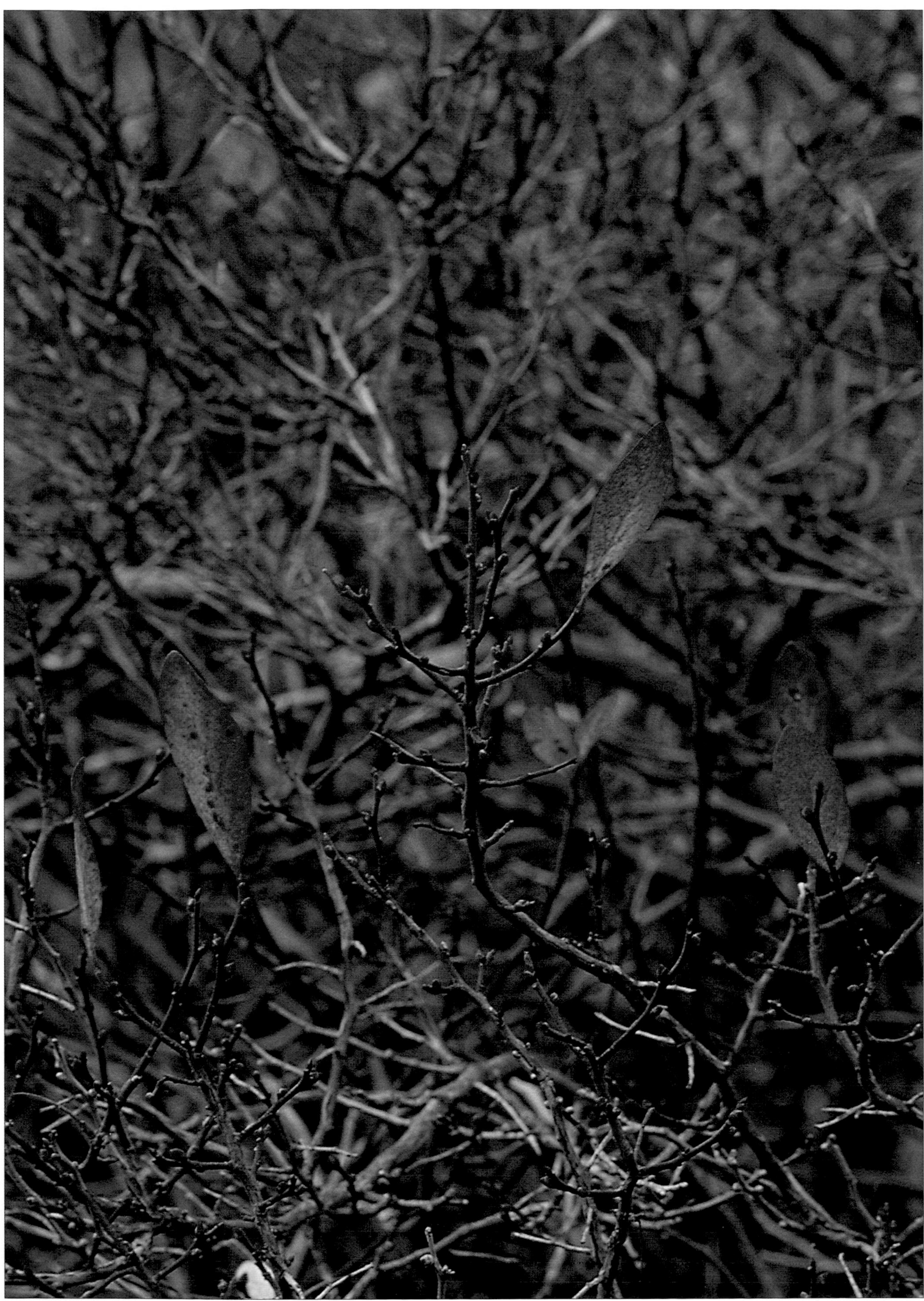

The Return

There was something about the coast town of Dunner which made it seem more attractive than other maritime villages of eastern Maine. Perhaps it was the simple fact of acquaintance with that neighborhood which made it so attaching, and gave such interest to the rocky shore and dark woods, and the few houses which seemed to be securely wedged and tree-nailed in among the ledges by the Landing. These houses made the most of their seaward view, and there was a gayety and determined floweriness in their bits of garden ground; the small-paned high windows in the peaks of their steep gables were like knowing eyes that watched the harbor and the far sea-line beyond, or looked northward all along the shore and its background of spruces and balsam firs. When one really knows a village like this and its surroundings, it is like becoming acquainted with a single person. The process of falling in love at first sight is as final as it is swift in such a case, but the growth of true friendship may be a lifelong affair.

From *The Country of the Pointed Firs*
Sarah Orne Jewett, 1896

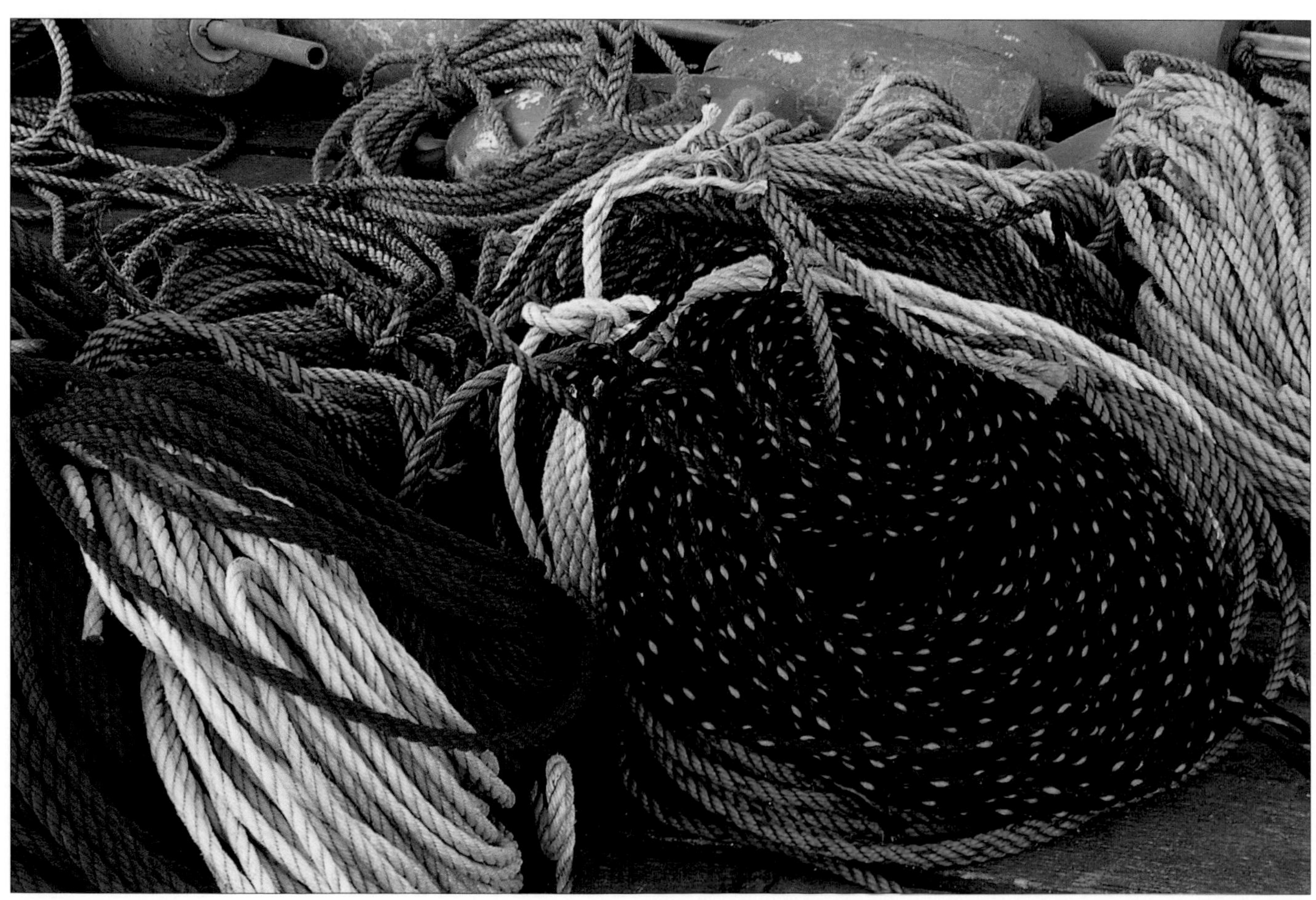

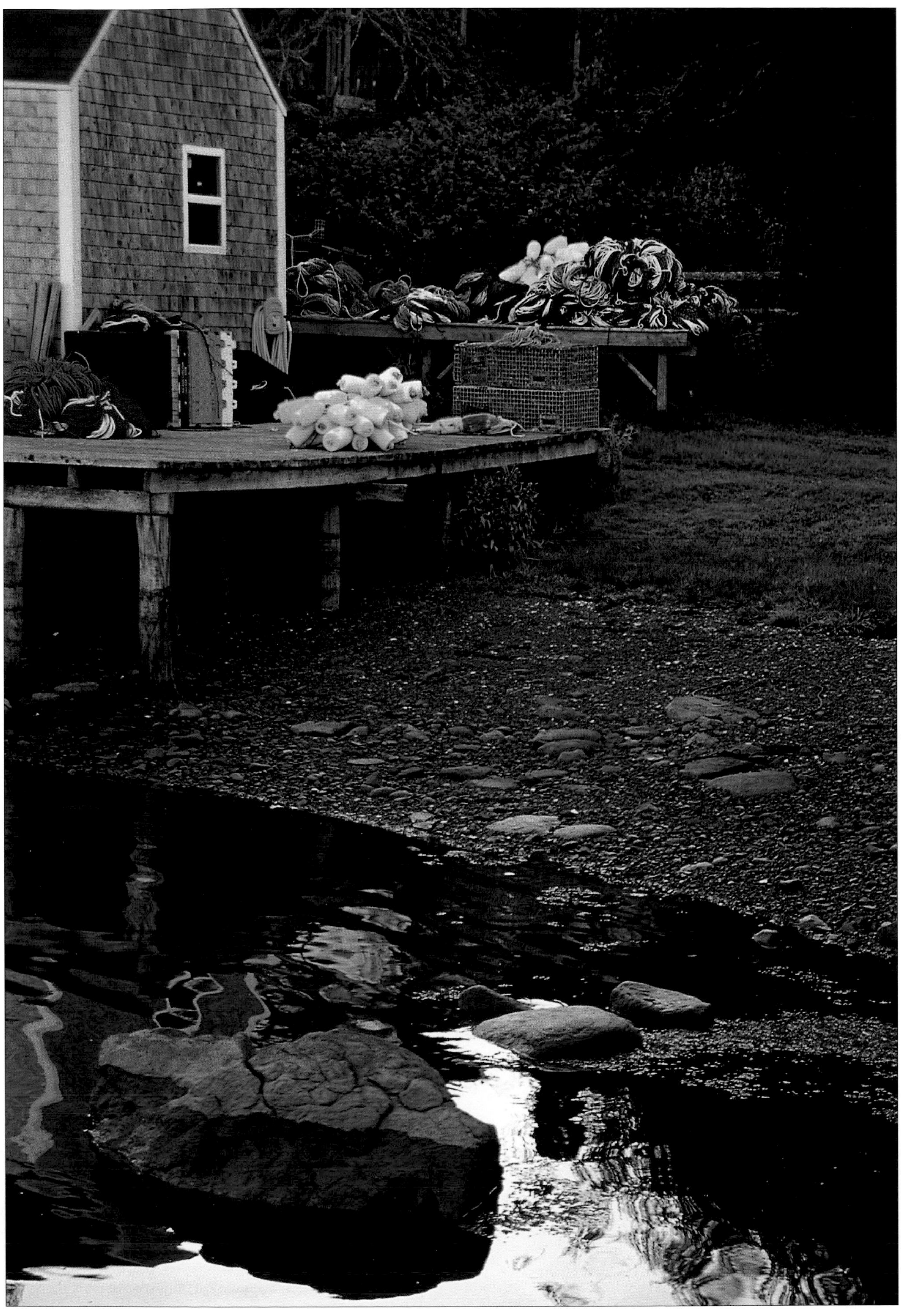

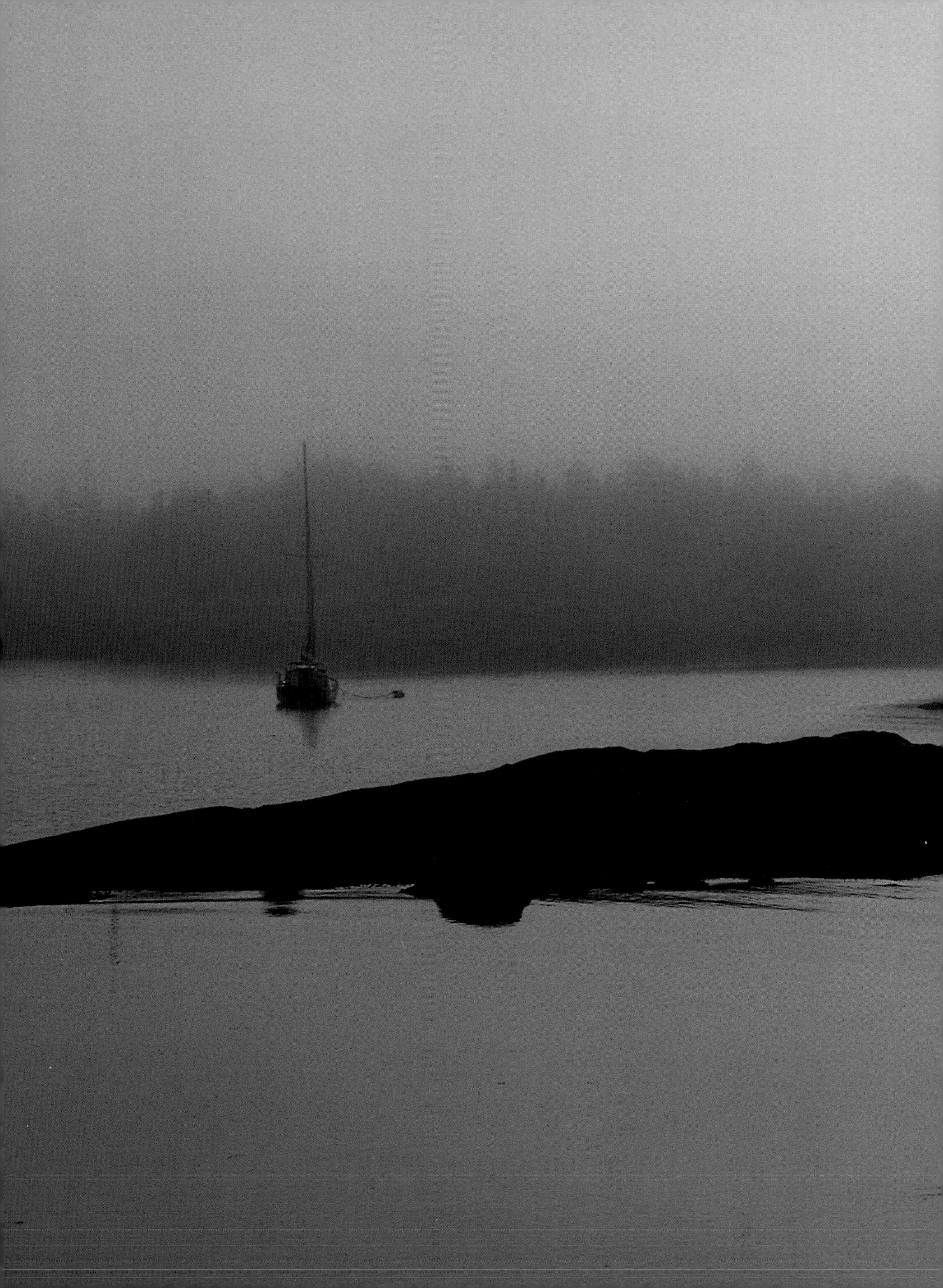

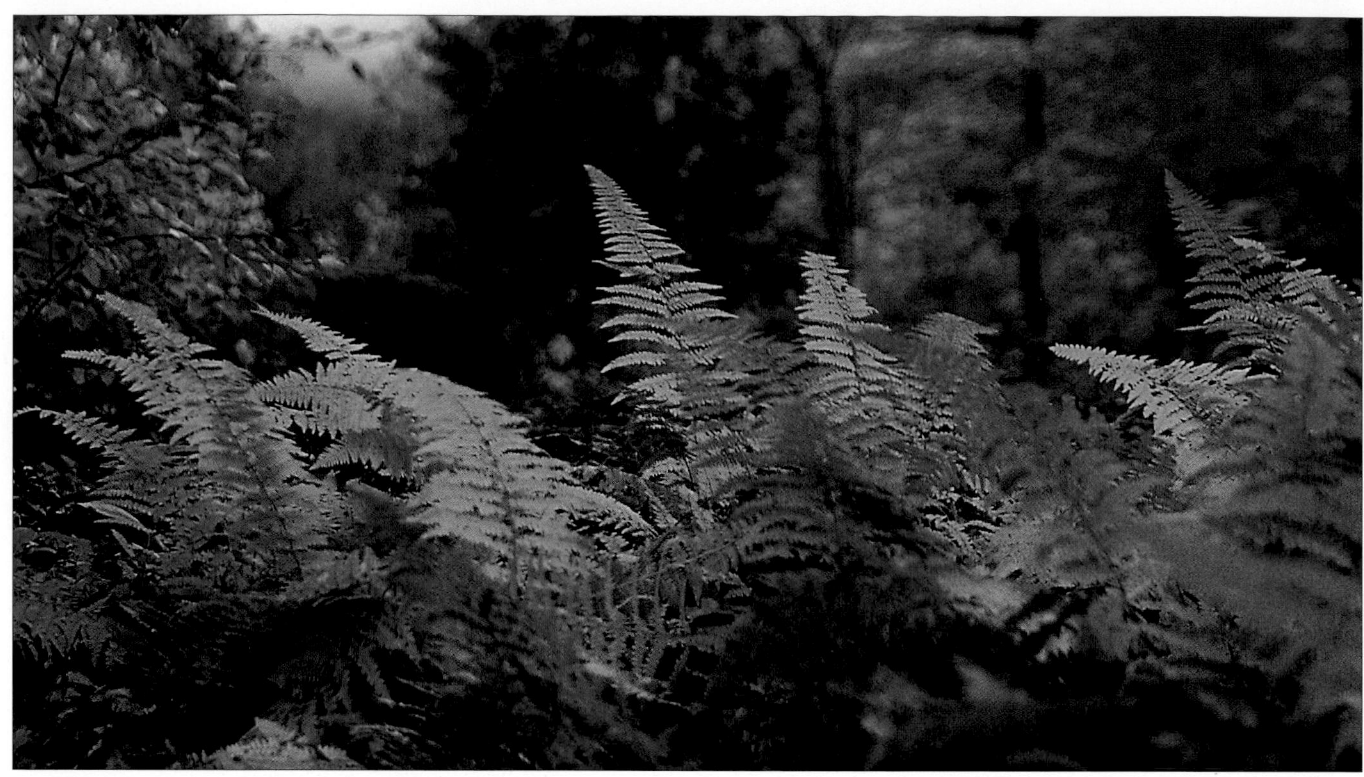

Sonnet VII

Dank fens of cedar, hemlock branches gray
With tress and trail of mosses wringing-wet
Beds of the black pitchpine in dead leaves set
Whose wasted red has wasted to white away,
Remnants of rain and droppings of decay,
Why hold ye so my heart, nor dimly let
Through your deep leaves the light of yesterday,
The faded glimmer of a sunshine set?
Is it that in your darkness, shut from strife,
The bread of tears becomes the bread of life?
Far from the roar of day, beneath your boughs
Fresh griefs beat tranquilly, and loves and vows
Grow green in your gray shadows, dearer far
Even than all lovely lights, and roses are?

Frederick Goddard Tuckerman, 1860

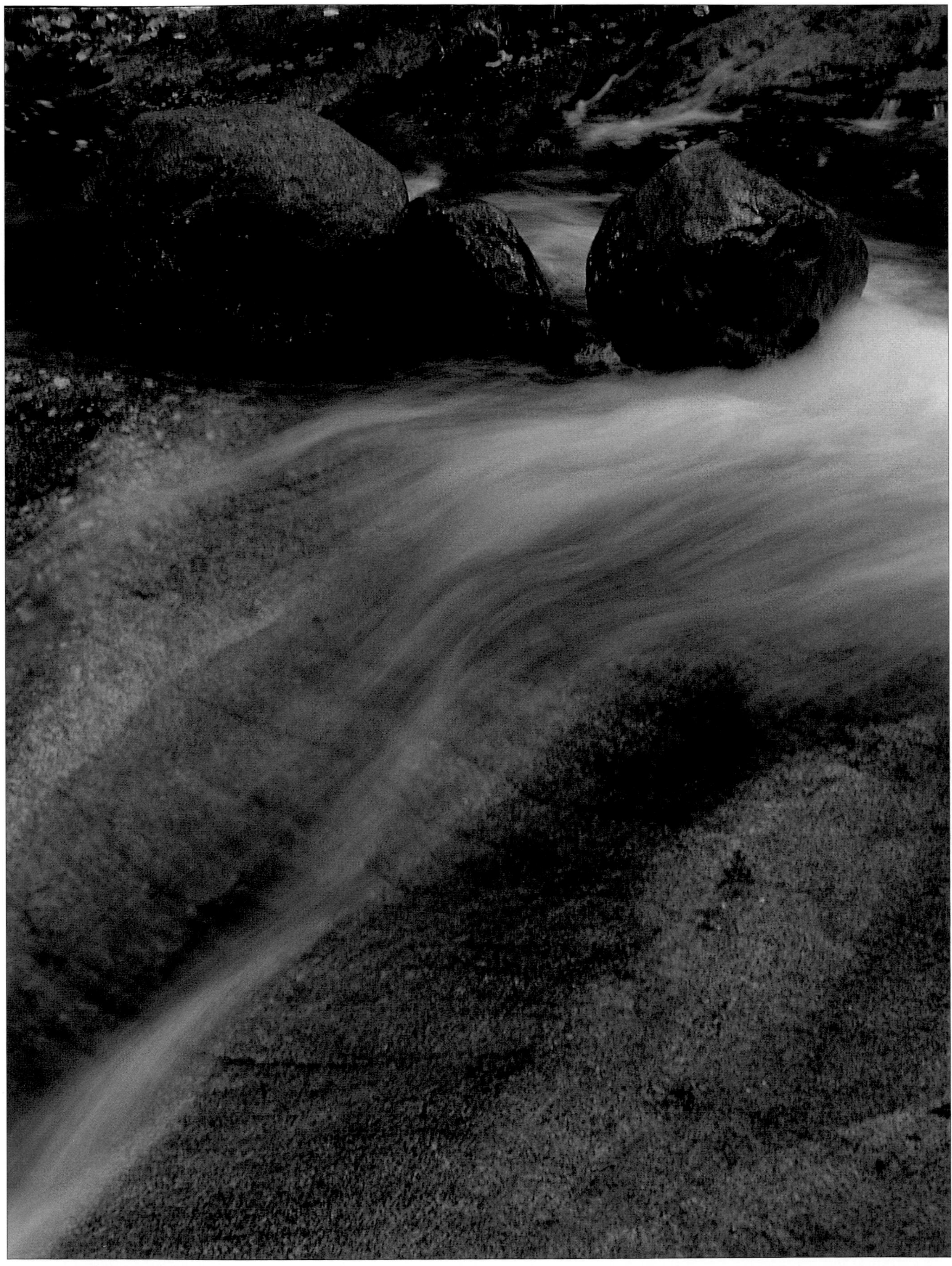

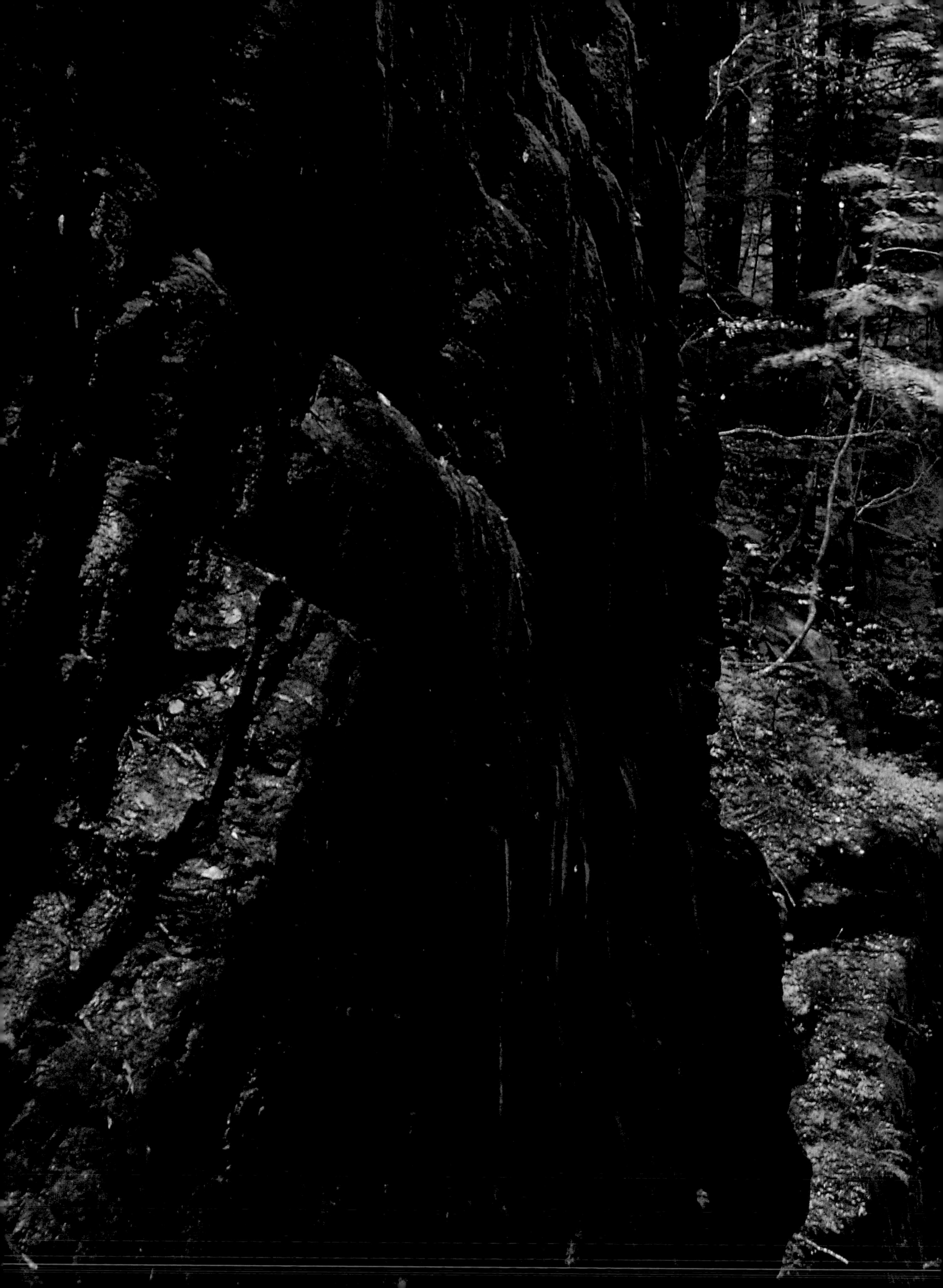

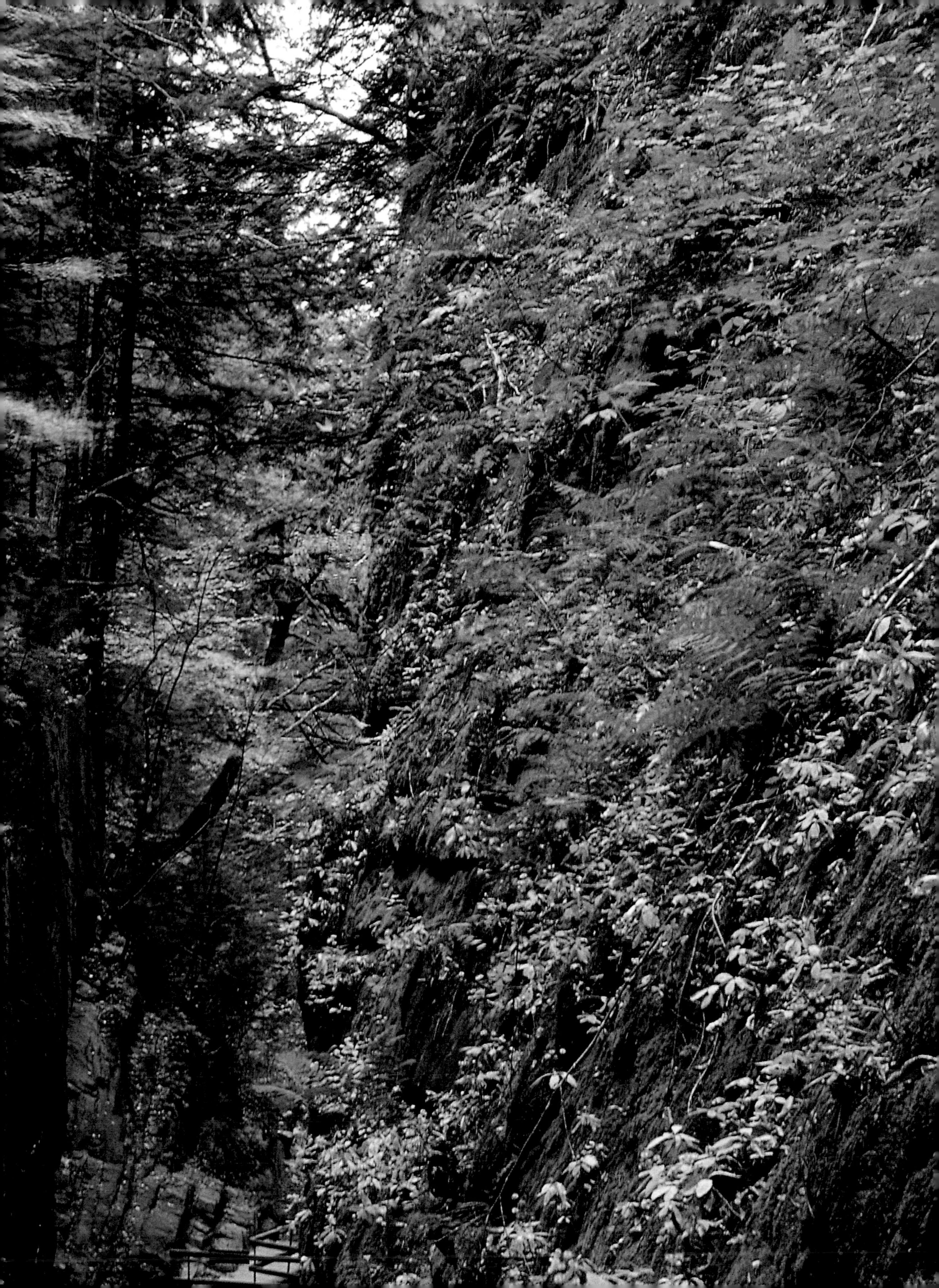

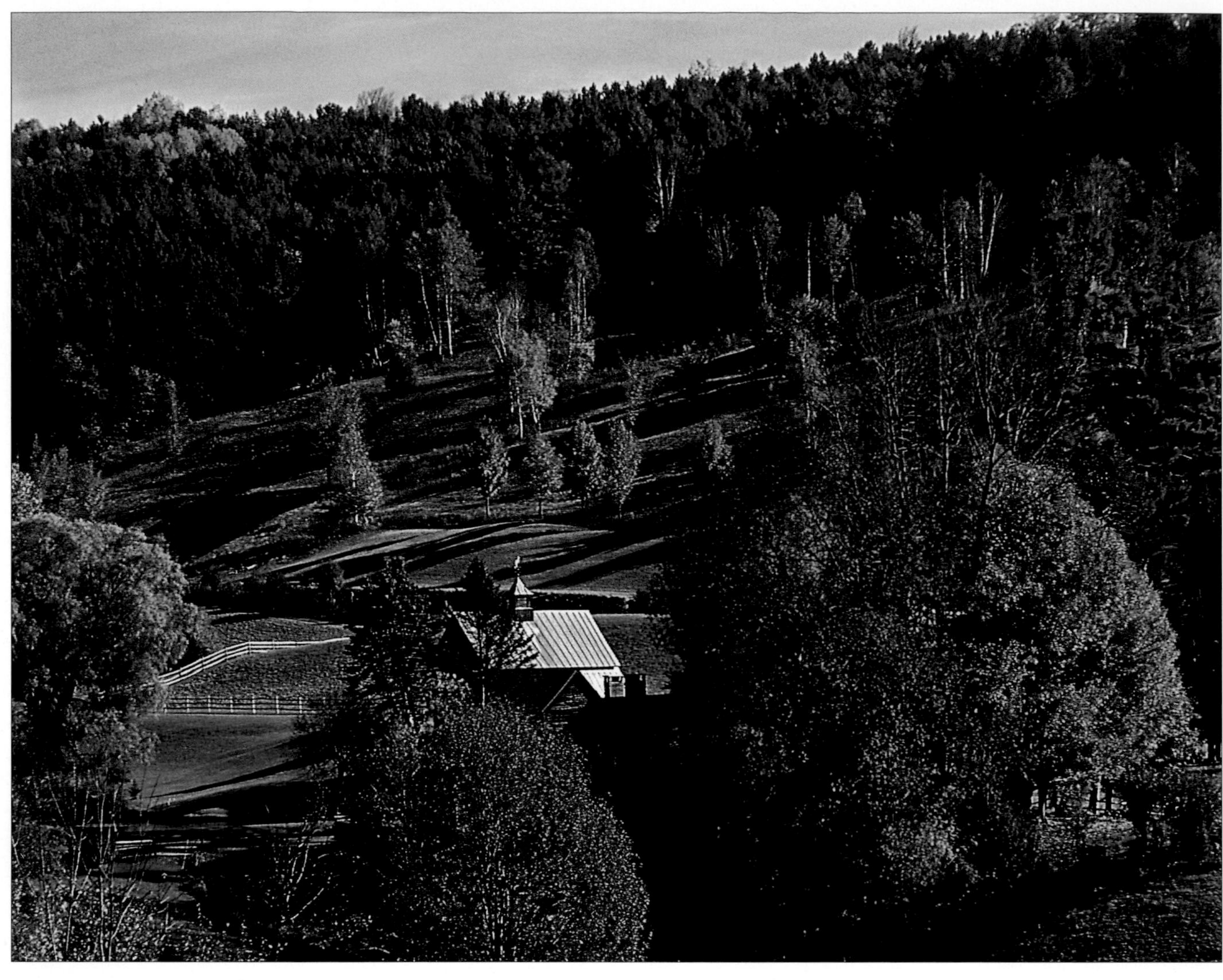

And the cost of a thing is the amount of what I will call life which is required to be exchanged for it, immediately or in the long run.

From *Walden*
Henry David Thoreau, 1854

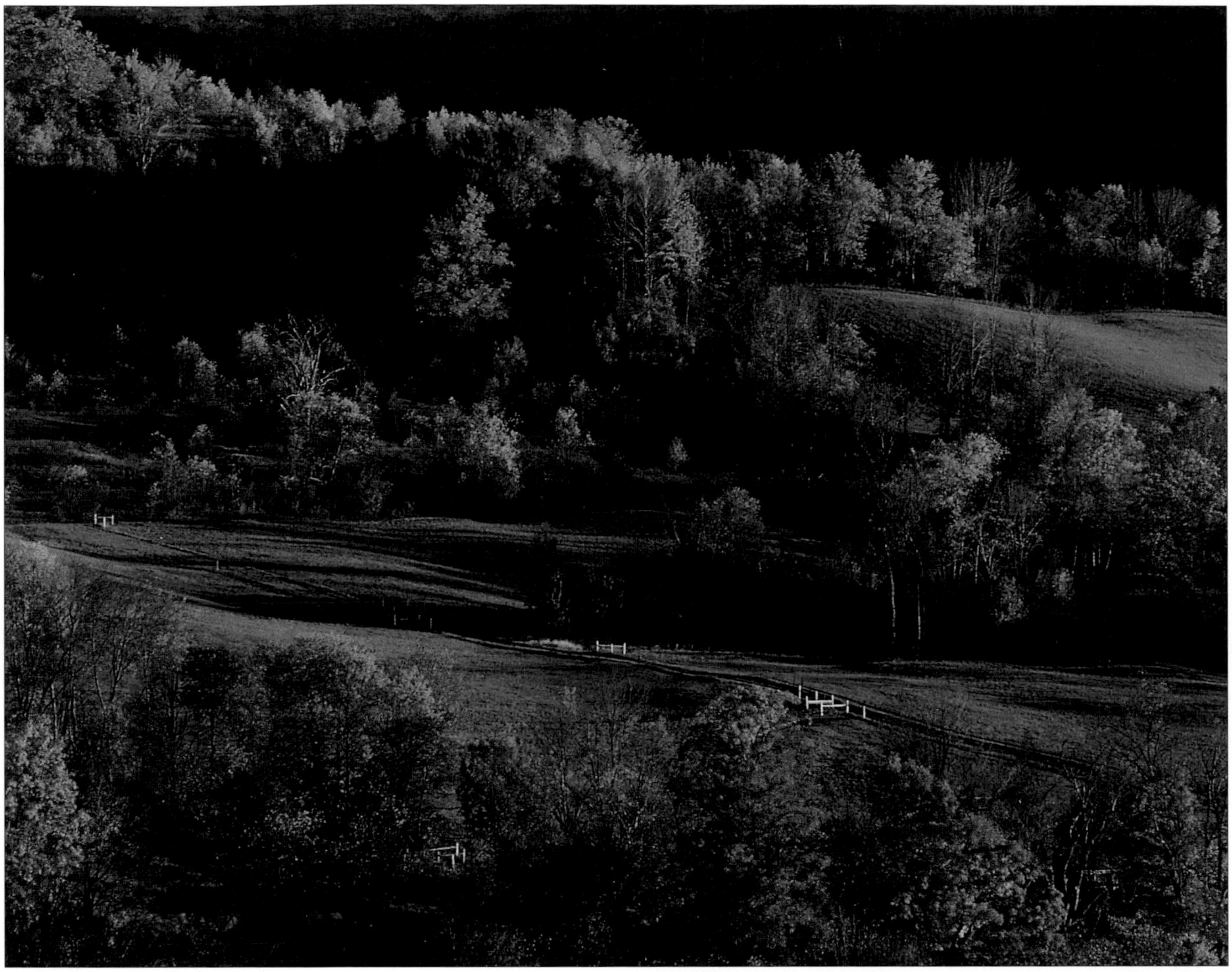

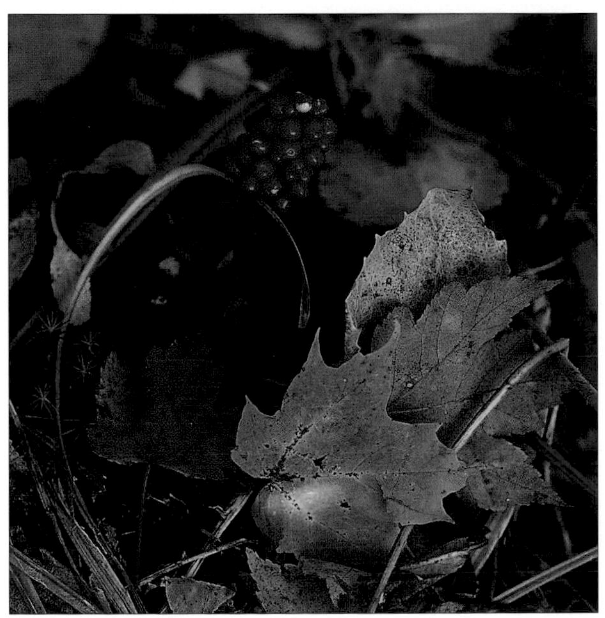

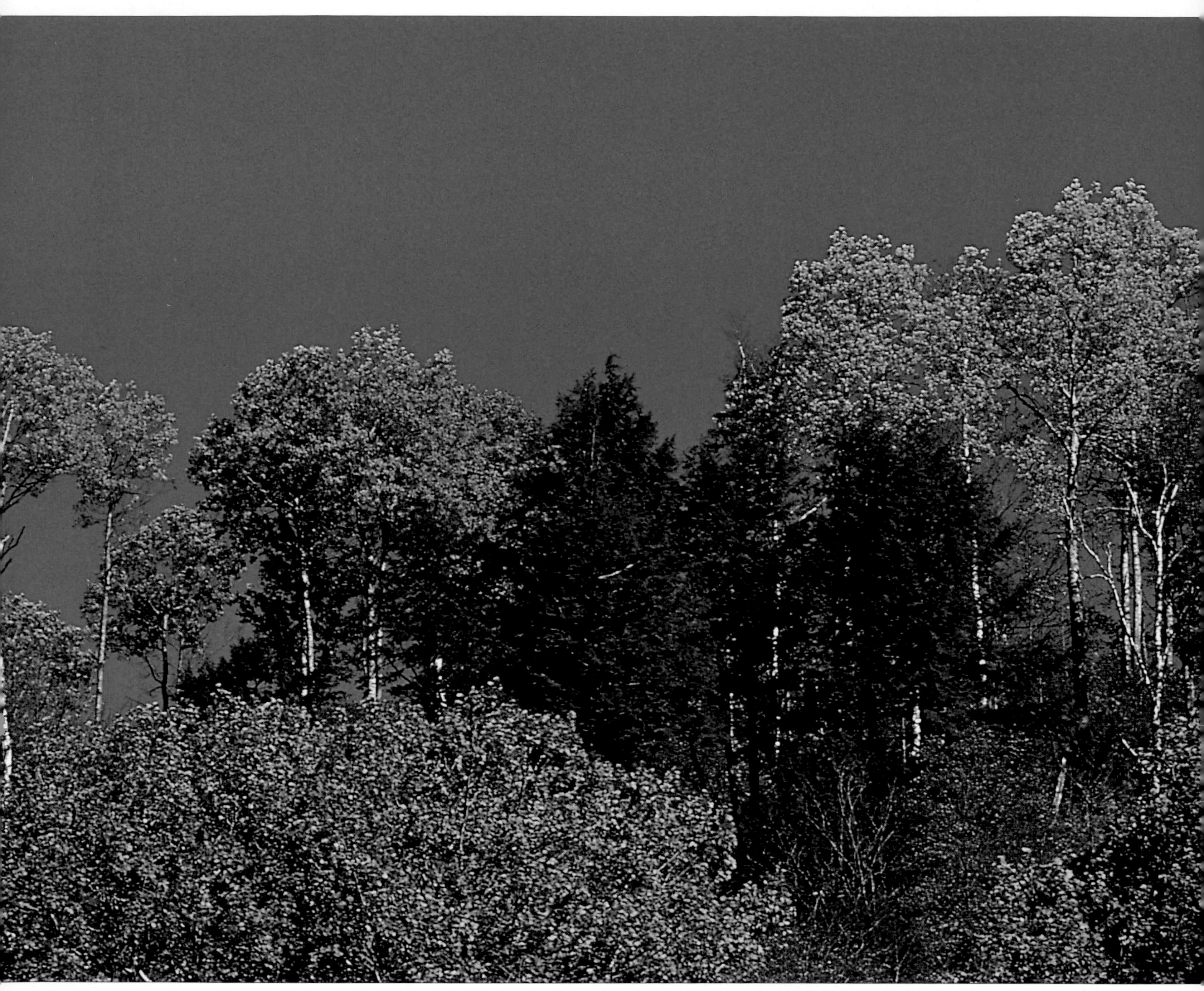

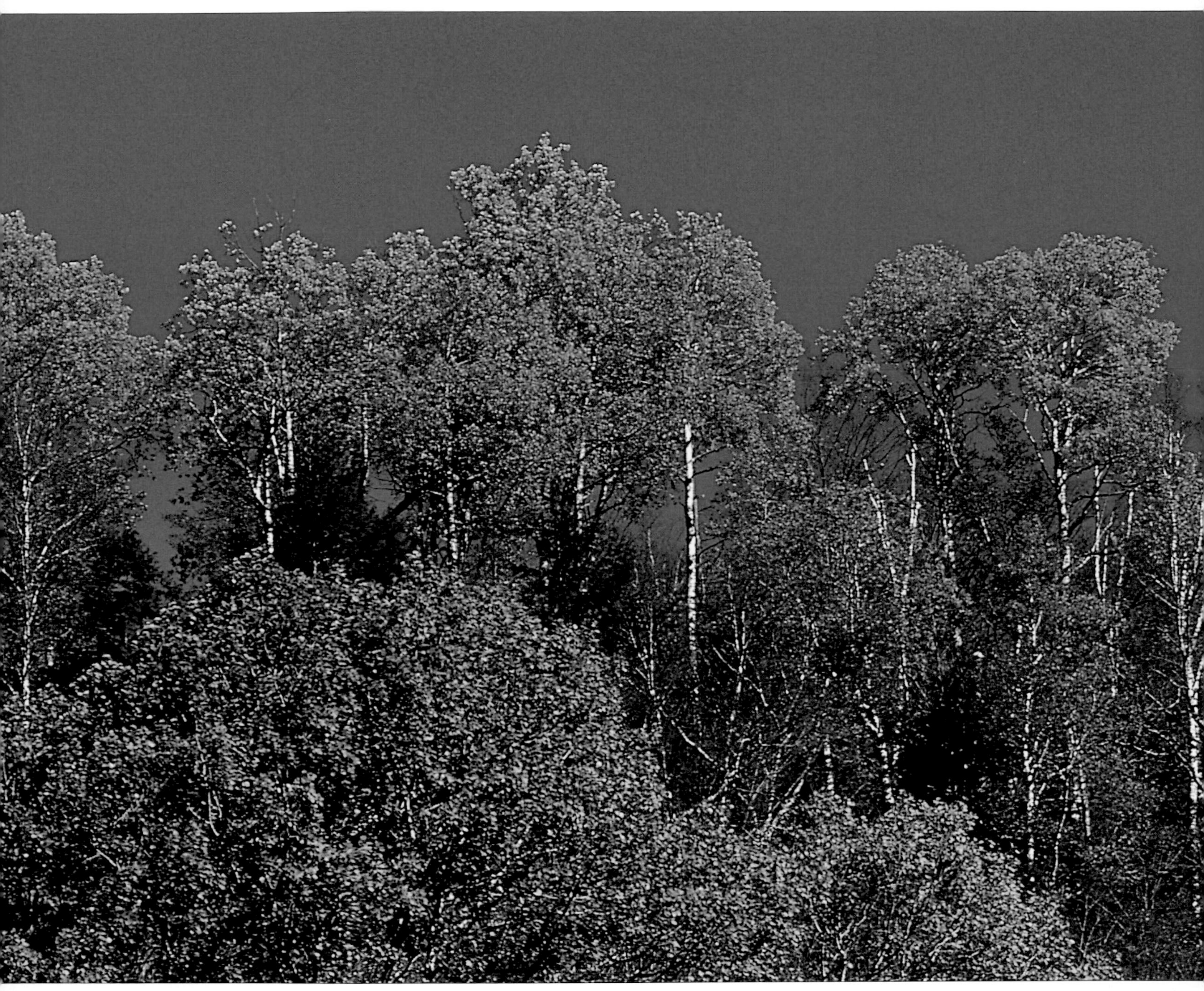

Our inventions are wont to be pretty toys, which distract our attention from serious things. They are but improved means to an unimproved end, an end which it was already but too easy to arrive at; as railroads lead to Boston or New York. We are in great haste to construct a magnetic telegraph from Maine to Texas; but Maine and Texas, it may be, have nothing important to communicate.

From *Walden*
Henry David Thoreau, 1854

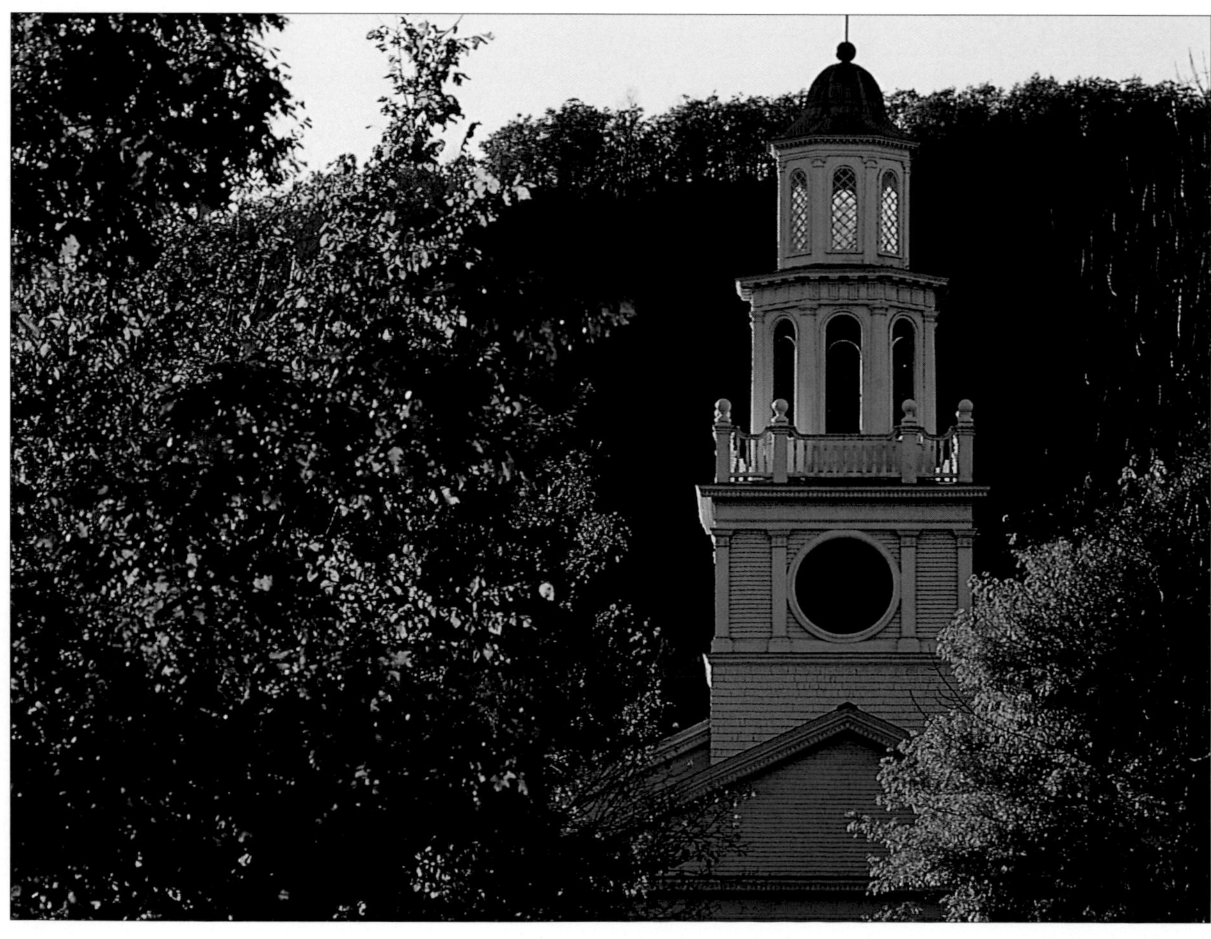

In such a day in September or October, Walden is a perfect forest mirror, set round with stones as precious to my eye as if fewer or rarer. Nothing so fair, so pure, and at the same time so large, as a lake, perchance, lies on the surface of the earth. Sky water. It needs no fence. Nations come and go defiling it. It is a mirror which no stone can crack, whose quicksilver will never wear off, whose gilding Nature continually repairs; no storms, no dust, can dim its surface ever fresh;—a mirror in which all impurity presented to it sinks, swept and dusted by the sun's hazy brush,—this the light dust-cloth,—which retains no breath that is breathed on it, but send its own to float as clouds high above its surface, and be reflected in its bosom still.

From *Walden*
Henry David Thoreau, 1854

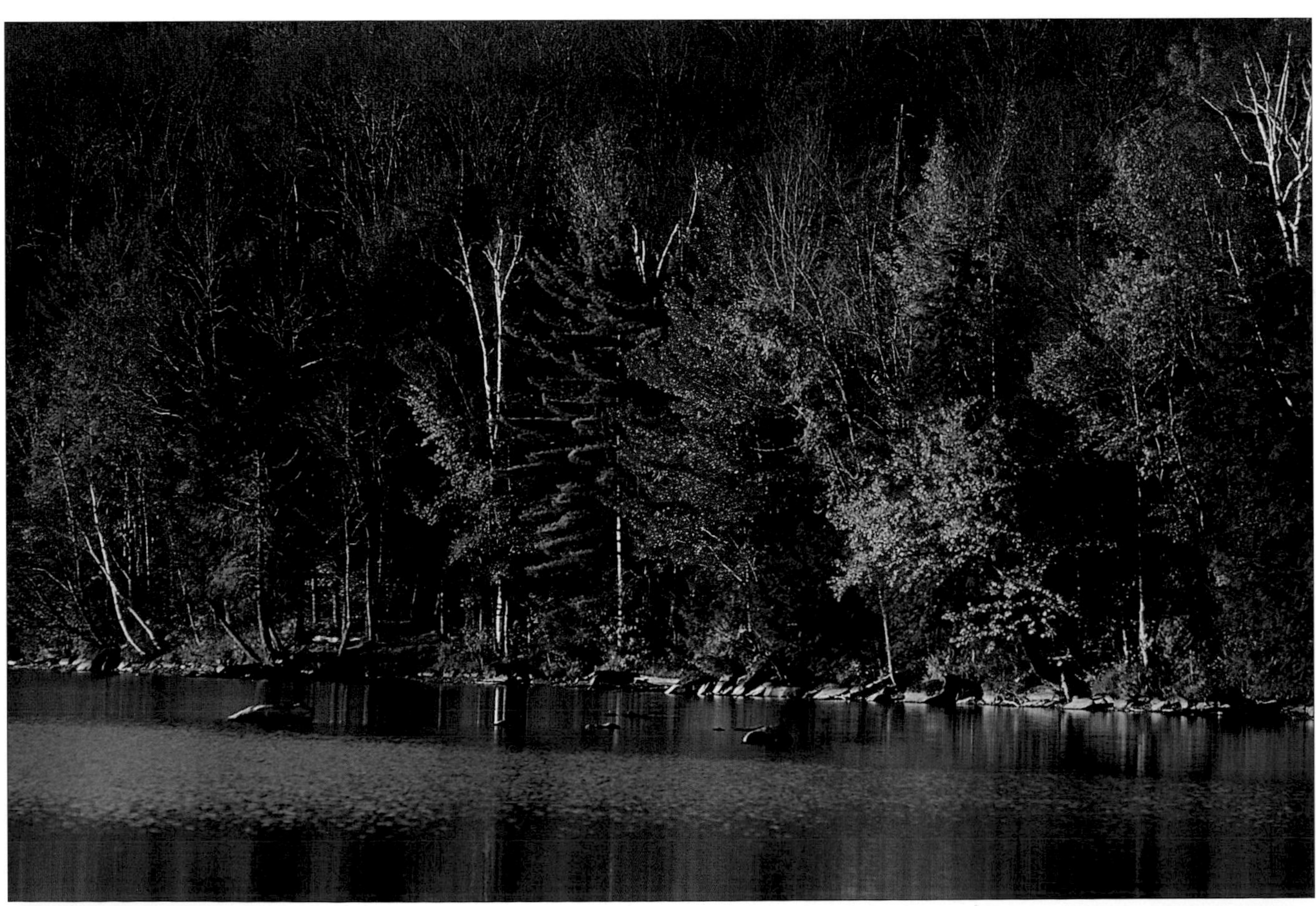

I love a broad margin to my life. Sometimes, in a summer morning, having taken my accustomed bath, I sat in my sunny doorway from sunrise till noon, rapt in a revery, amidst the pines and hickories and sumachs, in undisturbed solitude and stillness, while the birds sang around or flitted noiseless through the house, until by the sun falling in at my west window, or the noise of some traveller's wagon on the distant highway, I was reminded of the lapse of time. I grew in those seasons like corn in the night, and they were far better than any work of the hands would have been. They were not time subtracted from my life, but so much over and above my usual allowance.

My days were not days of the week, bearing the stamp of any heathen deity, nor were they minced into hours and fretted by the ticking of a clock; for I lived like the Puri Indians, of whom it is said that "for yesterday, to-day, and to-morrow they have only one word, and they express the variety of meaning by pointing backward for yesterday, forward for to-morrow, and overhead for the passing day." This was sheer idleness to my fellow-townsmen no doubt; but if the birds and flowers had tried me by their standard, I should not have been found wanting. A man must find his occasions in himself, it is true. The natural day is very calm, and will hardly reprove his indolence.

From *Walden*
Henry David Thoreau, 1854

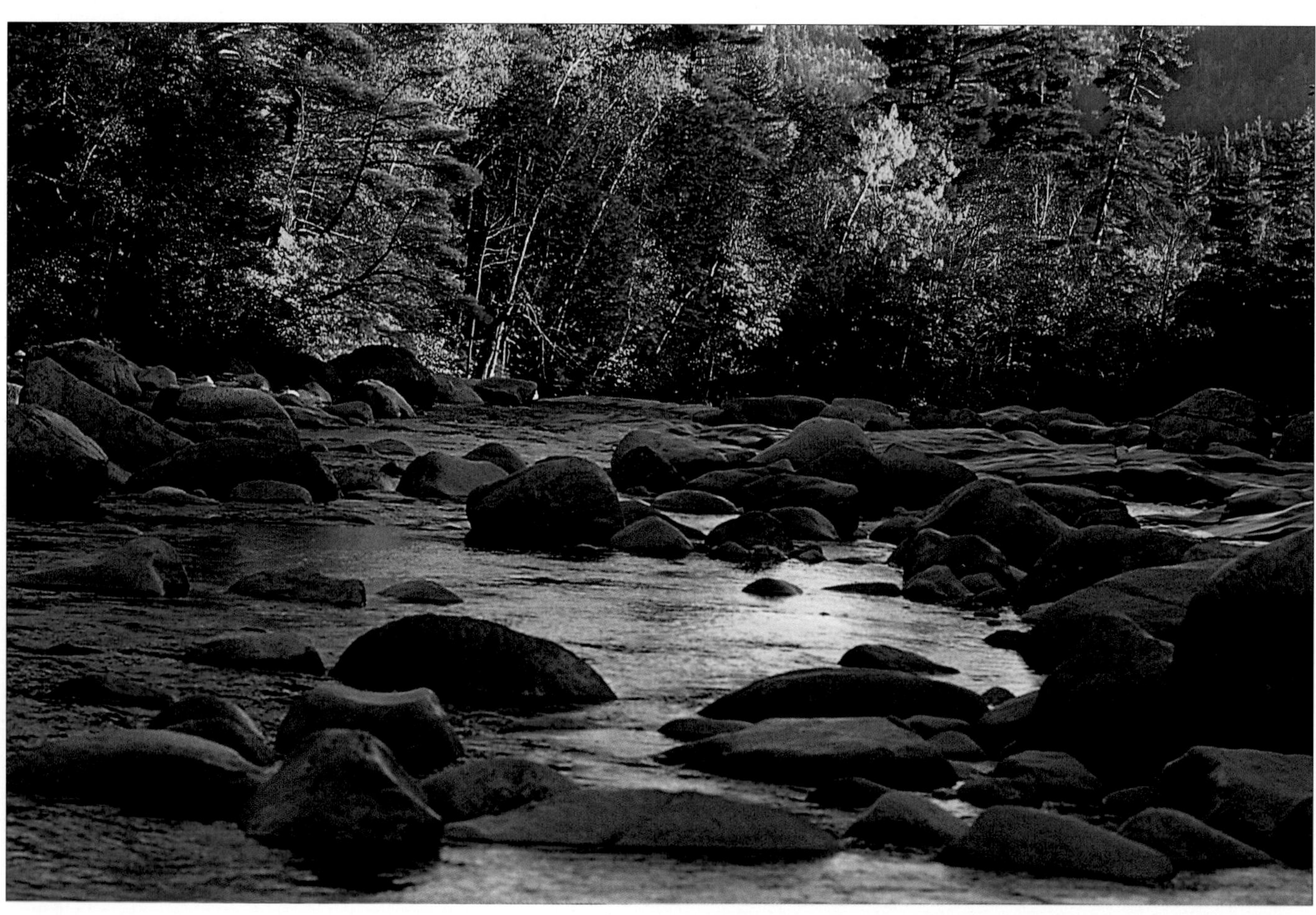

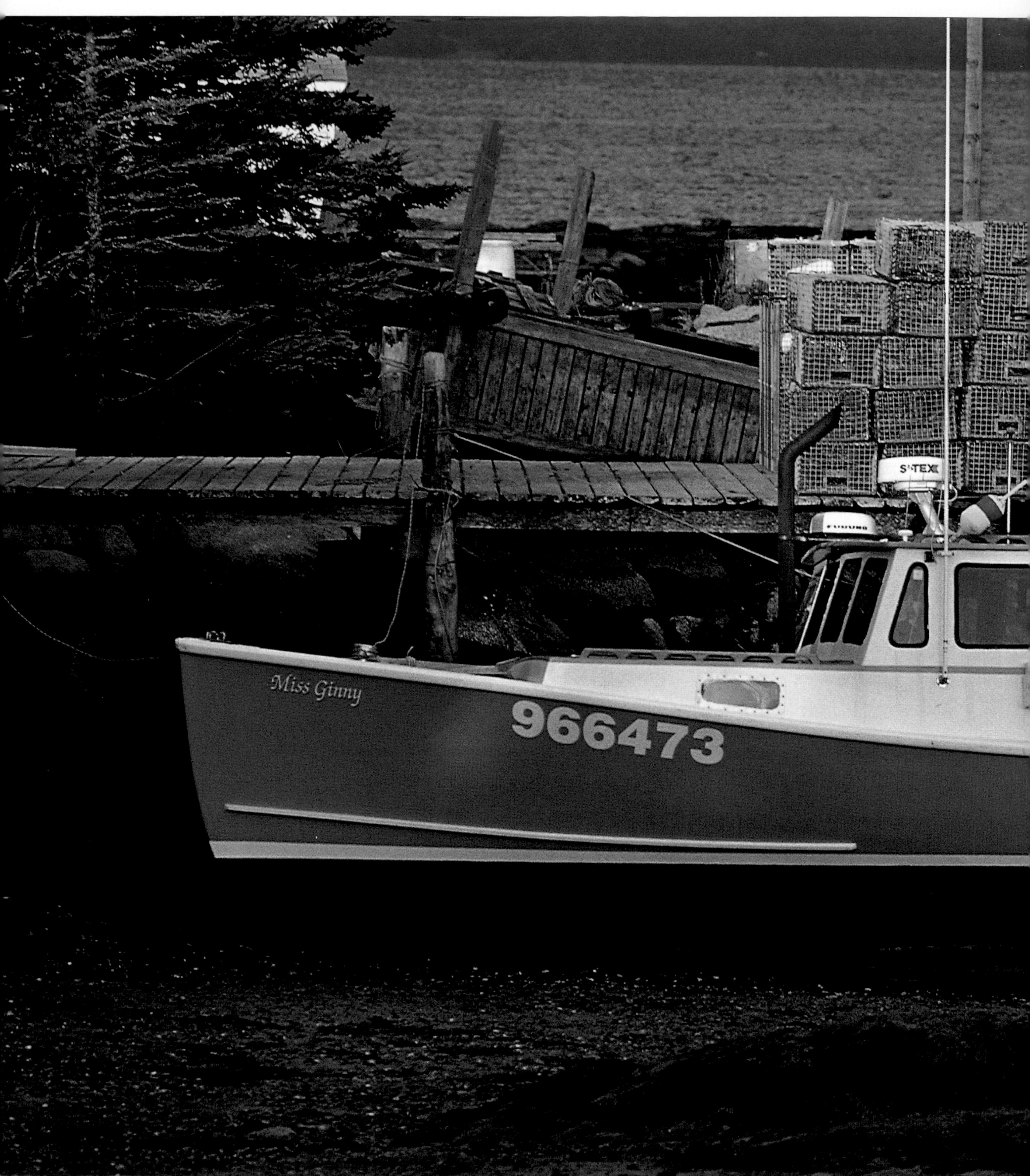
Miss Ginny
966473

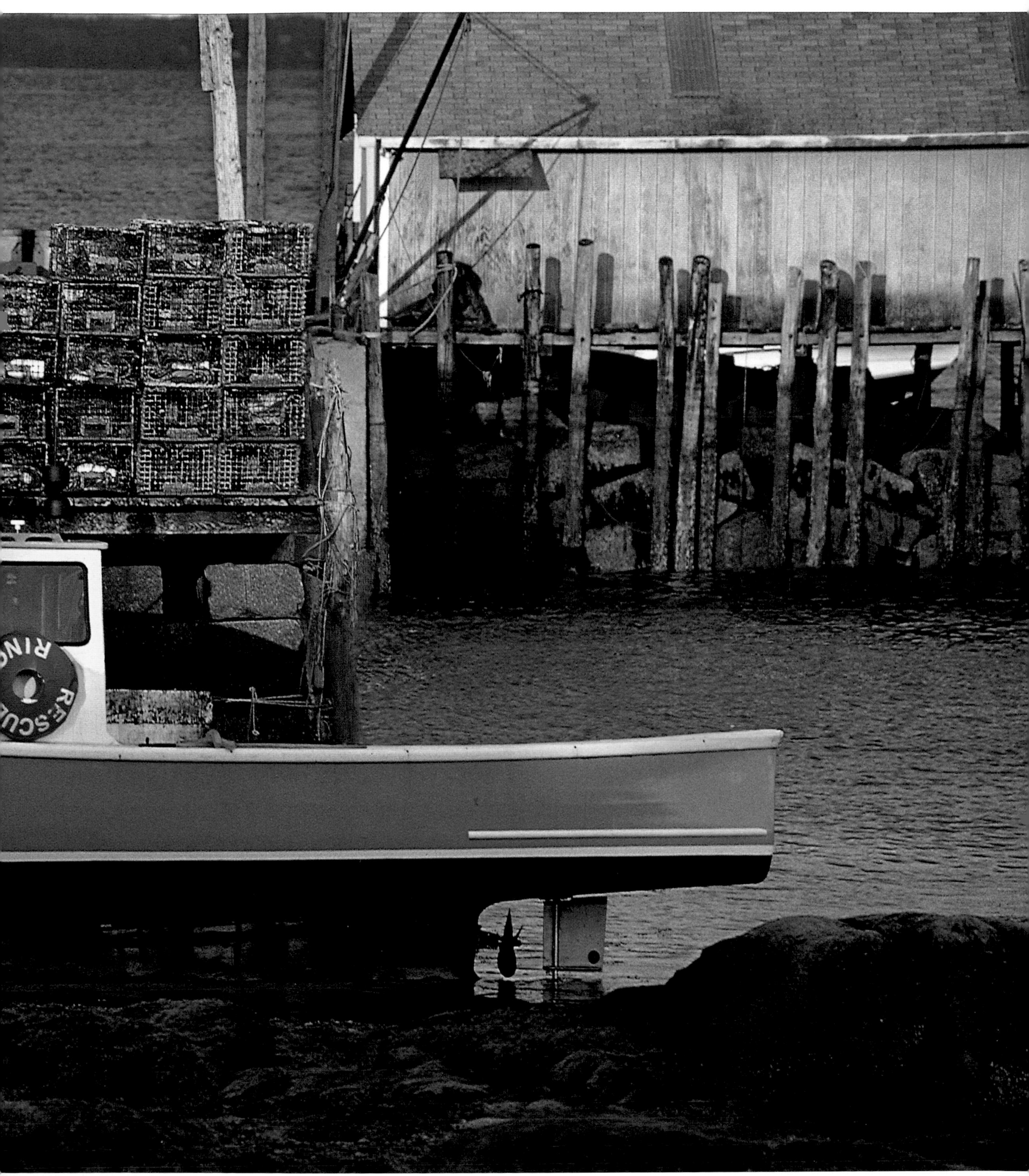

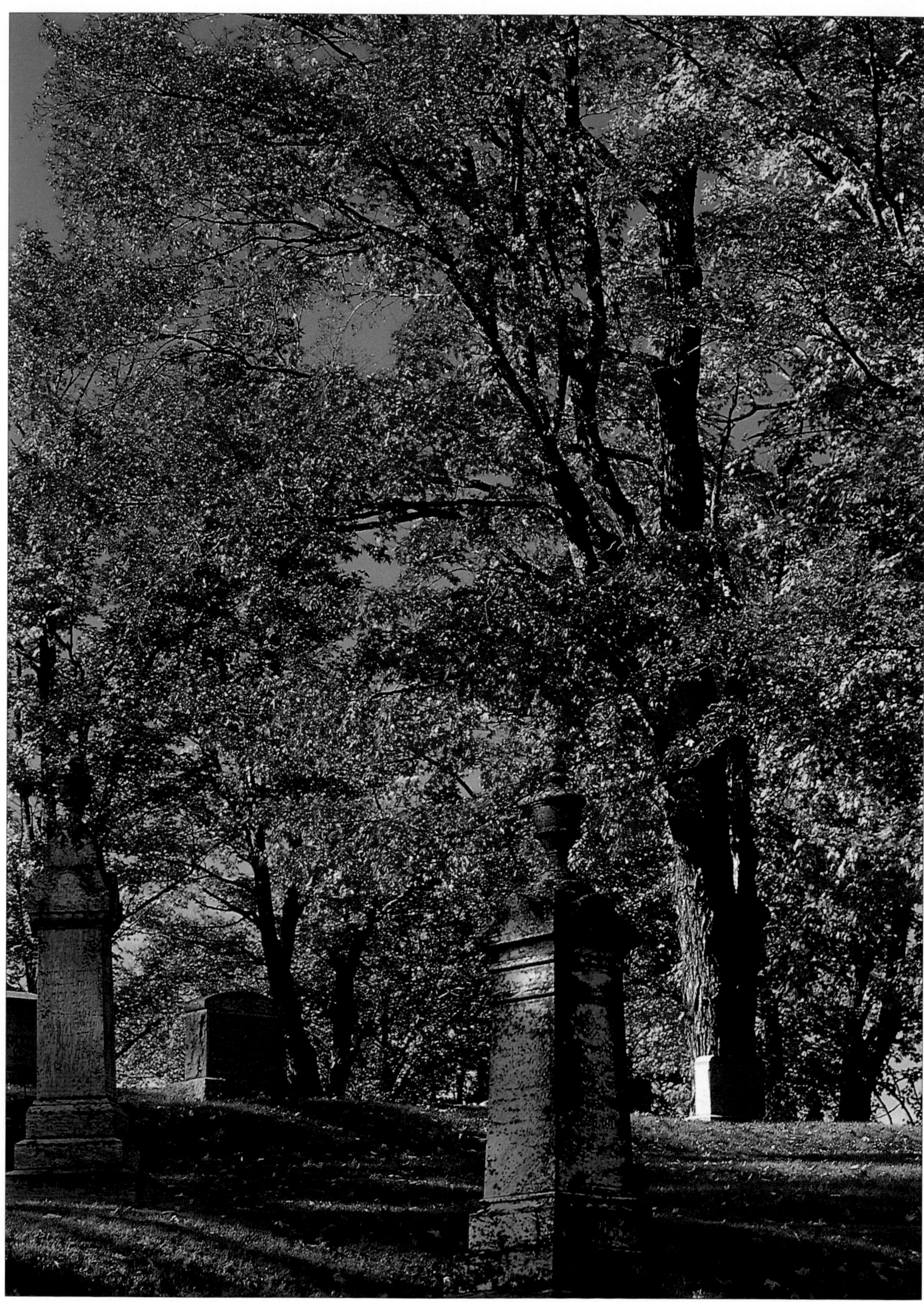

I died for Beauty—but was scarce
Adjusted in the Tomb
When One who died for Truth, was lain
In an adjoining Room—

He questioned softly "Why I failed"?
"For Beauty," I replied—
"And I—for Truth—Themself are One—
We Brethren are," He said—

And so, as Kinsmen met a Night—
We talked between the Rooms—
Until the Moss had reached our lips—
And covered up—our names—

Emily Dickinson, 1862

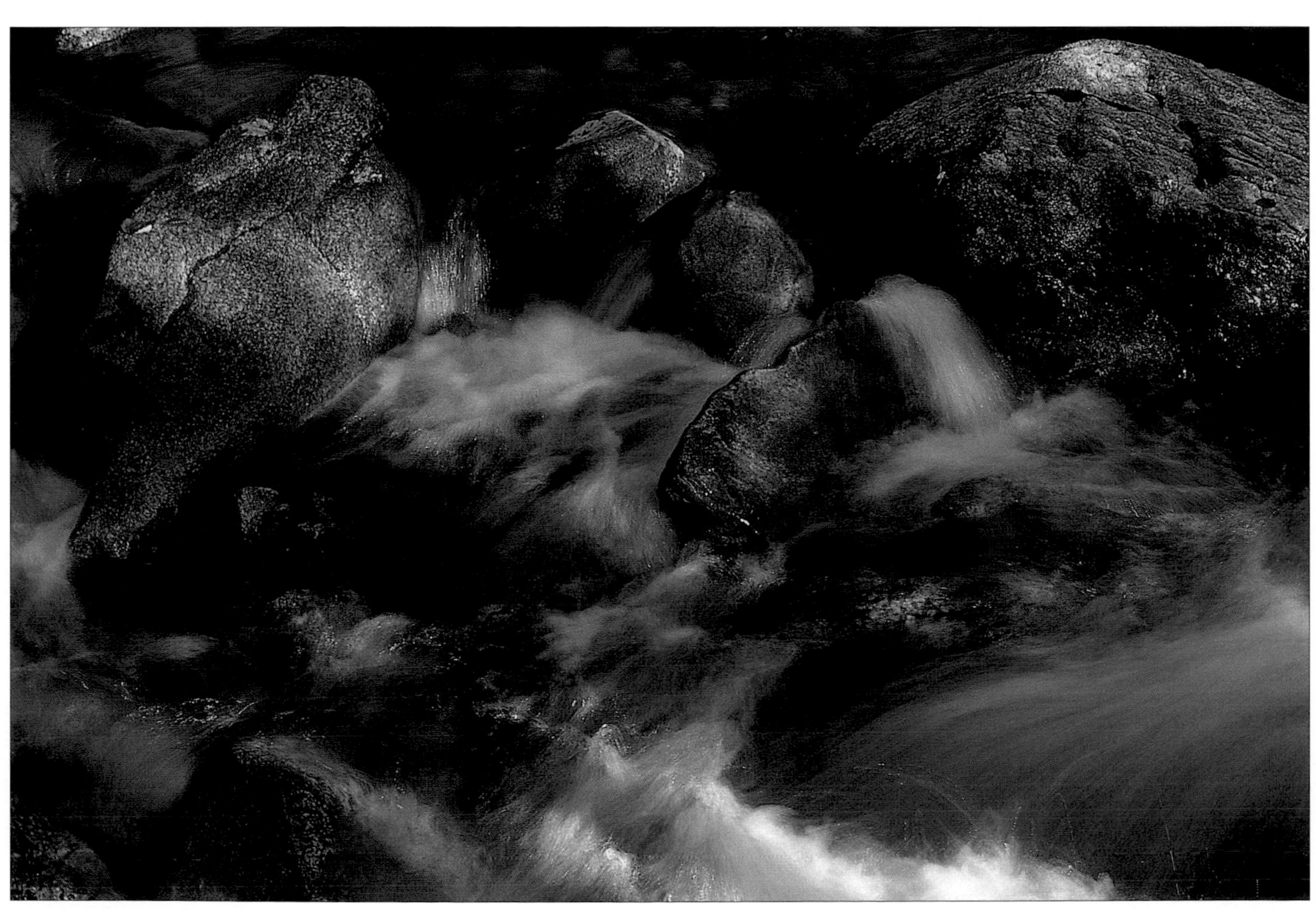

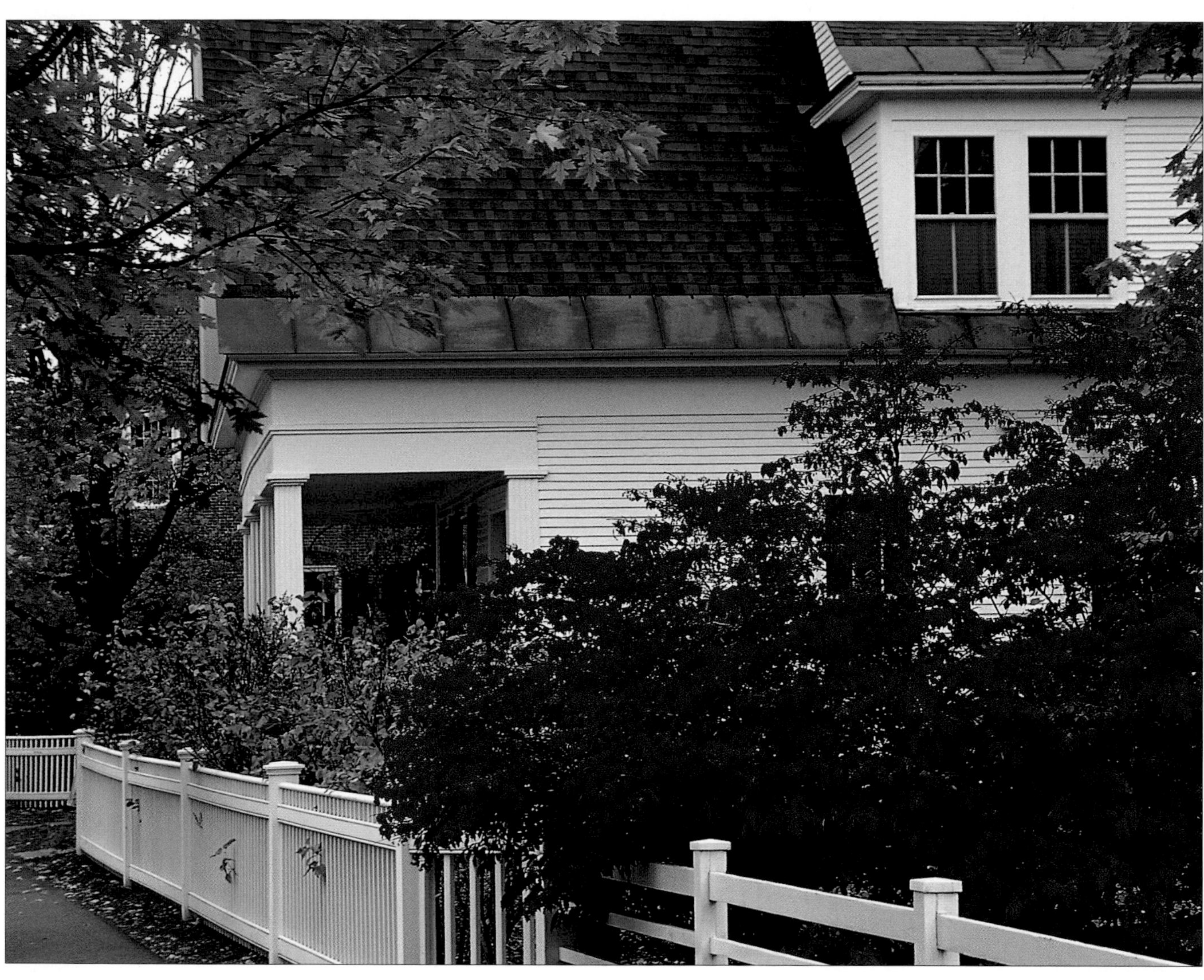

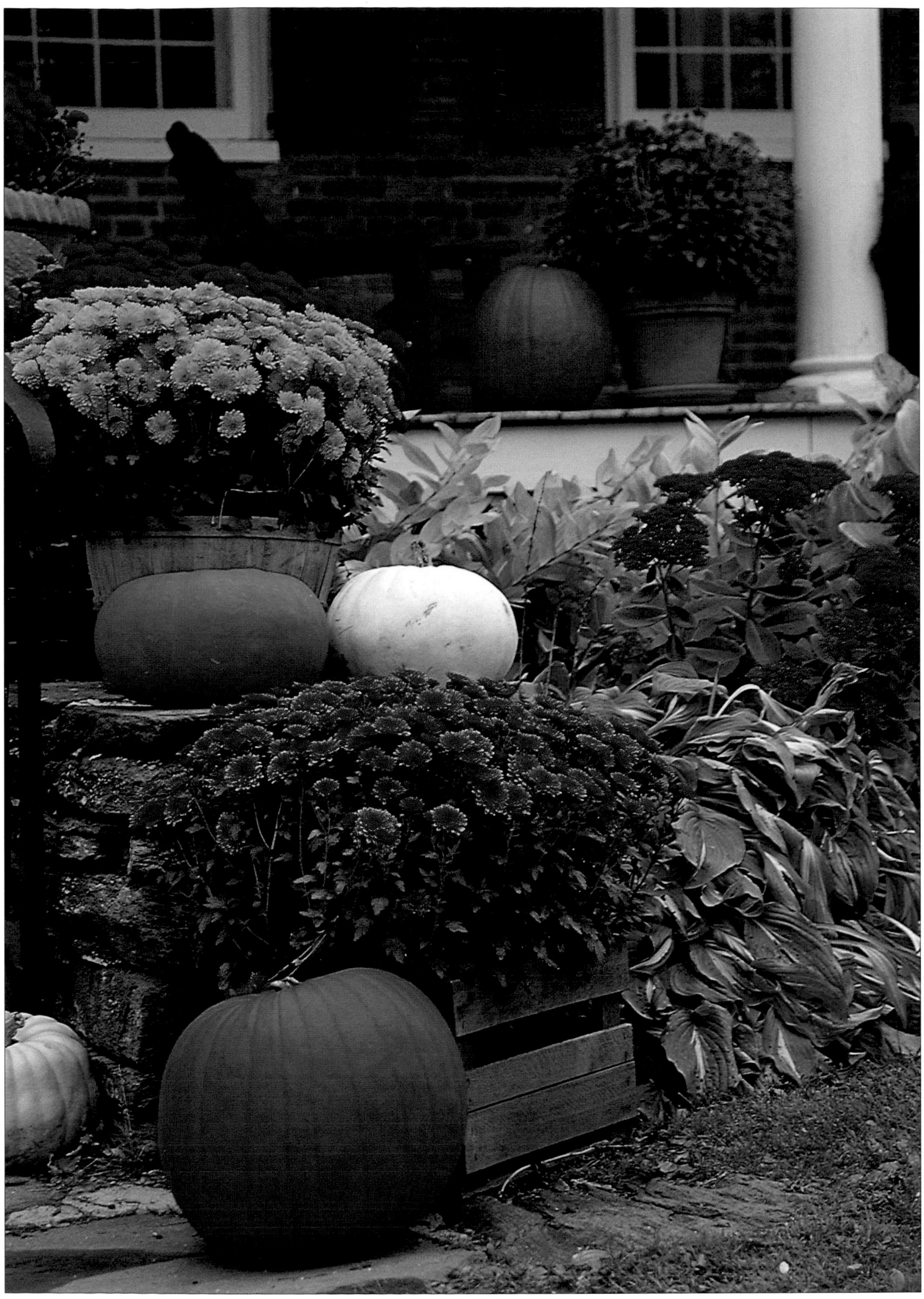

Luke Havergal

Go to the western gate, Luke Havergal,
There where the vines cling crimson on the wall,
And in the twilight wait for what will come.
The leaves will whisper there of her, and some,
Like flying words, will strike you as they fall;
But go, and if you listen she will call.
Go to the western gate, Luke Havergal—
Luke Havergal.

No, there is not a dawn in eastern skies
To rift the fiery night that's in your eyes;
But there, where western glooms are gathering,
The dark will end the dark, if anything:
God slays Himself with every leaf that flies,
And hell is more than half of paradise.
No, there is not a dawn in eastern skies—
In eastern skies.

Out of a grave I come to tell you this,
Out of a grave I come to quench the kiss
That flames upon your forehead with a glow
That blinds you to the way that you must go.
Yes, there is yet one way to where she is,
Bitter, but one that faith may never miss.
Out of a grave I come to tell you this—
To tell you this.

There is the western gate, Luke Havergal,
There are the crimson leaves upon the wall.
Go, for the winds are tearing them away,—
Nor think to riddle the dead words they say,
Nor any more to feel them as they fall;
But go, and if you trust her she will call.
There is the western gate, Luke Havergal—
Luke Havergal.

Edwin Arlington Robinson, 1896

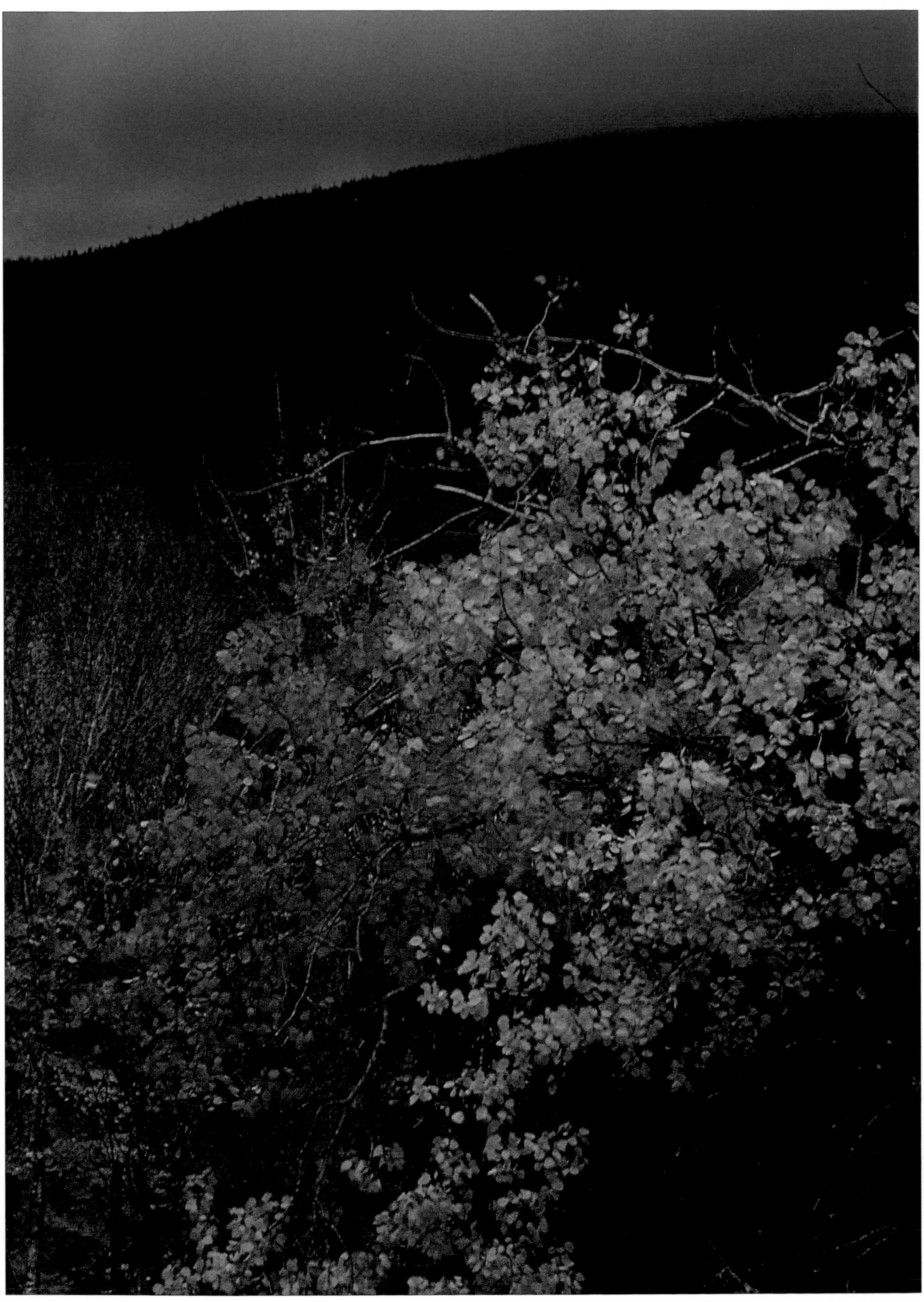

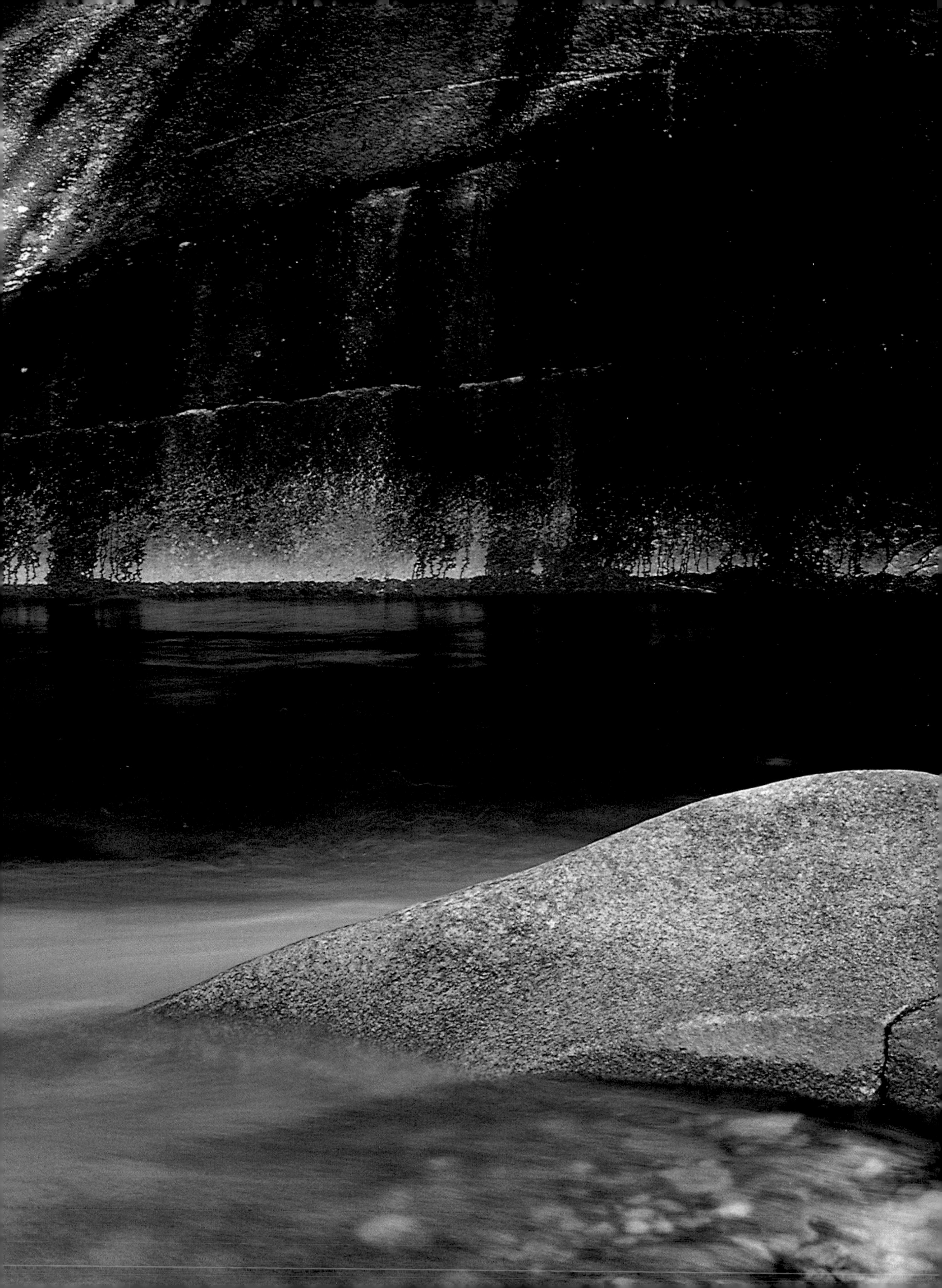

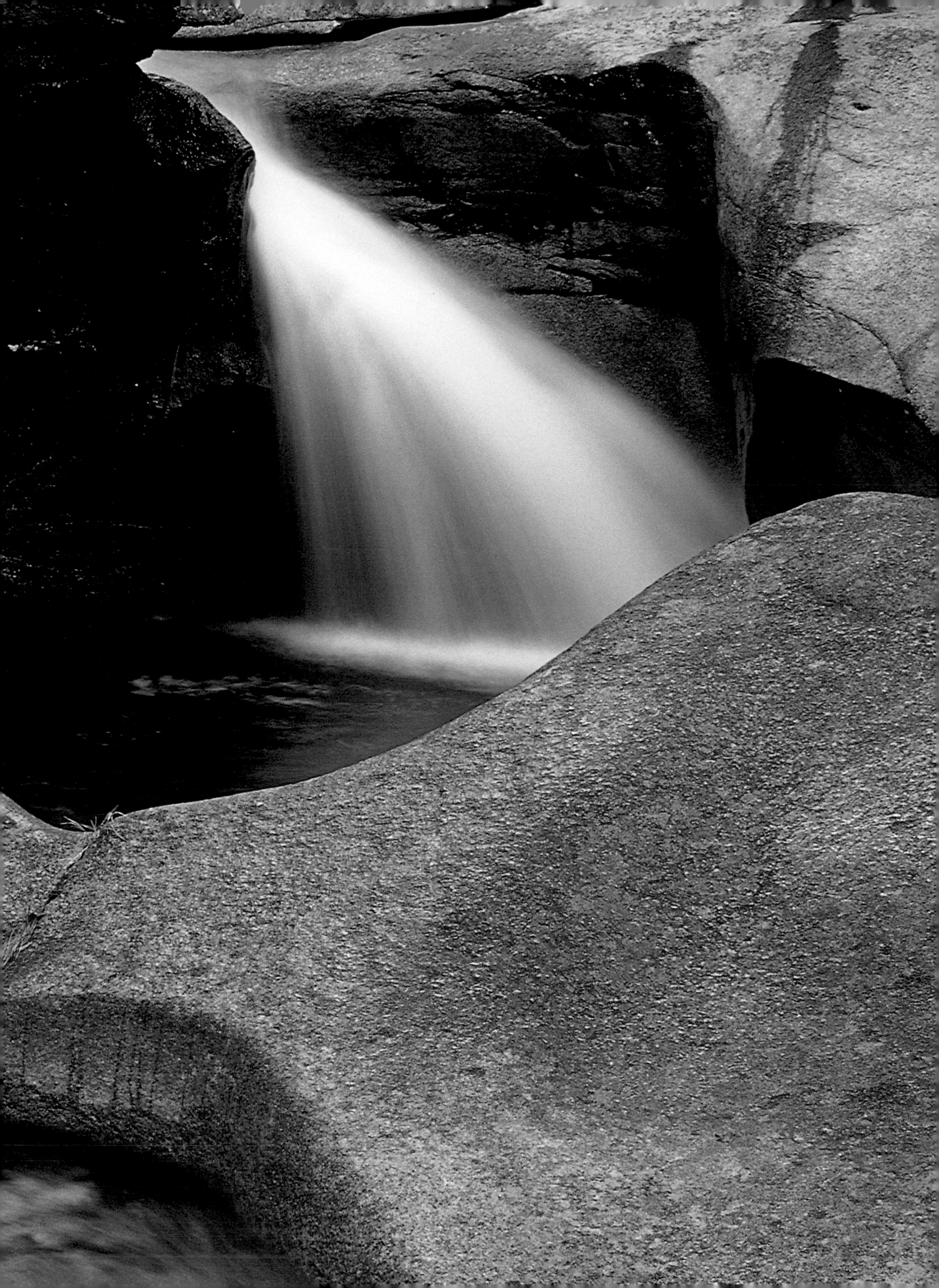

Along Shore

Mr. Elijah Tilley appeared to regard a stranger with scornful indifference. You might see him standing on the pebble beach or in a fish-house doorway, but when you came nearer he was gone. He was one of the small company of elderly, gaunt-shaped great fisherman whom I used to like to see leading up a deep-laden boat by the head, as if it were a horse, from the water's edge to the steep slope of the pebble beach. There were four of these large old men at the Landing, who were the survivors of an earlier and more vigorous generation. There was an alliance and understanding between them, so close that it was apparently speechless. They gave much time to watching one another's boats go out or come in; they lent a ready hand at tending one another's lobster traps in rough weather; they helped to clean the fish, or to sliver porgies for the trawls, as if they were in close partnership; and when a boat came in from deep-sea fishing they were never too far out of the way, and hastened to help carry it ashore, two by two, splashing alongside, or holding its steady head, as if it were a willful sea colt.

"Come right in an' set down. Come in an' rest ye," he exclaimed, and led the way into his comfortable kitchen. The sunshine poured in at the two further windows, and a cat was curled up sound asleep on the table that stood between them. There was a new-looking light oilcloth of a tiled pattern on the floor, and a crockery teapot, large for a household of only one person, stood on the bright stove. I ventured to say that somebody must be a very good housekeeper.

"That 's me," acknowledged the old fisherman with frankness. "There ain't nobody here but me. I try to keep things looking right, same 's poor dear left 'em. You set down here in this chair, then you can look off an' see the water. None on 'em thought I was goin' to get along alone, no way, but I wa'n't goin' to have my house turned upsi' down an' all changed about; no, not to please nobody. I was the only one knew just how she liked to have things set, poor dear, an' I said I was goin' to make shift, and I have made shift. I'd rather tough it out alone." And he sighed heavily, as if to sigh were his familiar consolation.

We were both silent for a minute; the old man looked out the window, as if he had forgotten I was there.

"You must miss her very much?" I said at last.

"I do miss her," he answered, and sighed again. "Folks all kep' repeatin' that time would ease me, but I can't find it does. No, I miss her just the same every day."

"How long is it since she died?" I asked.

"Eight year now, come the first of October. It don't seem near so long. I've got a sister that comes and stops 'long o' me a little spell, spring an' fall, an' odd times if I send after her. I ain't near so good a hand to sew as I be to knit, and she 's very quick to set everything to rights. She's a married woman with a family; her son's folks lives at home, an' I can't make no great claim on her time. But it makes me a kind o' good excuse, when I do send, to help her a little; she ain't none too well off. Poor dear always liked her, and we used to contrive our ways together. 'Tis full as easy to be alone. I set here an' think it all over, an' think considerable when the weather's bad to go outside. I get so some days it feels as if poor dear might step right back into this kitchen. I keep a-watchin' them doors as if she might step in to ary one. Yes, ma'am, I keep a-lookin' off an' droppin' o' my stitches; that's just how it seems. I can't git over losin' of her no way nor no how. Yes, ma'am, that's just how it seems to me."

I did not say anything, and he did not look up.

"I git feelin' so sometimes I have to lay everything by an' go out door. She was a sweet pretty creatur' long's she lived," the old man added mournfully. "There 's that little rockin' chair o' her'n, I set an' notice it an' think how strange 'tis a creatur' like her should be gone an' that chair be here right in its old place."

From *The Country of the Pointed Firs*
Sarah Orne Jewett, 1896

At the Fishhouses

Although it is a cold evening,
down by one of the fishhouses
an old man sits netting,
his net, in the gloaming almost invisible
a dark purple-brown,
and his shuttle worn and polished.
The air smells so strong of codfish
it makes one's nose run and one's eyes water.
The five fishhouses have steeply peaked roofs
and narrow, cleated gangplanks slant up
to storerooms in the gables
for the wheelbarrows to be pushed up and down on.
All is silver: the heavy surface of the sea,
swelling slowly as if considering spilling over,
is opaque, but the silver of the benches,
the lobster pots, and masts, scattered
among the wild jagged rocks,
is of an apparent translucence
like the small old buildings with an emerald moss
growing on their shoreward walls.
The big fish tubs are completely lined
with layers of beautiful herring scales
and the wheelbarrows are similarly plastered
with creamy iridescent coats of mail,
with small iridescent flies crawling on them.
Up on the little slope behind the houses,
set in the sparse bright sprinkle of grass,
is an ancient wooden capstan,
cracked, with two long bleached handles
and some melancholy stains, like dried blood,
where the ironwork has rusted.
The old man accepts a Lucky Strike.
He was a friend of my grandfather.
We talk of the decline in the population
and of codfish and herring
while he waits for a herring boat to come in.
There are sequins on his vest and on his thumb.
He has scraped the scales, the principal beauty,
from unnumbered fish with that black old knife,
the blade of which is almost worn away.

Excerpt
Elizabeth Bishop, 1955

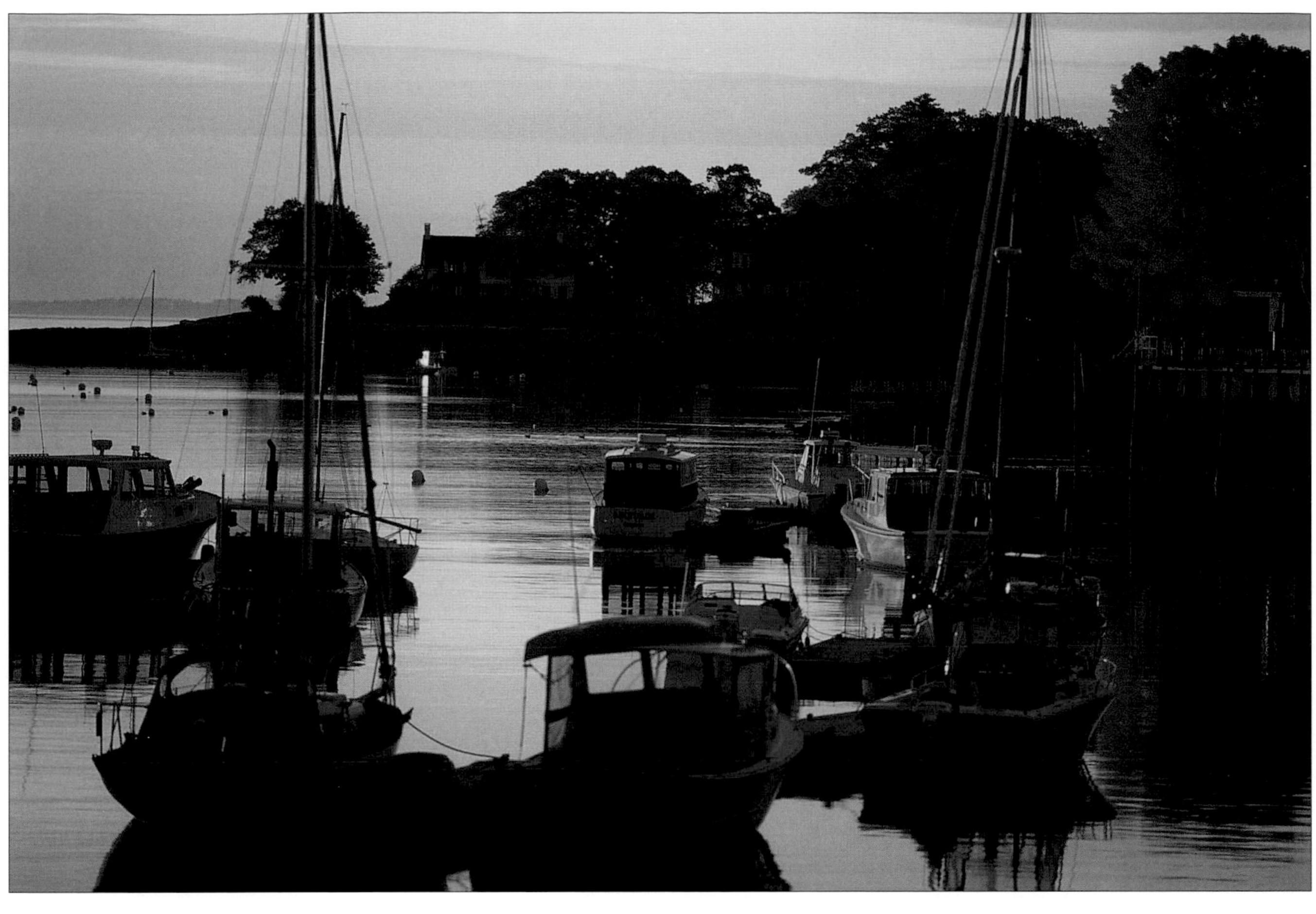

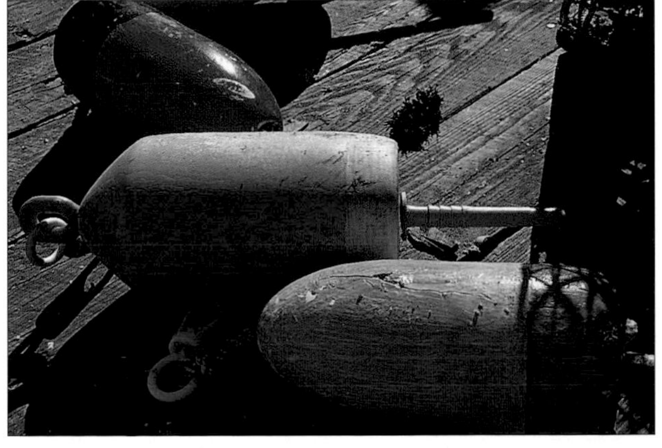

Mezzo Cammin

Half of my life is gone, and I have let
The years slip from me and have not fulfilled
The aspiration of my youth, to build
Some tower of song with lofty parapet.
Not indolence, nor pleasure, nor the fret
Of restless passions chat would not be stilled,
But sorrow, and a care that almost killed,
Kept me from what I may accomplish yet;

Though, half way up the hill, I see the Past
Lying beneath me with its sounds and sights,—
A city in the twilight dim and vast,
With smoking roofs, soft bells, and gleaming lights—
And hear above me on the autumnal blast
The cataract of Death far thundering from the heights.

Henry Wadsworth Longfellow, 1842

The Tide Rises, The Tide Falls

The tide rises, the tide falls,
The twilight darkens, the curlew calls;
Along the sea-sands damp and brown
The traveller hastens toward the town,
And the tide rises, the tide falls.

Darkness settles on roofs and walls,
But the sea, the sea in the darkness calls;
The little waves, with their soft, white hands,
Efface the footprints in the sands,
And the tide rises, the tide falls.

The morning breaks; the steeds in their stalls
Stamp and neigh, as the hostler calls;
The day returns, but nevermore
Returns the traveller to the shore,
And the tide rises, the tide falls.

Henry Wadsworth Longfellow, 1879

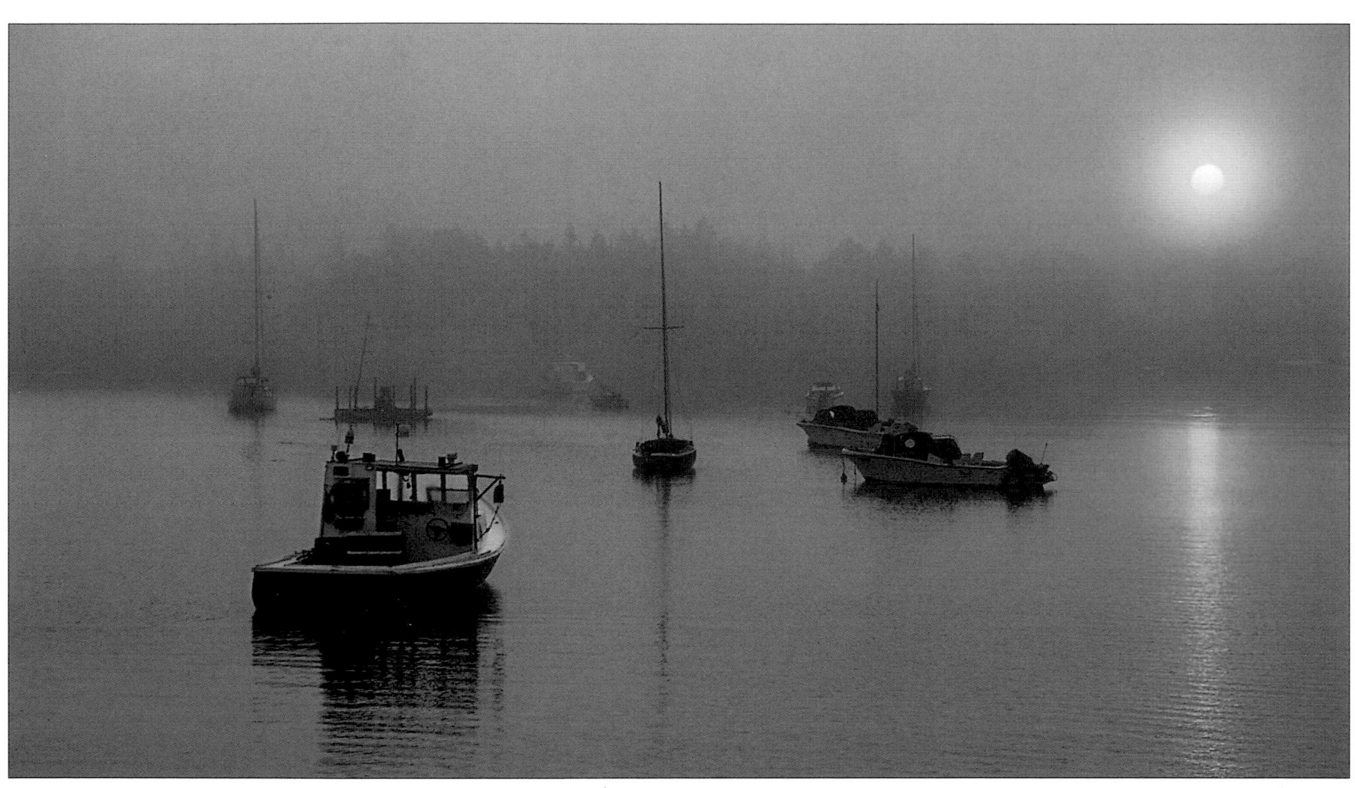

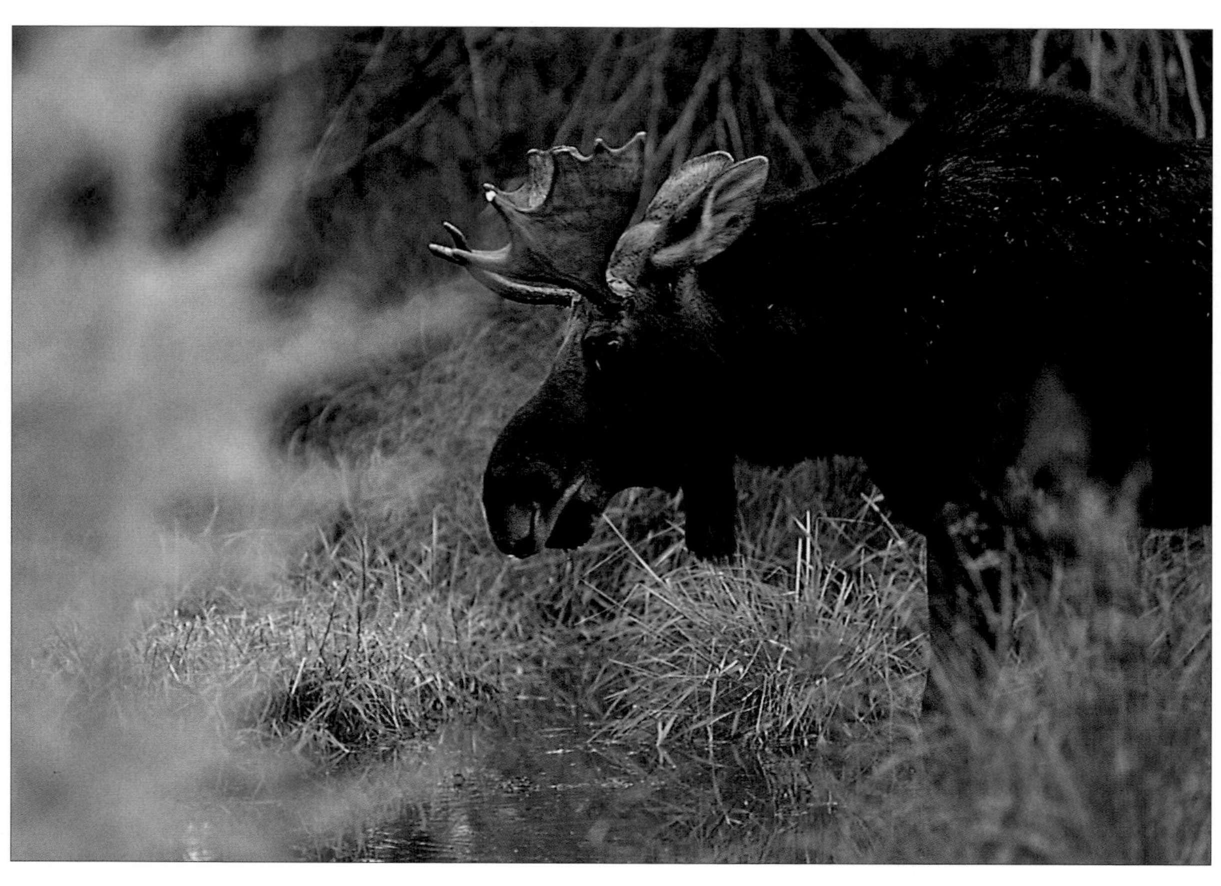

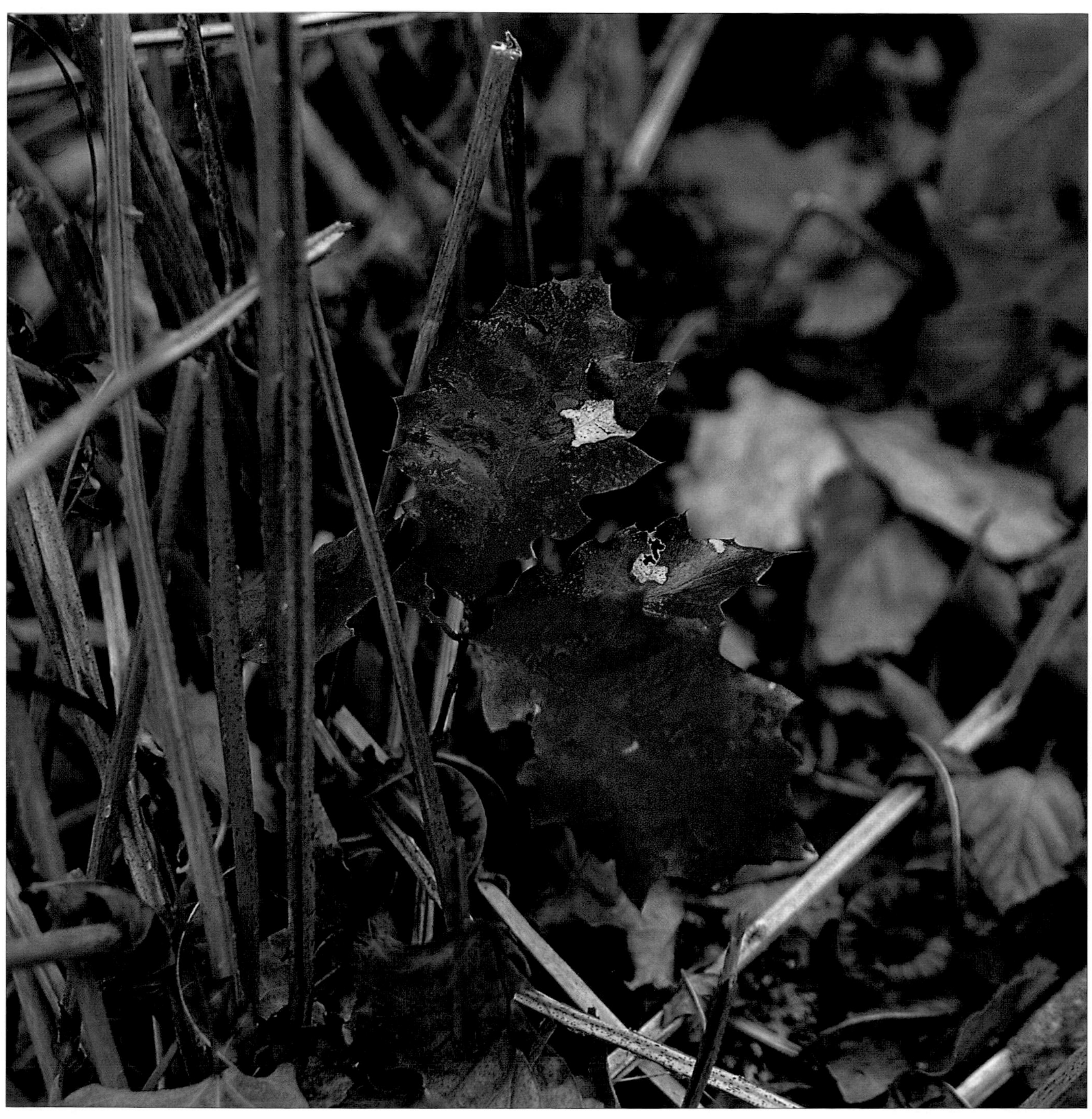

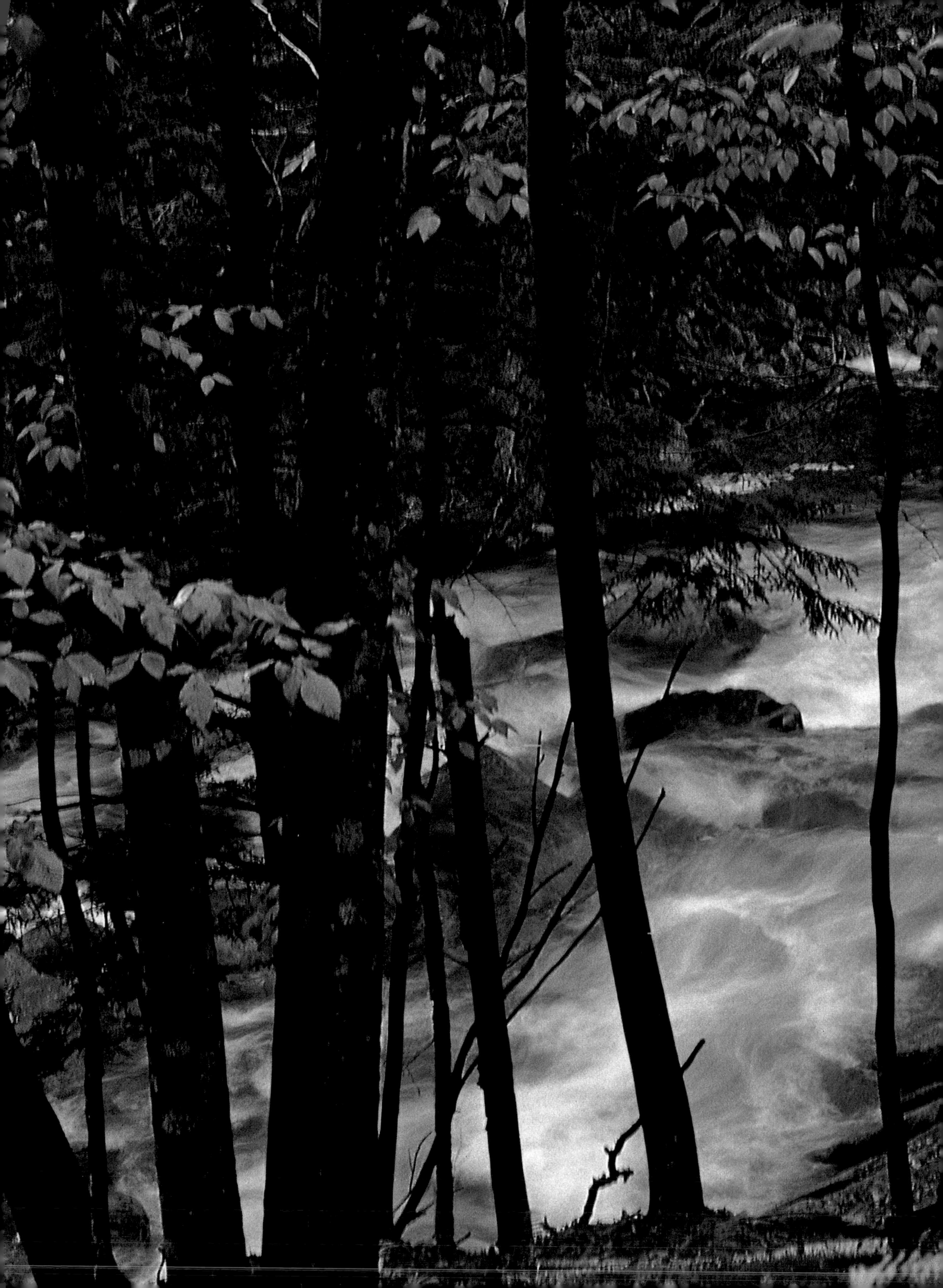

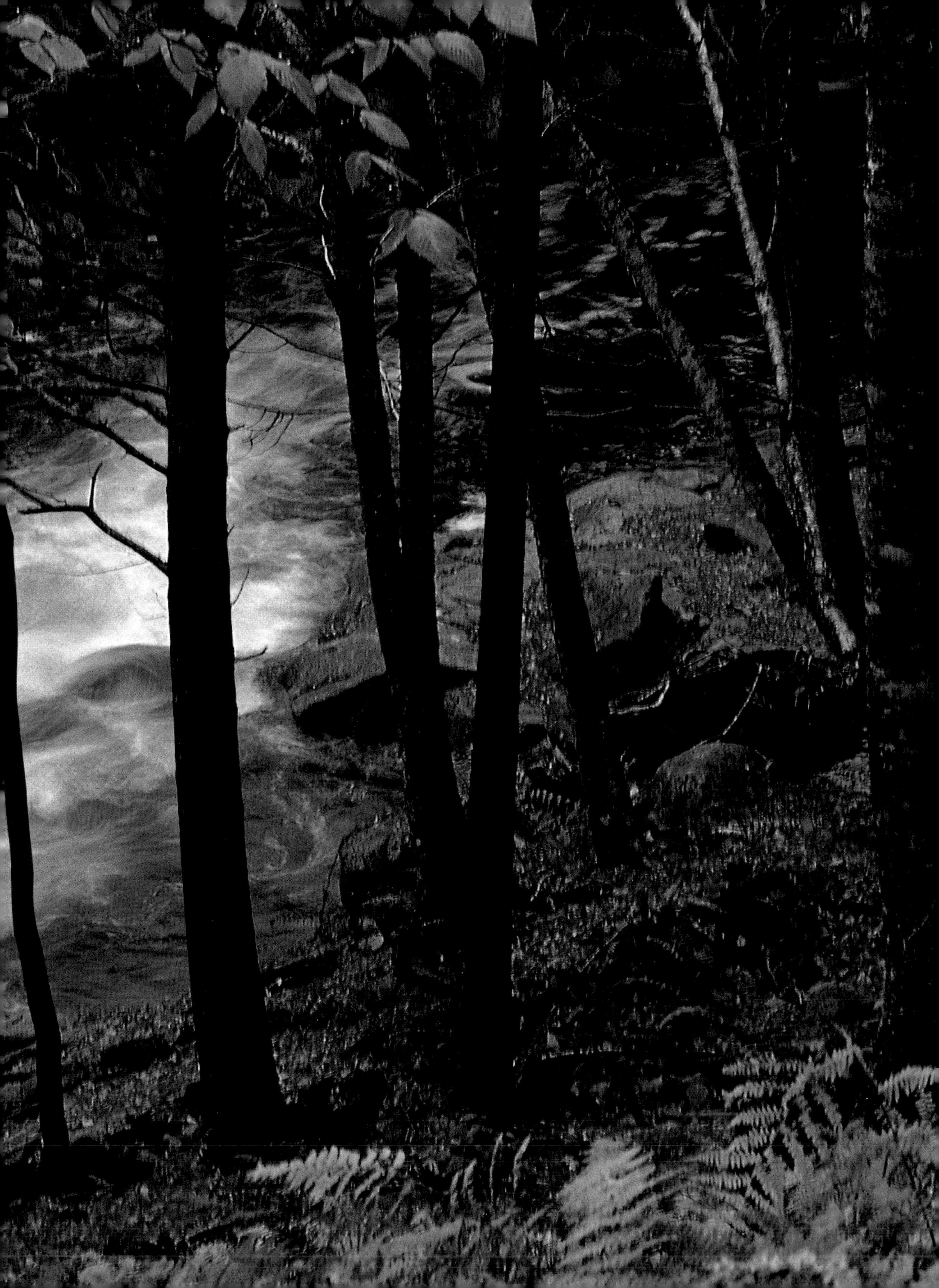

The Road Not Taken

Two roads diverged in a yellow wood,
And sorry I could not travel both
And be one traveler, long I stood
And looked down one as far as I could
To where it bent in the undergrowth;

Then took the other, as just as fair,
And having perhaps the better claim,
Because it was grassy and wanted wear;
Though as for that the passing there
Had worn them really about the same,

And both that morning equally lay
In leaves no step had trodden black.
Oh, I kept the first for another day!
Yet knowing how way leads on to way,
I doubted if I should ever come back.

I shall be telling this with a sigh
Somewhere ages and ages hence:
Two roads diverged in a wood, and I—
I took the one less traveled by,
And that has made all the difference.

Robert Frost

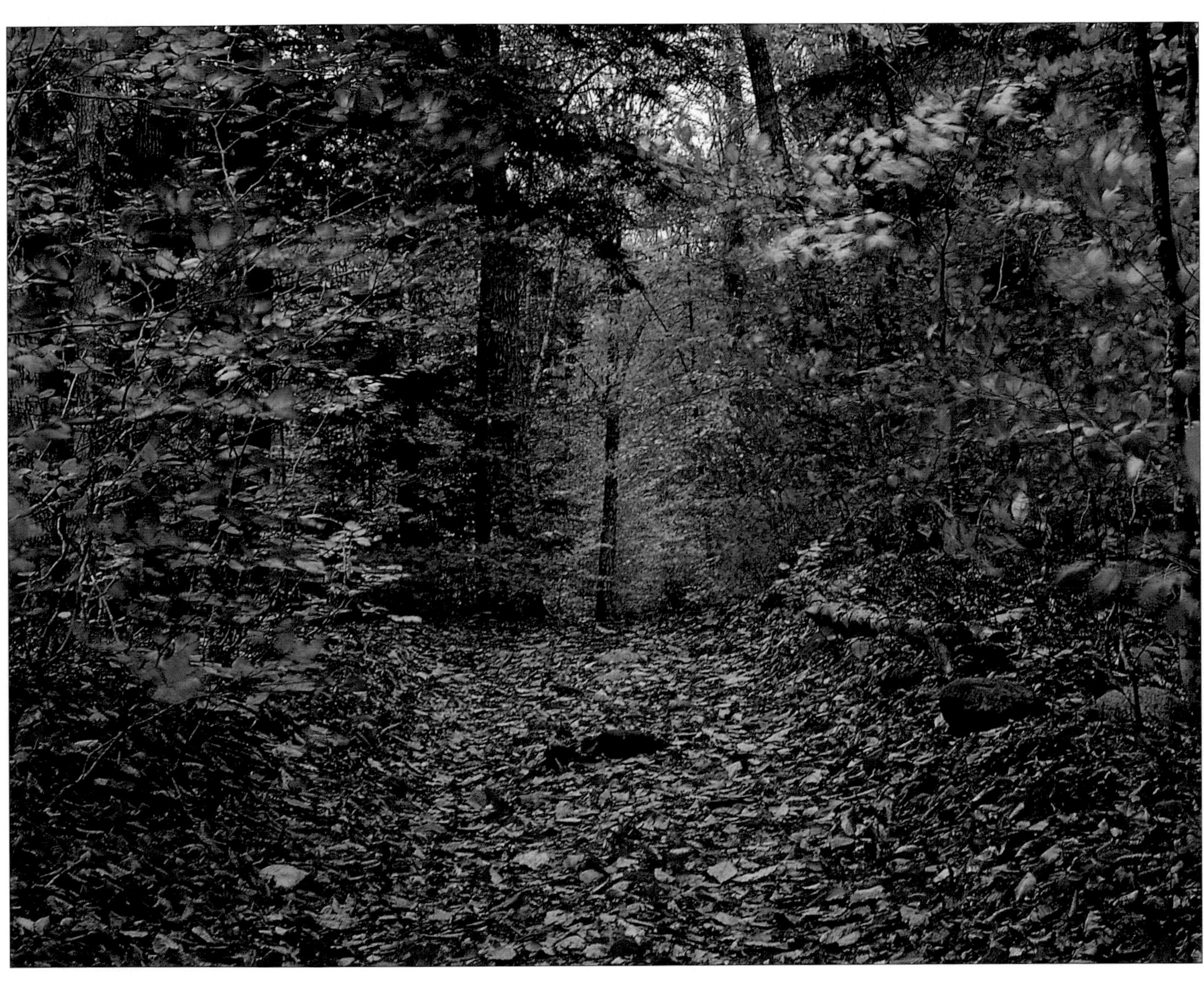

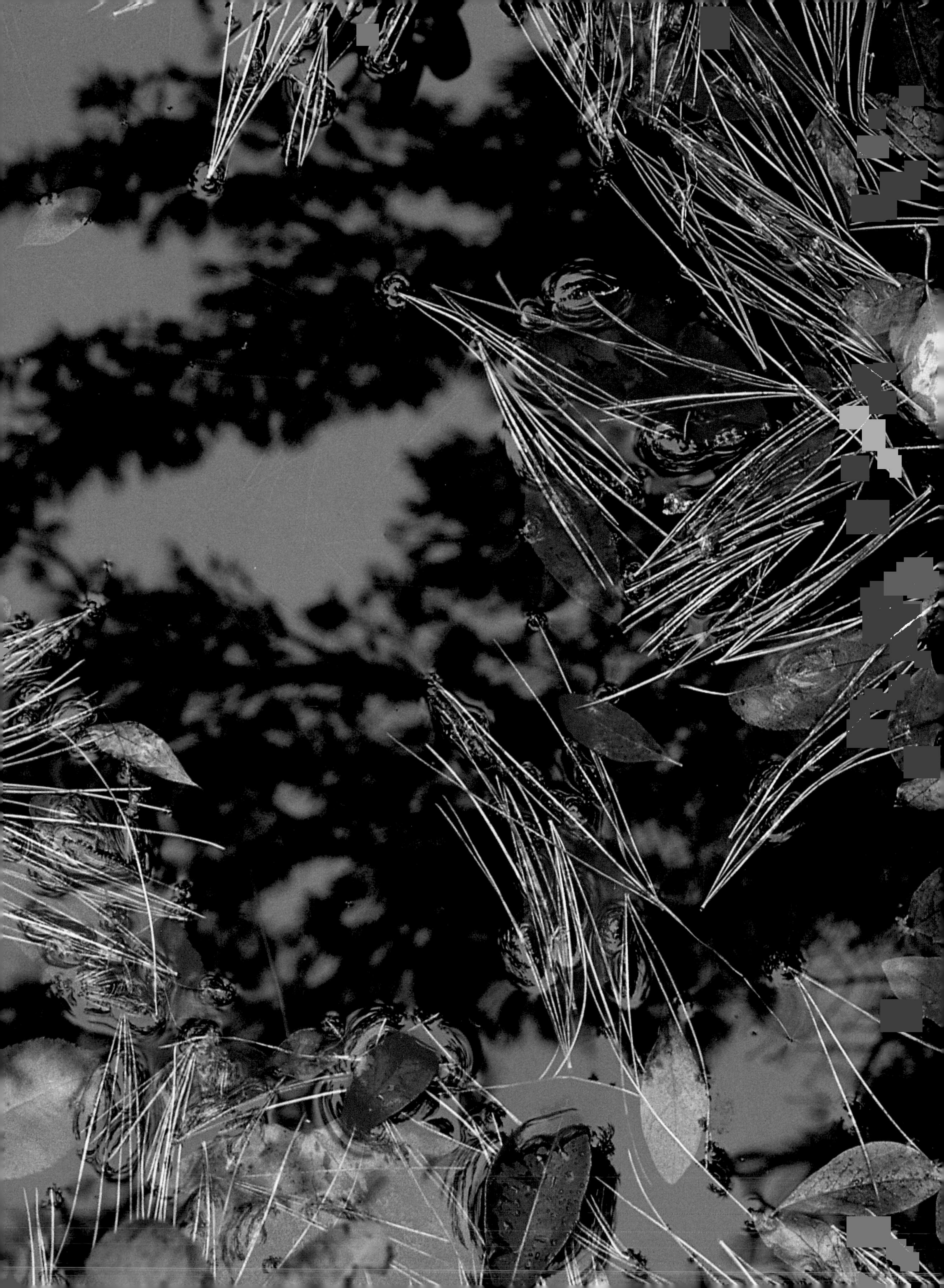

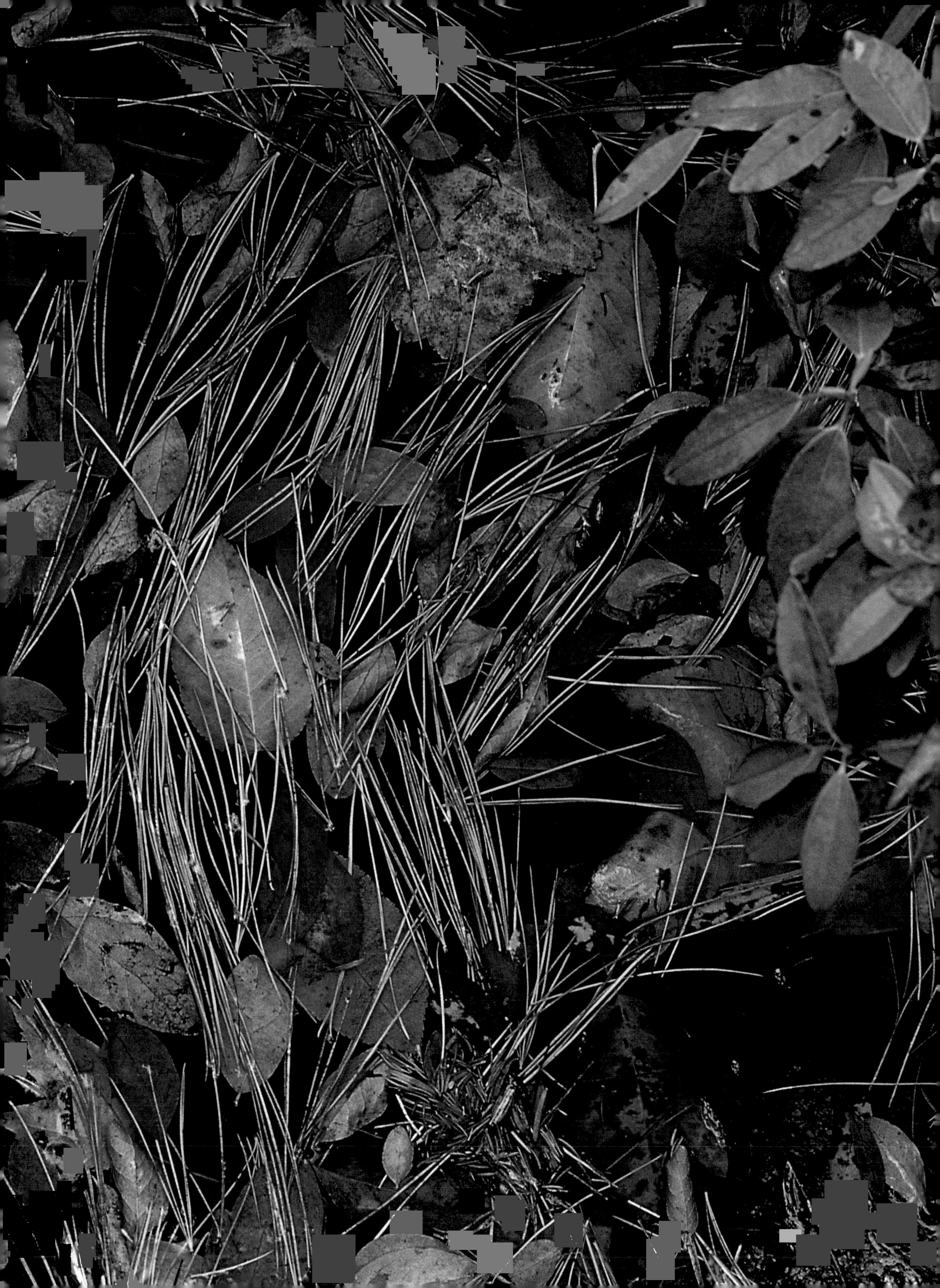

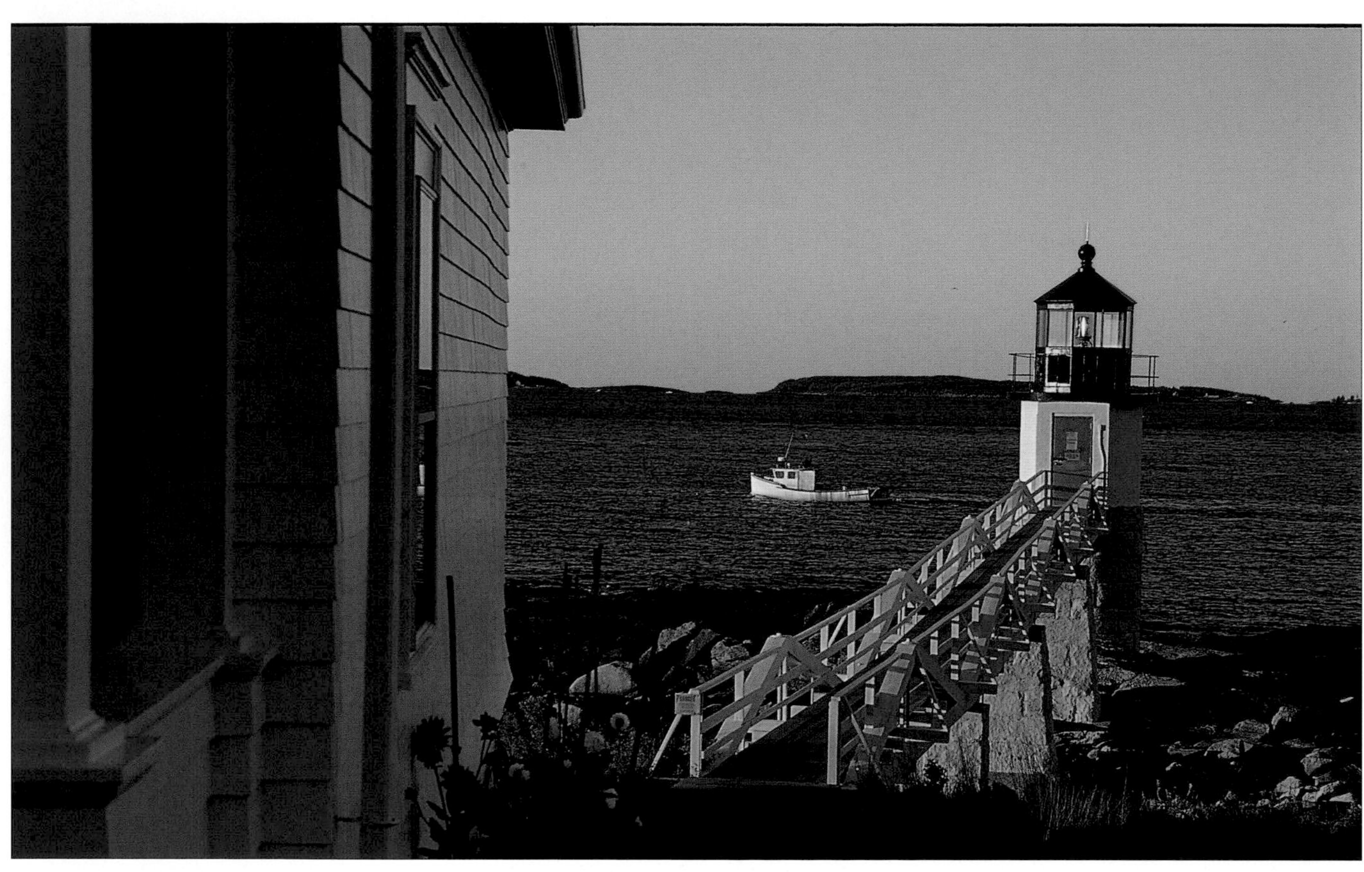

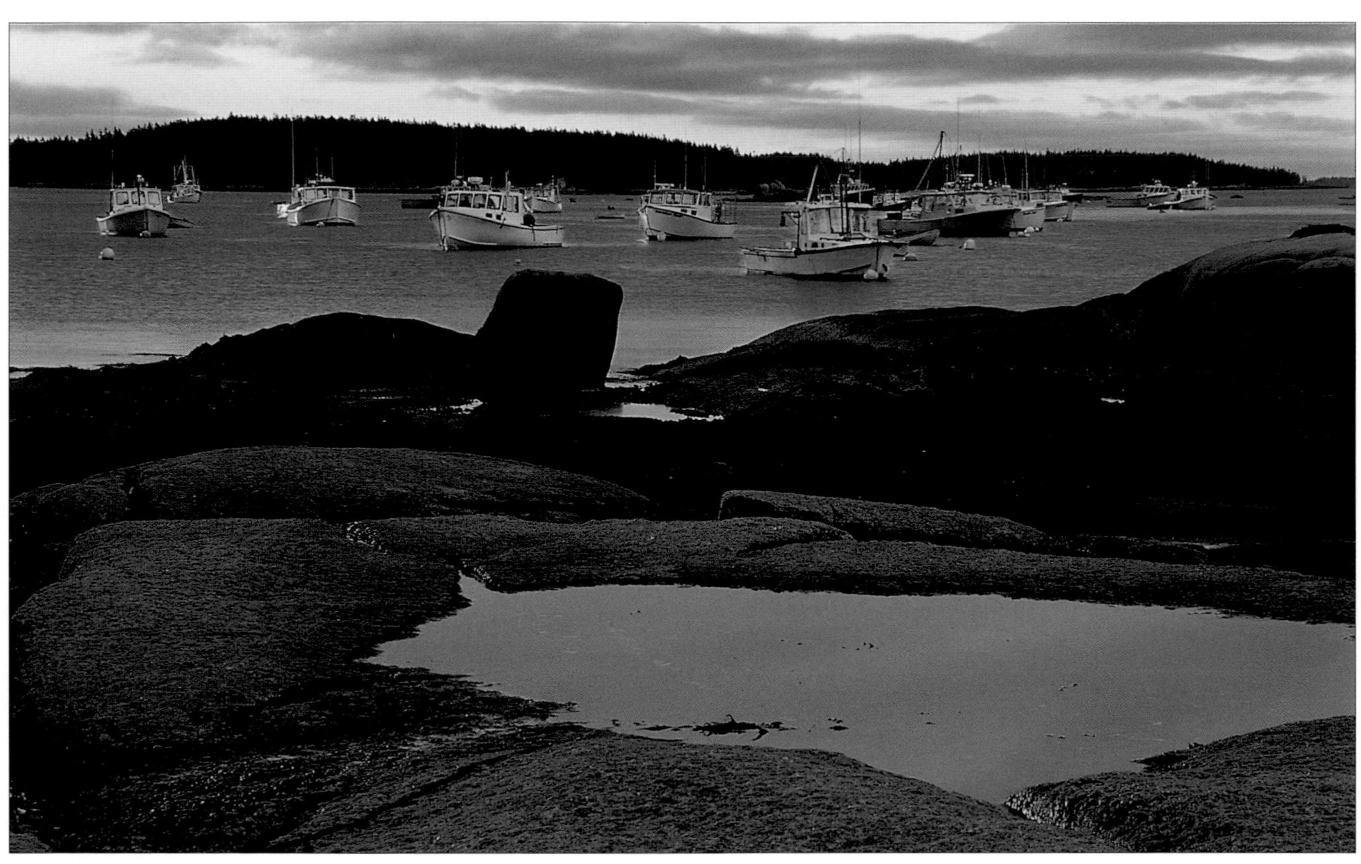

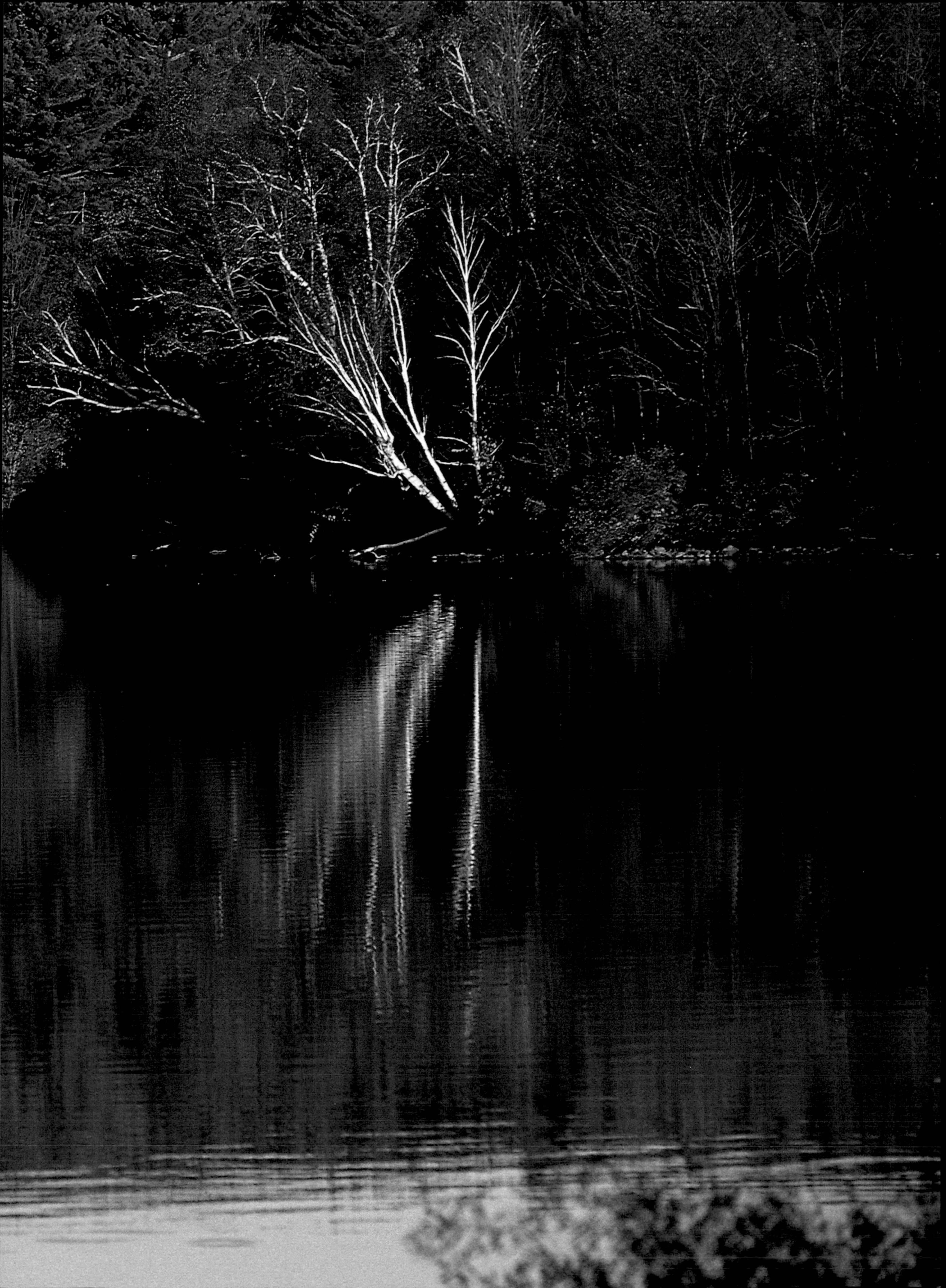

An Old Man's Winter Night

All out of doors looked darkly in at him
Through the thin frost, almost in separate stars,
That gathers on the pane in empty rooms.
What kept his eyes from giving back the gaze
Was the lamp tilted near them in his hand.
What kept him from remembering what it was
That brought him to that creaking room was age.
He stood with barrels round him—at a loss.
And having scared the cellar under him
In clomping there, he scared it once again
In clomping off;—and scared the outer night,
Which has its sounds, familiar, like the roar
Of trees and crack of branches, common things,
But nothing so like beating on a box.
A light he was to no one but himself
Where now he sat, concerned with he knew what,
A quiet light, and then not even that.
He consigned to the moon, such as she was,
So late-arising, to the broken moon
As better than the sun in any case
For such a charge, his snow upon the roof,
His icicles along the wall to keep;
And slept. The log that shifted with a jolt
Once in the stove, disturbed him and he shifted,
And eased his heavy breathing, but still slept.
One aged man—one man—can't fill a house,
A farm, a countryside, or if he can,
It's thus he does it of a winter night.

Robert Frost, 1916

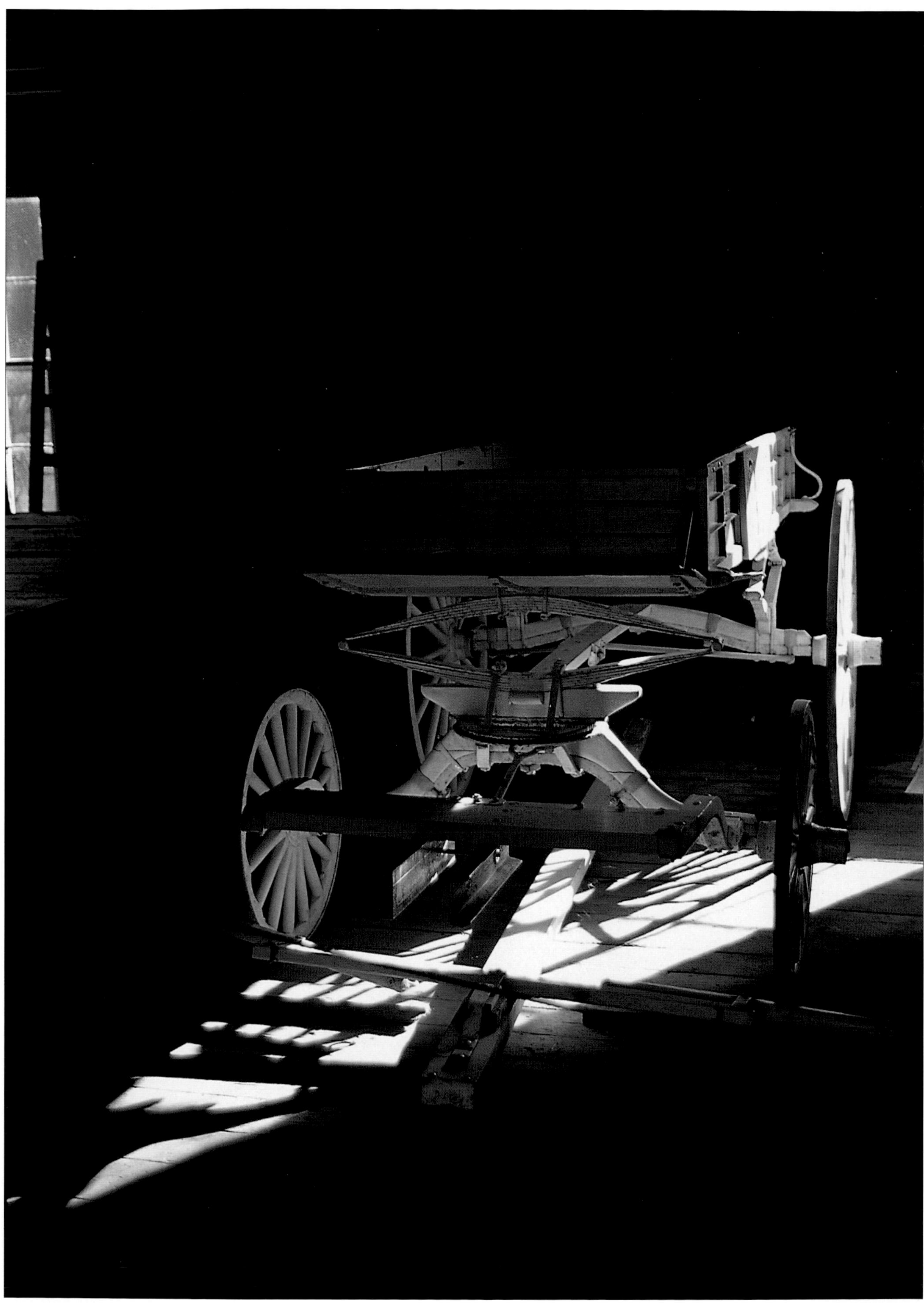

The Cross of Snow

In the long, sleepless watches of the night,
  A gentle face—the face of one long dead—
  Looks at me from the wall, where round its head
  The night-lamp casts a halo of pale light.
Here in this room she died, and soul more white
  Never through martyrdom of fire was led
  To its repose; nor can in books be read
  The legend of a life more benedight.
There is a mountain in the distant West
  That, sun-defying, in its deep ravines
  Displays a cross of snow upon its side.
Such is the cross I wear upon my breast
  These eighteen years, through all the changing scenes
  And seasons, changeless since the day she died.

Henry Wadsworth Longfellow, 1879

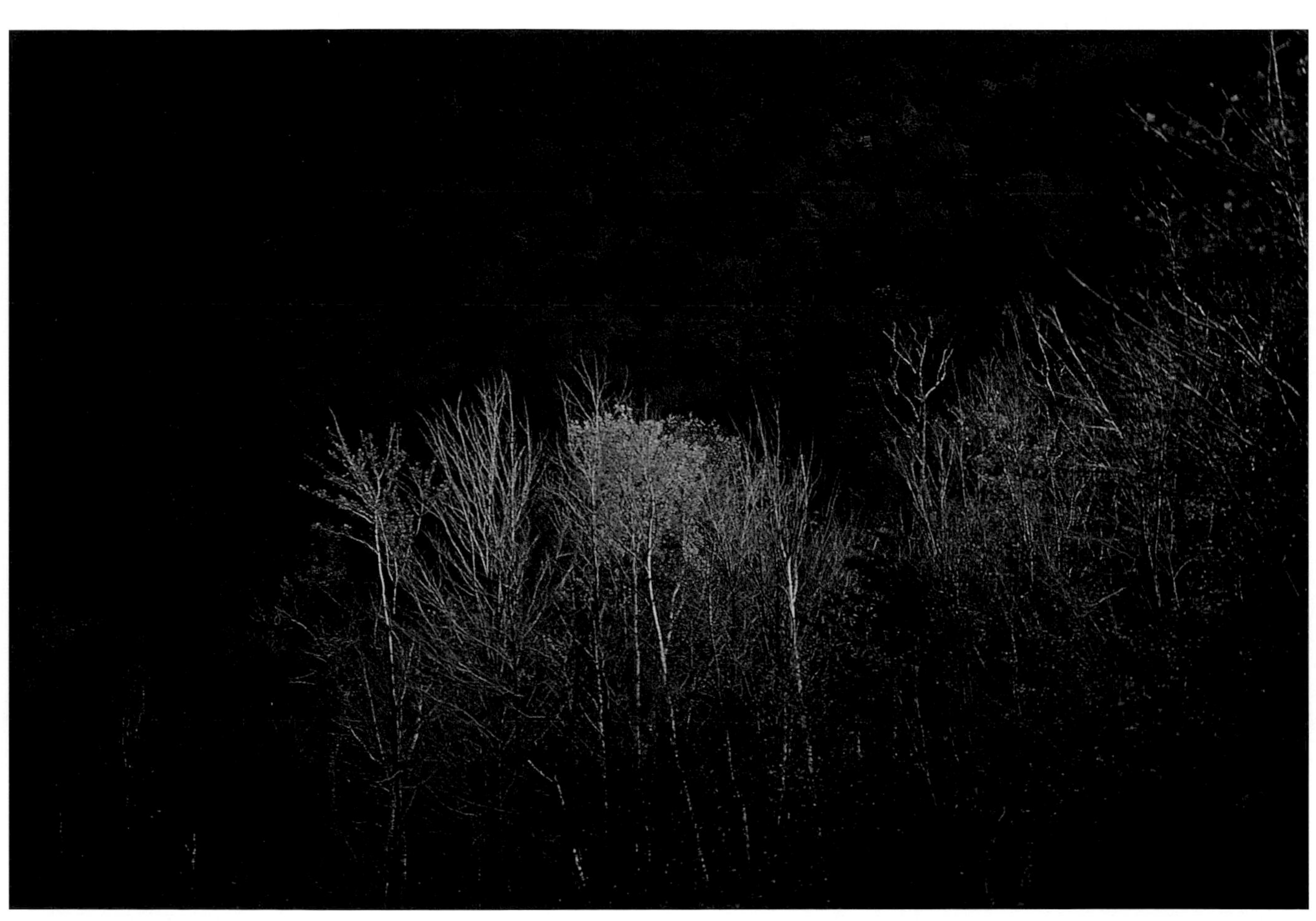

Ringing the Bells

And this is the way they ring
The bells in Bedlam
and this is the bell-lady
who comes each Tuesday morning
to give us a music lesson
and because the attendants make you go
and because we mind by instinct,
like bees caught in the wrong hive,
we are the circle of the crazy ladies
who sit in the lounge of the mental house
and smile at the smiling woman
who passes us each a bell,
who points at my hand
that holds my bell, E flat,
and this is the gray dress next to me
who grumbles as if it were special
to be old, to be old,
and this is the small hunched squirrel girl
on the other side of me
who picks at the hairs over her lip,
who picks at the hairs over her lip all day,
and this is how the bells really sound,
as untroubled and clean
as a workable kitchen,
and this is always my bell responding
to my hand that responds to the lady
who points at me, E flat;
and although we are no better for it,
they tell you to go. And you do.

Ann Sexton, 1960

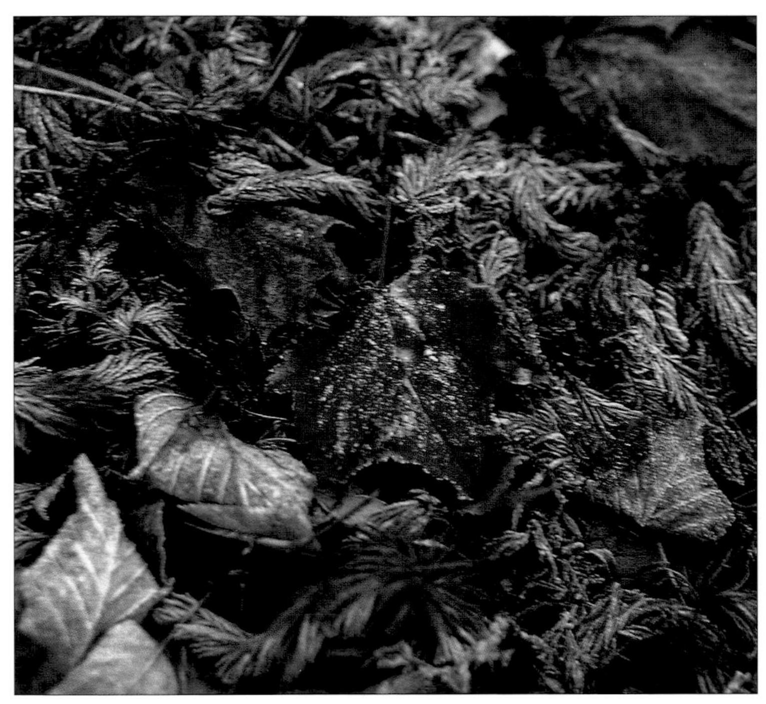

Stopping by Woods on a Snowy Evening

Whose woods these are I think I know.
His house is in the village, though;
He will not see me stopping here
To watch his woods fill up with snow.

My little horse must think it queer
To stop without a farmhouse near
Between the woods and frozen lake
The darkest evening of the year.

He gives his harness bells a shake
To ask if there is some mistake.
The only other sound's the sweep
Of easy wind and downy flake.

The woods are lovely, dark and deep,
But I have promises to keep,
And miles to go before I sleep,
And miles to go before I sleep.

Robert Frost, 1923

Dust of Snow

The way a crow
Shook down on me
The dust of snow
From a hemlock tree

Has given my heart
A change of mood
And saved some part
Of a day I had rued.

Robert Frost, 1920

Snowbound

Unwarmed by any sunset light
The gray day darkened into night,
A night made hoary with the swarm
And whirl-dance of the blinding storm,
As zigzag, wavering to and fro,
Crossed and recrossed the wingëd snow:
And ere the early bedtime came
The white drift piled the window-frame,
And through the glass the clothes-line posts
Looked in like tall and sheeted ghosts.

Shut in from all the world without,
We sat the clean-winged hearth about,
Content to let the north-wind roar
In baffled rage at pane and door,
While the red logs before us beat
The frost-line back with tropic heat;
And ever, when a louder blast
Shook beam and rafter as it passed,
The merrier up its roaring draught
The great throat of the chimney laughed;
The house-dog on his paws outspread
Laid to the fire his drowsy head,
The cat's dark silhouette on the wall
A couchant tiger's seemed to fall;
And, for the winter fireside meet,
Between the andirons' straddling feet,
The mug of cider simmered slow,
The apples sputtered in a row,
And, close at hand, the basket stood
With nuts from brown October's wood.

Excerpt
John Greenleaf Whittier, 1866

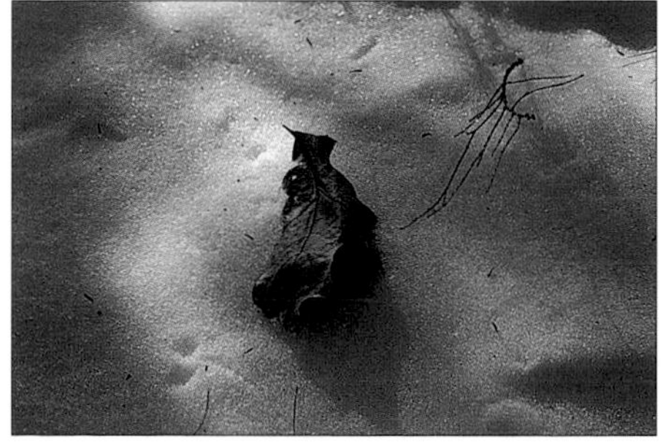

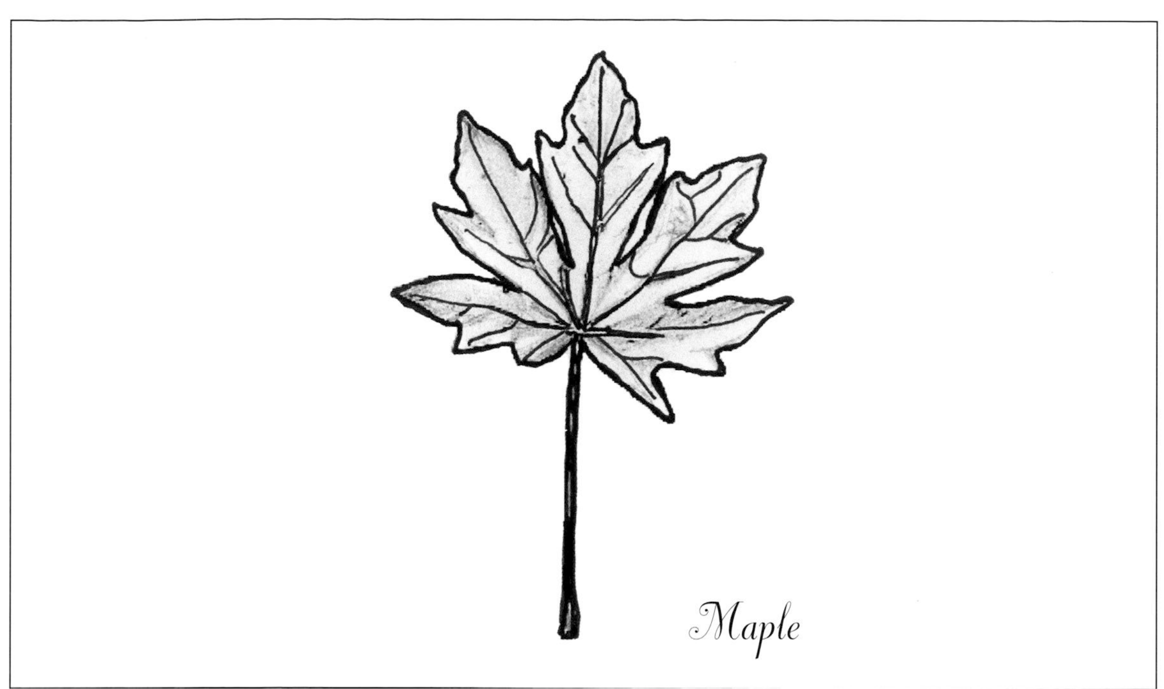

New England Tour Planner

Illustrations by Céline Little

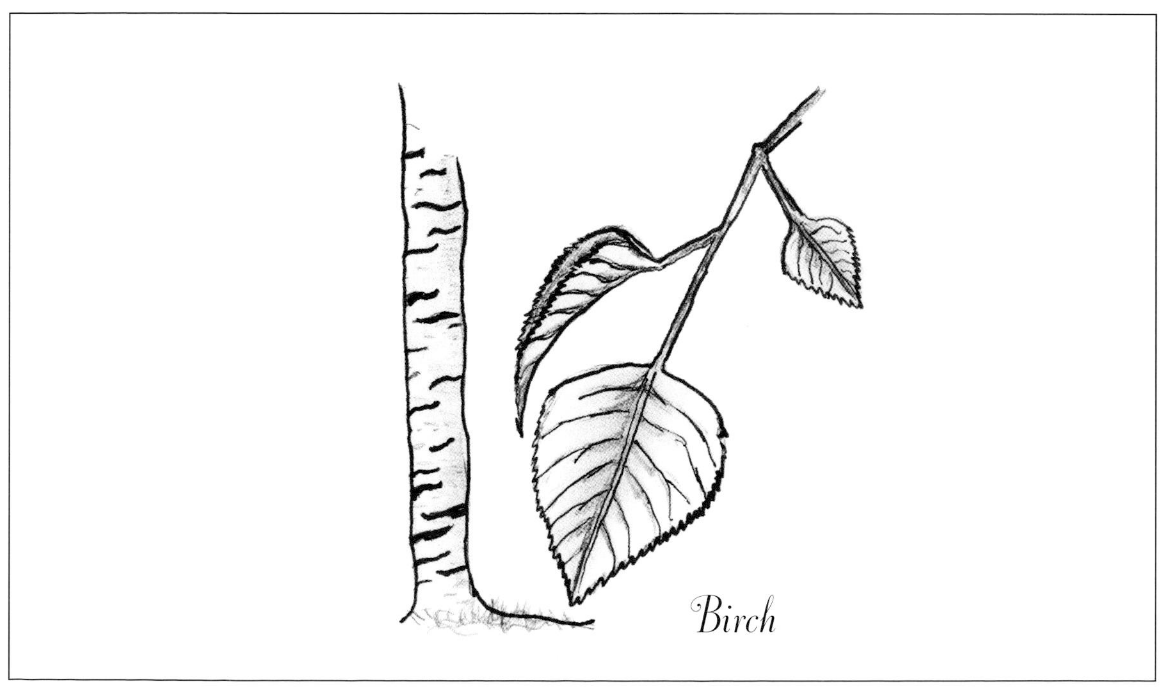

Maine

It's only 228 miles from Maine's northern most coastal point to its southern, but if you walk along its coastline you won't double on your footsteps for over three thousand miles. The thousands of rocky nooks and crannies, inlets and islets make for one of the most spectacular coastlines in the world. Here, along with the colors of autumn forests, you'll find the changing colors of bogs and marshes and brilliant clear autumn air. The northern part of the coast remains the most natural and in its bays and harbors you can lose yourself for weeks.

Three regions seem the most rewarding for the traveller—**Cobscook Bay**, **Mount Desert Island** and the **peninsulas and islands between Bucksport and Stonington.**

A day's visit is worthwhile to the northern most region, **Cobscook Bay**, the eastern-most point in the United States. The rocky beaches surrounding natural basins where the tides rise as much as 25 feet, offer stark, natural beauty. You will find mostly evergreens here but the island-dotted waters make up for the lack of color. Six miles south of Lubec is Quoddy Head State Park. An hour and a half walk on a shoreline path will reward you with beautiful views of the coast and sea. From Lubec do drive to Canada's **Campobello Island**, the highlight of a visit to this region. Here the 2,600 acre **Roosevelt International Park** offers a drive through magical landscapes of bluffs, ponds, beaches, bogs and woods with richly varied vegetation. **Con Robinson's Point** has sweeping vistas. There are many easy trails. Near the park, President Roosevelt's cottage is open to visitors.

The drive around the bay from Lubec to Eastport is almost 40 miles. If you turn off the road at West Pembroke, a 4 mile drive will bring you to the end of Leighton Neck to **Reversing Falls Park** where you'll see beautiful views of secluded coves and evergreen-shrouded islands. You can picnic here and, if you catch the tides at full run, you'll see a ½ mile long rapids formed by the hurtling waters.

Ninety miles to the southwest lies **Acadia National Park** on **Mount Desert Island**. If you only have a short time to spend in Maine, spend it here. Formed by Ice Age glaciers, the island abounds with extraordinary flora and fauna. Over 500 species of trees, shrubs and flowers have been counted in the region, and nearly 300 species of birds. Steep cliffs, booming surf, quiet, shaded ponds, woods and marshes, tranquil, weathered fishing villages and long, shell beaches make for some of North America's most unique scenery.

The best way to visit the park is on bicycle, the second best is by car. The highlight of the park is **Loop Road**, a 30 mile long drive running along magnificent open coastlines and island-sprinkled waters. A side road goes to the top of **Cadillac Mountain** where beautiful **views** can be had from trails along the bare, rocky summit. Allow a good half day for the Loop Road drive and its stops. Start your tour from the Visitor Center and make your first stop at **Frenchman Bay Overlook** for a spectacular view. Five miles further you'll come to Sieur de Monts Spring with a nearby Nature Center with a Wild Gardens where plants, flowers and trees are displayed in various natural settings. Farther along the main road is a sand beach, the only good one in the park. Another mile will bring you to **Thunder Hole** where the breaking surf at high tide booms into a narrow chasm. Another mile will bring you to **Otter Cliffs** rising over 100 feet above the sea rendering north and south views of the coast.

Other points of interest on Mount Desert Isle are **Somes Sound**, the longest fjord on the east coast and the views from Beech Cliff Trail—just south of Somesville at the end of Beech Cliff Road.

Nearby **Bass Harbor** and, across the bay from it, the village of **Bernard**, are quiet little fishing villages in the fall, with fishboats, fish houses and old, weathered docks. On the west side of **Bernard Mountain** a narrow desolate **fire-road** runs through woods of birches and maples whose autumn colors set off beautifully against the dark evergreens. There are fascinating bogs in here with mysterious plants.

Back on Rte 1, just before Bucksport, turn south on Rte 15 toward **Blue Hill**—a favorite of artists and craftsmen—and **Deer Isle**. This long quiet peninsula is studded with sparkling bays, little harbors and secluded woods. At **Deer Isle's** southernmost point is the picture-postcard pretty fishing village of **Stonington** where fisherman's shacks and houses dot the rocks and islets and a fishboat pier bustles with life. From here the mailboat runs daily to Isle au Haut with many hiking trails in its National Park.

About 5 miles north of Stonington on the west side of Deer Island is **Caterpillar Rest Area**. Try to be here for a magnificent sunset over the many islands. Halfway back to Bucksport along the road hugging the coast is the village of Castine with treelined streets and a pretty main street. Farther south along the coast, **Pemaquid Point**, with its dramatically set lighthouse and many tidal pools, is recom-

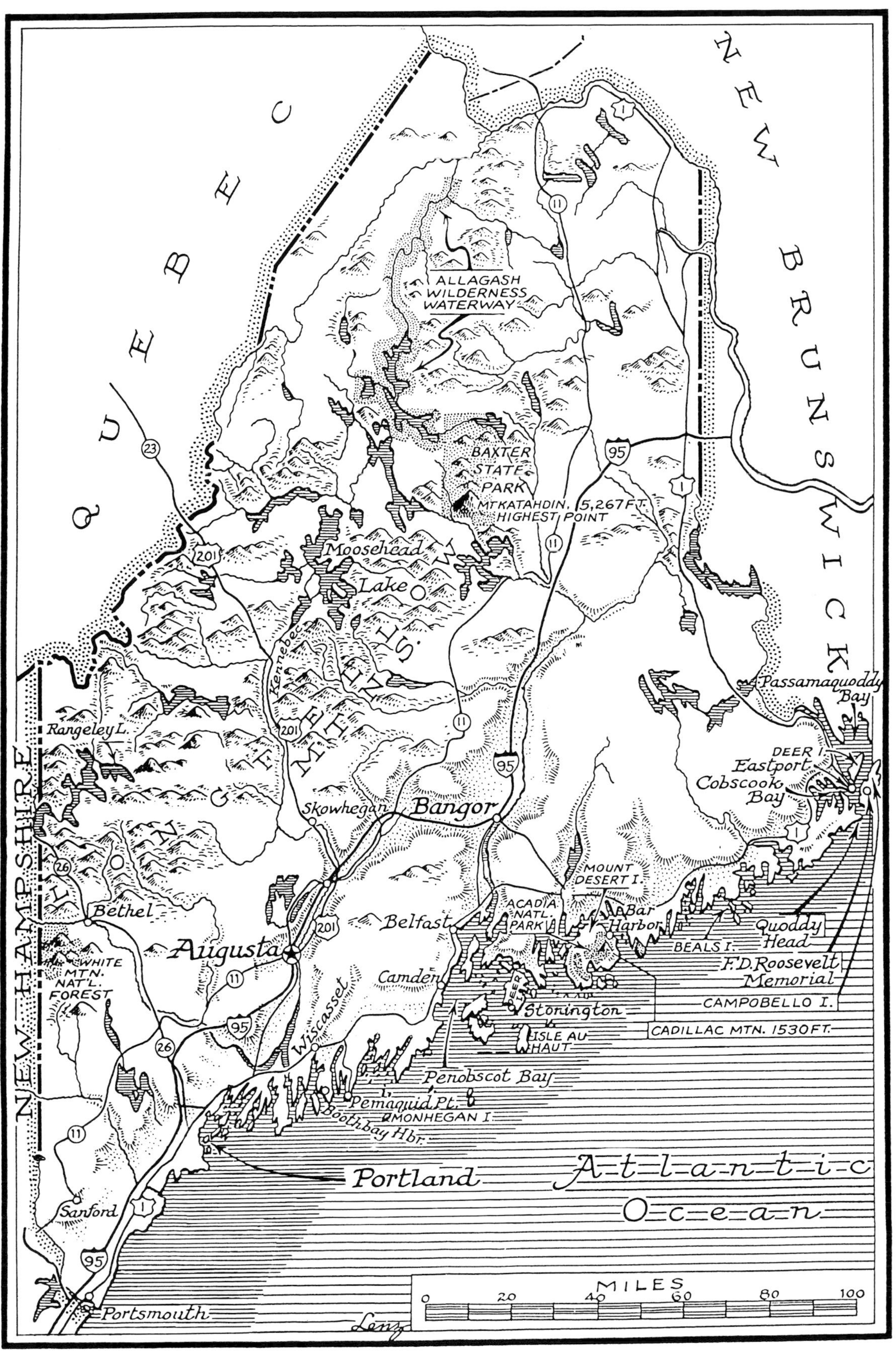
QUEBEC
NEW BRUNSWICK
NEW HAMPSHIRE
ALLAGASH WILDERNESS WATERWAY
BAXTER STATE PARK
MT KATAHDIN, 5,267 FT. HIGHEST POINT
Moosehead Lake
Kennebec
Rangeley L.
Skowhegan
Bangor
Passamaquoddy Bay
DEER I.
Eastport
Cobscook Bay
MOUNT DESERT I.
ACADIA NATL. PARK
Bar Harbor
Belfast
Bethel
Augusta
WHITE MTN. NAT'L. FOREST
Camden
Wiscasset
Stonington
ISLE AU HAUT
Quoddy Head
BEALS I.
F.D. Roosevelt Memorial
CAMPOBELLO I.
CADILLAC MTN. 1530 FT.
Penobscot Bay
Pemaquid Pt.
MONHEGAN I.
Boothbay Hbr.
Portland
Atlantic Ocean
Sanford
Portsmouth
MILES
0 20 40 60 80 100
Lenz

mended by almost everyone. **Boothbay Harbor** is a favorite of boaters and lobster eaters. If you have time, you might take a mailboat out to **Monhegan Island** lying ten miles offshore. The boat runs from Port Clyde only three times in the fall so check the schedules. The trails on the island are well numbered leading to spectacular headlands of which Burnt Head and White Head are the best.

Even the most fervent avoiders of civilization should plan a visit to **Camden** with its beautiful old schooners and pretty harbor, if only to catch the sunrise from **Mount Battie** right behind the town. There is a road that leads to the top but it doesn't open until after sunrise so you'll have to scramble up a tough path from the end of a street right in town. The way up—one would be hardpressed to call it a trail—is rocky, and slippery with autumn leaves, so give yourself a half hour for the ascent.

Farther down the coast, the town of **Bath** has a fine **Marine Museum**; the town of **Wiscasset**, some fine dead schooners and a Musical Wonder House full of ancient instruments, phonographs and music boxes; **York**, a colonial village; and **Portland**, a rejuvenated old waterfront district with interesting l9th century architecture.

Inland, in the White Mountain National Forest, **Evans Notch** offers beautiful valley views. Well north, **Baxter State Park**, is a 200,000 acre wildlife sanctuary for—among others—deer, bear and moose. There are no commercial facilities. The roads are unpaved and narrow. Heaven. You'll have to hike to see spectacular views.

For **fall foliage**, the Maine Auto Touring Association recommends the following five tours ranging from two to five hours.

Southern Circle (85 miles, 2 hours)
From Sanford, east on US 202 through Alfred to Bar Mills; north on 35 to Standish; west on 25 through Kezar Falls to Porter; south on 160 to Limerick; south on 11 to Sanford. This is the southern corner of Maine, known for its superb apple orchards where you may pick your own apples.

Western Loop (130 miles, 3¼ hours)
From Fryeburg, east on US 302 to Naples; north on 35 to Harrison; north on 117 to near Norway; north on road along shore of Lake Pennesseewassee to Greenwood; east on 219 to 26; north on 26 to Bethel; west on US 2 Gilead; south on 113 to Stowe; east and around Lake Kezar to North Lovell; south on 5 through Lovell to Fryeburg. Passing through western Maine, you can sense the peaceful quiet of life here.

Mountain Tour (108 miles, 2½ hours)
From Rumford, west on US 2 to Newry; north on 26 to Errol, N.H.; east on 16 to Oquossoc; south on 17 to Mexico (the town, not the country) cross bridge to Rumford. As towns become further apart you'll encounter many miles of untouched mountains and forests.

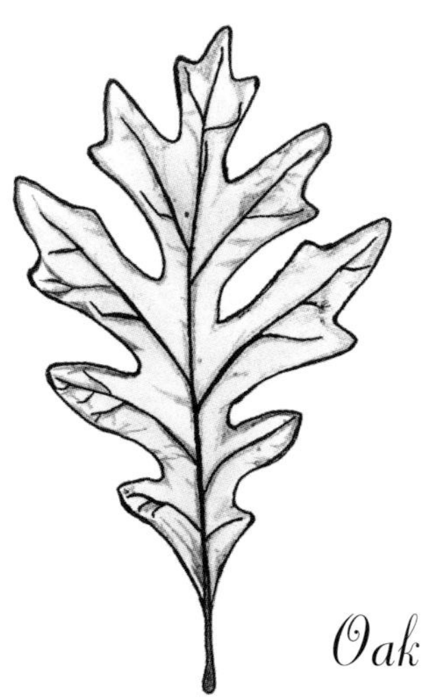
Oak

Ski Region (132 miles, 3½ hours)
From Farmington, west on US 2 to Wilton; northwest on 156 to Weld; north on 142 to 4; northwest on 4 to Rangeley; southeast on 16 through Kingfield to North Anson; south on US 201 to Norridgewock; west on US 2 to Farmington.

Moosehead Trip (210 miles, 5½ hours)
From Skowhegan on US 201 through Bingham to near Jackman; southeast on 15 through Greenville to Dover-Foxcroft; south on 7 to Newport; west on 151 to Coston's Corner; west on 43 to Athens; south on 150 to Skowhegan. This route brings you to the southern reaches of the Great North Maine Woods and to Moosehead Lake, the largest lake in the northeastern United States.

New Hampshire

Foliage begins to peak in New Hampshire's North Country near the Canadian border towards the end of September until about October 10. The northern slopes of the White Mountains usually reach their peak colors between October 1-10. The Southern Hill Country will be at its most brilliant between October 7-15. Last to turn is the Merrimack River Valley and the southeastern corner of the state.

The North Country

Here all the roads are backroads. Dixville Notch (a notch is a narrow mountain pass) State Park on Rte 26 between Colebrook and Errol sits among rugged mountain cliffs and dense evergreen forests. There are two picnic areas right off the highway. On Lake Gloriette, the Balsams Hotel, one of the last 19th Century grand resort hotels, rules over the highest point in the notch. Just east of the hotel two paths near the road afford short easy walks to waterfalls. The Sanquinary Ridge hiking trail offers long panoramas of the Maine Mountains.

Just north of Colebrook, on Rte 3, turn right onto Rte 145 to Pittsburg. A 13 mile **scenic drive** will bring you to the Connecticut Lake region, a paradise for fishermen. Eight miles from Pittsburg you can camp or picnic on the shores of Lake Francis in the state park of the same name.

The White Mountains

A few days in the White Mountains, among its waterfalls and quiet slopes is one of the highlights of any New England journey. The **White Mountain National Forest** covers three quarters of a million acres, has over a thousand miles of trails, forty-five lakes and ponds and over six-hundred fishing streams. From Errol, scenic Rte 16 leads south into the great peaks of the White Mountains where the blazing colors of autumn are set off beautifully by the rich darkness of evergreens. Higher up, the rugged, treeless peaks, named after the snow that covers them most of the year, were revered by the natives long before the white man came. They called them the province of the gods and never climbed them.

The best scenery will be south of Gorham around 6,288 foot **Mount Washington**, the coldest and windiest place in the region. In April of 1934 the strongest winds ever recorded (231 mph) howled across the summit. As a precaution, the summit buildings of wood and stone are anchored to the ground by great chains. Snow has been known to fall year round. Only hardy, tiny plants and gnarled dwarf spruce and fir survive among the boulders above the timberline. **The view** from the top extends fifty miles on a clear autumn day. On the horizon the Atlantic shimmers. Distant lakes sparkle like jewels. The mountains are everywhere—all below your feet.

You can either take a train or you can drive, to the top. The 3-½ mile long **Mount Washington Cog Railway** is a small steam train built in 1869. The steepest grade on the run is 37%. During the 1-½ hour ascent, drastic changes in the vegetation can be seen. The train station is on the west side of the mountain off Rte 302. After Labor Day it operates only on weekends from 10 AM to 2 PM.

The 8 mile long *toll road* to the top begins at Glen House on the east side of the mountain off Rte 16. You can take your own car or take a van with a driver. The road is mostly gravel and very steep in places with abrupt, sharp curves. Beware. If you are a good hiker take one of the many hiking trails. Or leave the place to the gods.

Across Rte 16 from Mount Washington is a Gondola lift leading to the top of the ski area of **Wildcat Mountain** which yields a nice view. From here, driving south, you're in **Pinkham Notch**. The mountains close in. On the west side of the road you'll see a sign for **Glen Ellis Falls**. These are prettiest in early morning with the sun shining into the cut, lighting up the spray and backlighting the blazing colors of the forest on the mountainslopes.

Ten miles south, off the main road, is the quiet little village of **Jackson** with a pretty covered bridge and some beautiful old hotels. This is the ideal place to stay and use as a base for visiting Mount Washington and Crawford Notch. There is a fine Irish pub serving excellent pizza. You read right.

The 38 mile **scenic drive** along Rte 302 from Glen to Fabyan and the Mount Washington Cog Railway Station is along the Saco River. The valleys are wider with much pretty foliage along the way. A noteworthy stop is **Arethusa Falls** west of the road. A pleasant two hour hike will get you to the falls and back. Just north of the falls on Rte 302 **Crawford Notch** begins. For six miles you're in a rugged, unspoiled mountain pass with many wooded trails and a campsite.

The Kancamagus Highway between Conway and Lincoln is one of New England's most spectacular drives during foliage season. It leads through the White Mountain National Forest, (no gas stations, no billboards, no junk-food stands) along crystal clear mountain streams with white water rapids and shaded waterfalls. For a spectacular morning, stay in Lincoln and try to catch the **sunrise** at the large roadside pullout near **Kancamagus Pass** about 10 miles east of Lincoln. If you're lucky there will have been a cold night or a storm and the sun will rise before you over valleys thick with mist below. As the mist begins to burn off it will rise and screen the sun and enormous beams of light will pour into the valley. The trees before you will be backlit and on fire.

Farther east, stop at **Sabbaday Falls**, south of the road. A broad, leaf-strewn trail will lead you through the woods along a stream into the dark shadowy falls hidden from the morning sun. The falls tumble from ledge to ledge into a giant pothole, then fall some more into a great slowly eddying pool at your feet, then away through a narrow, hissing flume. A damp path leads to the top of the falls. Allow an hour for a meditative return trip.

A few miles to the east, not far off the road, you will come across **Rocky Gorge Scenic Area**. The best view is from the wooden footbridge over the chasm where, after a good rain, the water boils through the narrow gorge below you. There is much thick moss in the forest across the bridge, and fallen leaves, and sparkling early morning light. In the great smooth rocks beside the gorge are dark pools reflecting the color of the sunlit trees above.

Farther east still, stop at **Lower Falls** Scenic Area where a short stroll through the woods will bring you upon great glacier and water-rounded boulders. You can walk out on them into the middle of the stream. The sun will be high by now and you'll be warm.

If you are a good hiker who can keep going for five or six hours (lunch and return included) you can hike to the top of **Mount Chocorua** from the Champney Falls Trail parking area just off Rte 112, a couple of miles east of the turnoff to Bartlett. From the summit are *spectacular views* of the White Mountains to the north and Lake Chocorua to the south. You're advised to follow the trails with care for there are many Get a hiking map at an information booth before you go. If you don't want to hike, you can still get a good view of Mount Chocorua and Lake Chocorua if you drive south from Conway on Rte 16. About ten miles from Conway you'll pass the lake. You can stop right beside the lake and see the reflection of the mountain with its colored leaves or go a ways up the hill into a pasture and get a more interesting view. If you continue west on Rte 113 you'll pass through **Center Sandwich**, one of the most picturesque and unspoiled New England villages with modest whitewashed houses and pretty churches.

The drive through **Franconia Notch** can be spectacular on a stormy day (see book jacket). **The Basin** is an interesting 30 foot wide water-carved bowl. **The Flume** is a natural gorge extending 800 feet at the base of Mount Liberty. Granite walls rise to 70 feet and are only 12 to 20 feet apart. Closeup views can be had of rare mountain flowers and rich mosses growing on the moist walls.

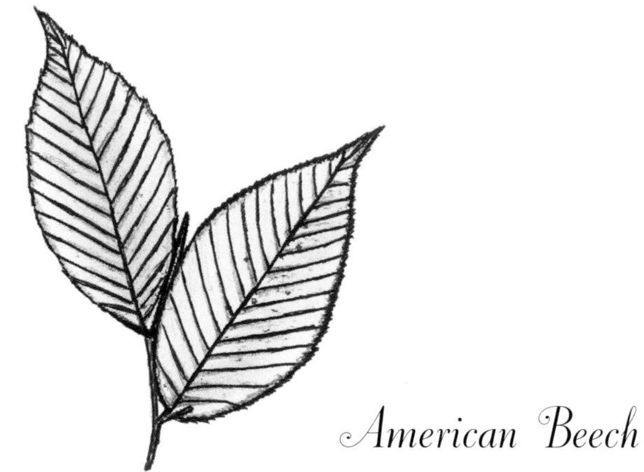
American Beech

Southern New Hampshire

After the second week in October the southern part of the state reaches its peak. A **scenic drive** along Rte 9 of about 50 miles can be taken from Concord to Keene. You'll pass through picturesque villages. A short side trip to **Hillsborough Center** is recommended.

The Mount Monadnock region has the mountain itself to recommend it—numerous four to six hour return trails with a spectacular all-around **views** from a bare rock ledge at its summit. Stops at Cathedral of the Pines, and the villages of Harrisville and Hancock are worthwhile.

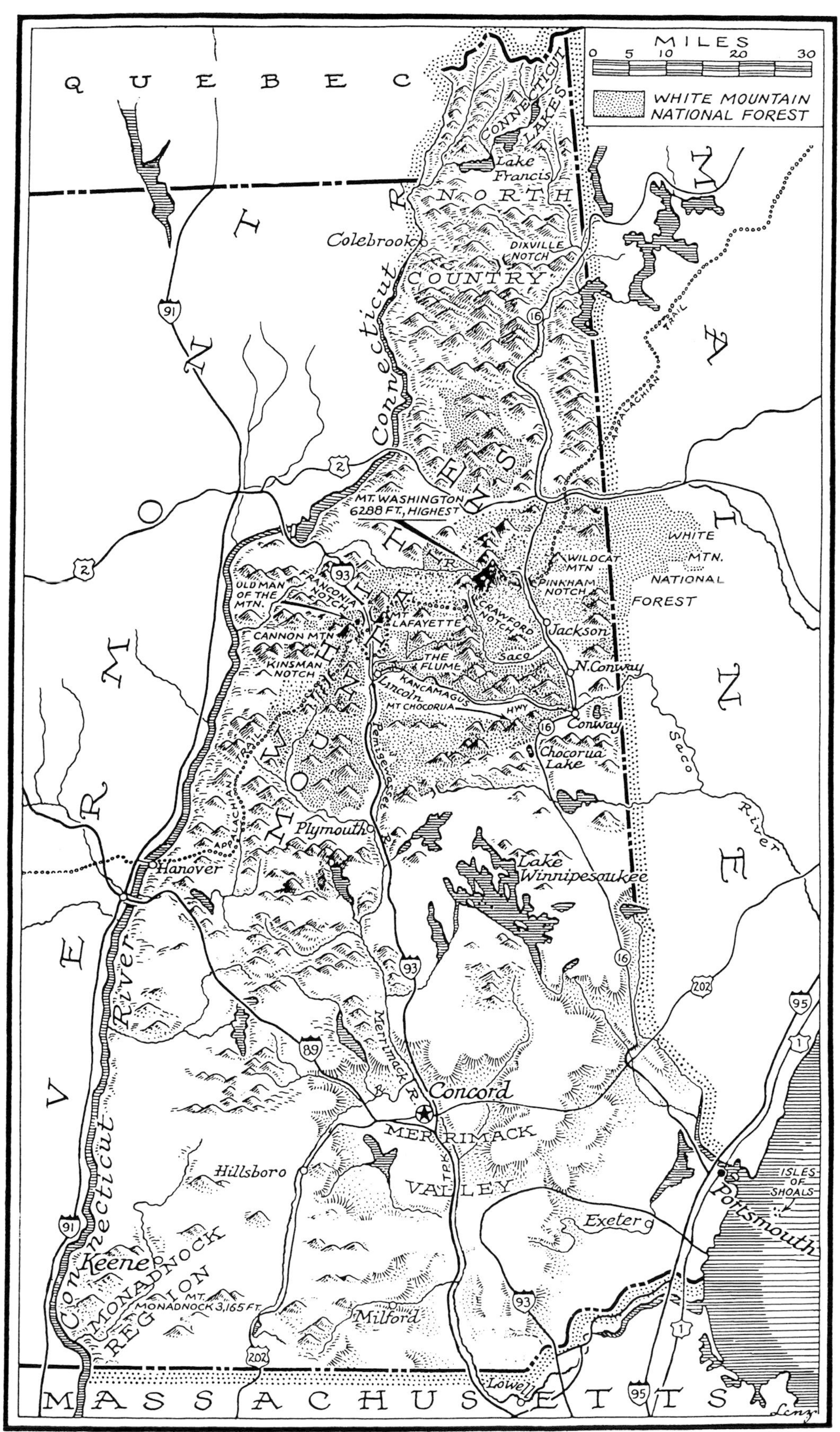
MILES
0 5 10 20 30
WHITE MOUNTAIN NATIONAL FOREST
QUEBEC
VERMONT
MAINE
NEW HAMPSHIRE
CONNECTICUT LAKES
Lake Francis
NORTH COUNTRY
Colebrook
DIXVILLE NOTCH
Connecticut R.
APPALACHIAN TRAIL
MT. WASHINGTON 6288 FT., HIGHEST
WILDCAT MTN
PINKHAM NOTCH
WHITE MTN. NATIONAL FOREST
OLD MAN OF THE MTN.
FRANCONIA NOTCH
MT. LAFAYETTE
CRAWFORD NOTCH
Jackson
CANNON MTN
KINSMAN NOTCH
THE FLUME
Saco
N. Conway
KANCAMAGUS HWY
Lincoln
MT CHOCORUA
Conway
Chocorua Lake
Saco River
Plymouth
Hanover
Lake Winnipesaukee
Connecticut River
Merrimack R.
Concord
MERRIMACK VALLEY
Hillsboro
ISLES OF SHOALS
Portsmouth
Exeter
Keene
MONADNOCK REGION
MT. MONADNOCK 3,165 FT.
Milford
Lowell
MASSACHUSETTS

VERMONT

For pure autumn colors, quiet backroads and pastoral countryside, there is no better place to visit than Vermont. It's one of the few states with no large cities; Burlington is the largest with only 40,000 souls. Vermont lacks the dramatic waterfalls, notches, and mountains of New Hampshire, but it makes up with its small farms, covered bridges and rolling hills whose birches, maples and beeches come ablaze in autumn.

We have broken Vermont into three tours—north, central and southern. *Vermont Life* magazine publishes an excellent 60 page pocket-sized book called *Guide to Fall Foliage* which has other tours as well, each tour described in detail with its own map. The Guide has fine drawings and photos to help you identify foliage, as well as writings by naturalist Gale Lawrence. This book is highly recommended for an autumn journey into New England.

The Northeast Kingdom (about 250 miles)

The cool northern climate causes fall colors to appear early here. You may as well start the tour in **Peacham**, for it's one of the most picturesque villages in Vermont, nestled as it is among rolling hills. The local Congregational Church has been acclaimed as one of the most beautiful country churches in the nation. From here, head north to West Danville to begin the tour. Head west to Hardwick. (From here you could make a side trip to **Smugglers Notch** and **Mount Mansfield** for some exciting mountain scenery and **summit views**.) From Hardwick head north on Rte 14 to Irasburg, and west on 58 to Lowell and **Montgomery Center**. Here you'll find six covered bridges within the immediate area. Next, take Rte 242 to Jay, Rte 101 to North Troy, Rte 105 to Newport, then to West Charleston on 5A then south to Lyndonville with a stop at **Lake Willoughby** under Mount Pisgah. Rte 114 to Island Pond. Then Rte 105 to Bloomfield, Rte 102 to Guildhall, then 102 and 2 to St. Johnsbury, a maple sugaring center.

Central Vermont

Woodstock is a good beginning for two central tours. One of about 150 miles takes you west to Fort Ticonderoga and back. The other takes a backroads loop north and south of **Woodstock**. Woodstock has well preserved churches and old buildings and lovely countryside. The backroads loop is a rectangle with Windsor at its southeast corner. Going clockwise, connect Tyson, Randolf, South Strafford and then back to Woodstock.

For the Ticonderoga loop, head northwest on Rte 12 then left on Rte 107. Take Rte 100 to Hancock, then 125 to Middlebury. Follow Rte 30 to Cornwall then Rte 74 to Fort **Ticonderoga**, a restored 18th century fort complete with soldiers, muskets and drills. Head back along Rte 73 through the pretty village of Brandon and through **Brandon Gap** which offers a good **view** of the region. From Rochester, head south to pick up Rte 100; stop at **Plymouth**, a lovely hamlet isolated in the hills. Old buildings here have been restored and are open to visitors.

Southeast Vermont

Head south from Plymouth into the southeast corner of Vermont for the third tour. **Weston** (there is a nice view of the town from the hill behind the small reservoir) is an excellent place to start. Head east on Rte 11 to Chester, then south on Rte 35 through the pretty, polished village of **Grafton**, then to **Newfane**, considered by many as the prettiest Vermont village of them all. Here the County Historical Society Museum shows what life was like 200 years ago. Double back to Rte 30 and head west to Jamaica and the Green Mountain National Forest. Heading west past Jamaica you'll pass a turn-off to the 4,000 foot Stratton Mountain, home of the Fall Arts Festival featuring arts and crafts from all over the state. When you hit Rte 11, head back toward Weston.

Although it is tempting to follow a prepared route, the best thing to do for really serene touring is to follow back roads. Don't be afraid of getting lost. It usually turns out to be the best part of a trip. Anyway, the earth is round.

For the lovers of civilization, Vermont has two interesting sites. The first is **Bennington** in the southwest corner with its Revolutionary Battle Memorial, and the oldest Stars and Stripes in existence. The best parts are the spectacularly simple paintings of Grandma Moses, and Robert Frost's grave with the headstone that reads, "I had a lover's quarrel with life."

The second is **Shelburne Museum** just south of Burlington near Lake Champlain. This is a great amalgam of thirty-seven well-restored buildings spread over 100 acres. Exhibits include art, furniture, glass, toys, coaches, clothes and figureheads. There are also covered bridges, paddlewheelers, railroad stations complete with steam locomotives, a lighthouse and a slew of motels. Up to you.

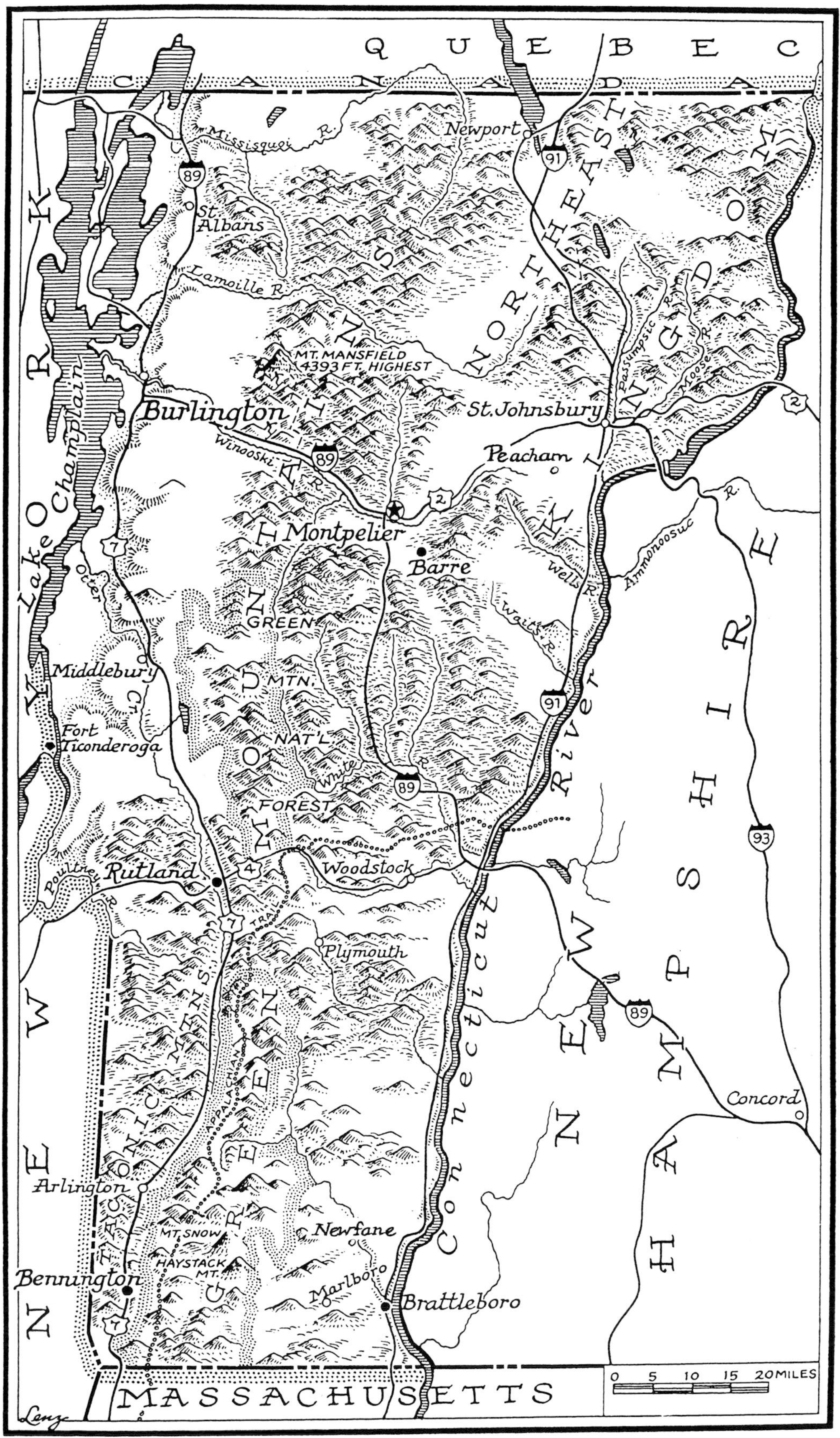
QUEBEC
CANADA
NEW YORK
Lake Champlain
Missisquoi R.
Newport
St. Albans
Lamoille R.
MT. MANSFIELD 4393 FT. HIGHEST
NORTHEAST KINGDOM
Burlington
St. Johnsbury
Peacham
Winooski R.
Montpelier
Barre
Otter Cr.
GREEN MTN. NAT'L FOREST
GREEN MOUNTAINS
Middlebury
Fort Ticonderoga
Wells R.
Waits R.
Ammonoosuc R.
Passumpsic R.
Moose R.
White R.
Rutland
Woodstock
Poultney R.
Plymouth
APPALACHIAN TRAIL
TACONIC MTNS.
Connecticut River
NEW HAMPSHIRE
Concord
Arlington
MT. SNOW
HAYSTACK MT.
Newfane
Bennington
Marlboro
Brattleboro
MASSACHUSETTS
0 5 10 15 20 MILES
Lenz

Rhode Island

As small, crowded and industrialized as Rhode Island is, you can still find seclusion in the autumn on the quiet, desolate shores of **Block Island**, and relative quiet in the northern portion of the state. On the other hand if you like cities, Newport's colonial part has some of the nation's best preserved architecture—Trinity Church, Touro Synagogue, Bowen's Wharf and the Brick Market being some of the highlights. A three to four hour walk will suffice for the sites.

The Newport Mansions—"summer cottages" with up to seventy rooms—were built in the last century by highly esteemed families, mostly with money made from the labor of men, women and children who worked and often died under inhuman conditions in their plantations and coal-mines. The Mansions' most celebrated social event was "the master and pet banquet" where all sat at the same table with their favorite animal, eating caviar and drinking champagne.

The following is a backroads tour of one of the quieter regions. We know it reads a bit more like a rally map than a guide to serene touring, but it might at least give you some hints. If you get lost, enjoy it.

Blackstone Valley and Northwestern Rhode Island

The tour route begins on Rte 295 in Cumberland. Access Rte 295 from Rte 95 North/South. Proceed to Exit 11 on Rte 295; at the exit turn right then go north on Rte 114 for 2.9 miles, then right onto Reservoir Road. Along the way a winery, gift shop and fresh apples are available. Follow Reservoir Road to Tingley Road (a left fork). Then take the first left (2 miles) on to Sumner Brown Road. Turn left again at the end of Sumner Brown Road. This is Rte 121, (unmarked); continue to the intersection of Rte 114, proceed straight; this is Wrentham Road. Take first left on to West Wrentham Road, then take first right on to Elder Balou Meeting House Road. (An iron mine stood at this site many years ago). Then proceed left onto Mendon Road. Follow Mendon Road 1-½ miles to the intersection. Proceed left and stay on Mendon Road (Rt 122S). Continue for 1-½ miles to the traffic light. Go right on to Manville Hill Road. Proceed down the hill, cross the Blackstone River, continue through the traffic light and bear to the left going up the hill. Look for sign for Rte 126 and proceed right. Go one block and follow signs to Rte 146 on Sayles Hill Road. Proceed straight through the traffic signal. At the top of the hill is Iron Mine Hill Road. Follow to the end, then turn left on to Rte 104 (unmarked at this point). Stay on Rte 104 through the town of Primrose. (Close to Pole #165 is an old country store). Go right on Rte 7 at the intersection. Proceed for 3 miles to Tarkiln Road on left. Follow through winding country road setting to the Village of Mapleville; go right on to the Victory Highway to the Village of Oakland, then left on to Rte 107. Follow for about 2-½ miles then right on to Rte 98 (Sherman Farm Road). Turn left on to Brook Road then cross Round Top Road on to West Road, (just before Round Top Road is a wonderful reproduction homestead). (West Road will turn into Stone Barn Road.) Proceed on to East Wallum, Lake Road (look for the cow passage tunnel built by the Providence and Springfield RailRoad for the local farmer's cattle in the 1800's. It is between Poles #39 and 38), then left onto Rte 100. As you enter the village, take a right turn Rte 100 and then first right onto Reservoir Road. Continue until reaching the end of the road, then proceed left on to Rte 44. Follow for about 7 miles through Greenville Village then enter Rte 116 N on left. Continue on Rte 116; it will join with Rte 5 at the intersection; take a left here. Rte 116 continues as your first right. Watch for Stillwater Road on the right about 1 mile ahead. Turn right onto Stillwater Road. You will pass through a former mill village which once had its own post office, general store and other supporting businesses when the Stillwater Mills were in operation. Follow to Limerock Road on left, (signs are not well marked; look for Pole #5—this is Limerock Road). Continue straight through two intersections then at the next intersection you will cross over Rte 146 and The Conklin Limestone Quarry will be on your right. This quarry is the oldest mining operation in America today. After passing by Conklin Quarry proceed to Great Road, your next left. Then cross on to Rte 116S, then on to Rte 146N and then to Rte 295N heading back to Rte 1-95.

If you have made it this far without a divorce or nervous breakdown then go directly to desolate **Block Island** with its moors, sand dunes and spectacular cliffs; you've earned it. The ferries leave from Point Judith Galilee Pier once or twice a day in the fall. Call for a schedule (401) 783-4613. The island is small so you can leave your car and rent a bicycle. You'll see more.

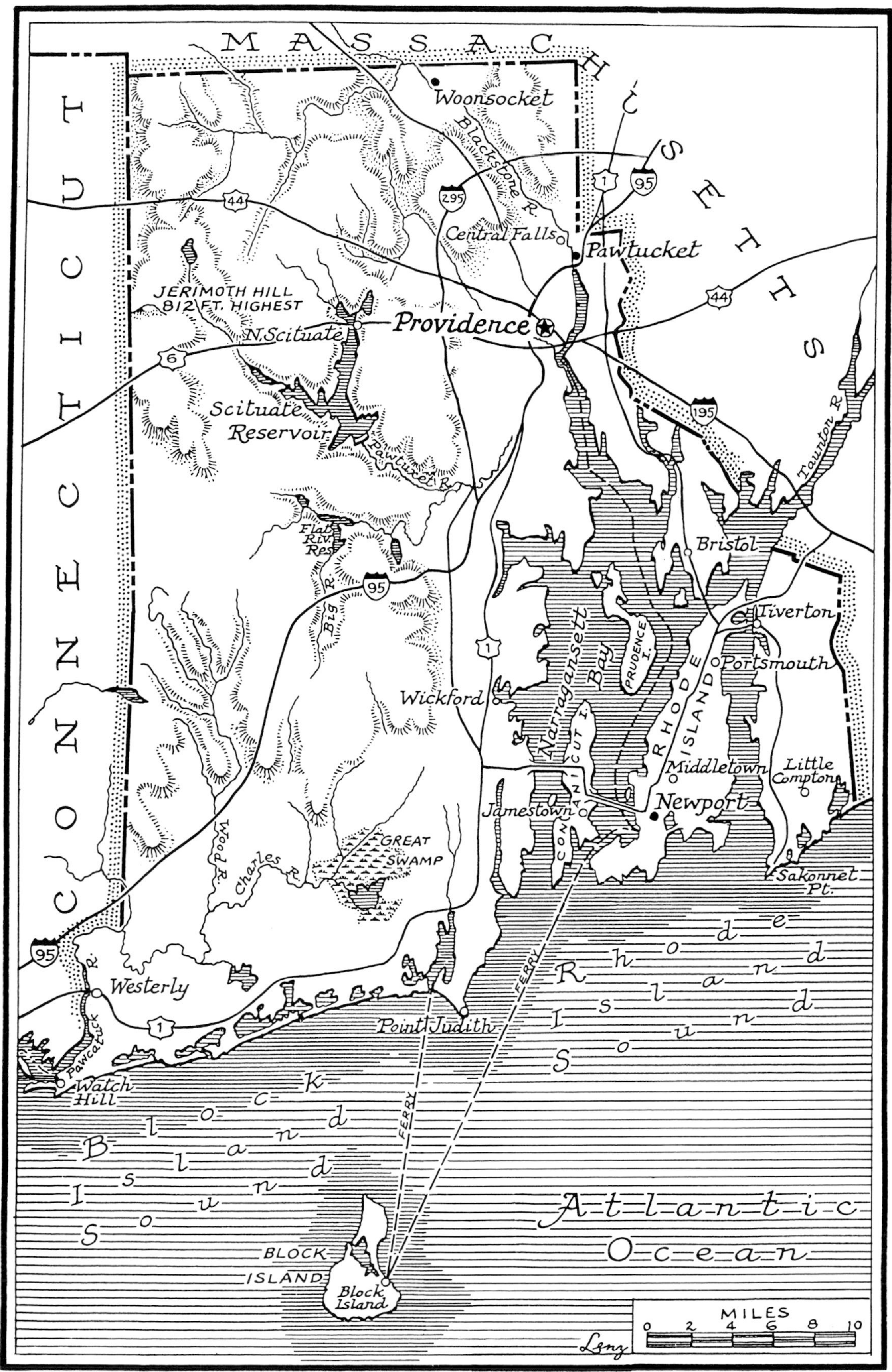
MASSACHUSETTS
CONNECTICUT
Woonsocket
Blackstone R.
Central Falls
Pawtucket
JERIMOTH HILL
812 FT. HIGHEST
N. Scituate
Providence
Scituate
Reservoir
Pawtuxet R.
Flat Riv. Res.
Big R.
Bristol
Tiverton
Portsmouth
PRUDENCE I.
Narragansett Bay
RHODE ISLAND
Wickford
CONANICUT I.
Middletown
Little Compton
Jamestown
Newport
GREAT SWAMP
Wood R.
Charles R.
Sakonnet Pt.
Rhode Island Sound
Westerly
Pawcatuck R.
Point Judith
Watch Hill
FERRY
Block Island Sound
Atlantic Ocean
BLOCK ISLAND
Block Island
MILES
0 2 4 6 8 10
Lenz

MASSACHUSETTS

Because it traverses all the New England states longitudinally, Massachusetts contains a little of each. In the west the Berkshires are forested and hilly, yielding in the middle to the Connecticut River Valley which reaches the coast of rugged rocky shores in the north and flat sandy beaches in the south. Its 50 mile long **Cape Cod**, rocky **Cape Ann** and the islands of **Martha's Vineyard** and **Nantucket** have become part of the nation's legends.

History abounds. **Boston's Freedom Trail**—specially marked for walkers—connects sixteen sites important to the history of Boston and America. It includes Paul Revere's house; the Old North Church ("One if by land, two if by sea"); the Old South Meeting House where the Boston Tea Party was born; Faneuil Hall, where public meetings helped define the revolution; and the U.S.S. Constitution, "Old Ironsides," a triumphant victor in numerous encounters against the British fleet in the War of 1812.

Salem's Heritage Trail takes visitors back to the port's clipper ship era when trade with the far east flourished.

There are four major "living history" museums in the state, where visitors can wander through 300 years of America's past. **Old Sturbridge Village** recreates a rural New England settlement of the 1830's Interpreters in period clothing farm the fields and go about their daily chores in forty restored buildings. **Plimoth Plantation** takes on the character of the 1627 Plymouth community where a visitor can chat with pilgrims such as Captain Standish. **Hancock Shaker Village** offers a fascinating glimpse at the life of the Shakers, (who for two centuries practiced a form of communal living) their buildings and starkly graceful furniture and furnishings. Nestled in the heart of Pioneer Valley, **Historic Deerfield** is a time capsule of the 18th and 19th centuries with twelve houses of antiques, ceramics and period furnishings.

Massachusetts has been home to great figures of literature. Visitors can view the houses of Emily Dickinson in Amherst, and Nathaniel Hawthorne, Thoreau and Emerson in **Concord**.

In the fall, the islands take on a special serenity. **Martha's Vineyard**, 45 minutes by ferry from Cape Cod, offers unspoiled dramatic coastal cliffs, sandy beaches, quiet harbors and six nicely different small towns. (Oak Bluffs boasts The Flying Horses, America's oldest wooden carousel). The island is dotted with romantic inns and guest houses. Nantucket is even more remote and serene. Lying 30 miles off **Cape Cod** it is three hours by a ferry that departs daily, year round from Woods Hole. It is a wide horseshoe of sand, moor, and heath that retains the air of its bygone days when whaling ships roamed the world from this island haven. Sea captains' houses with their roof walks dot cobblestone streets, and the Whaling Museum reflects the islands seafaring days. The island is small, only 14 miles long, so the best way to get around is by bicycle. You can rent one at the ferry dock. You can also rent a car.

On the North Shore, **Plum Island** offers miles of unspoiled beaches and sand dunes. Much of the island is a wildlife preserve—a haven for birdwatchers and nature lovers.

For enjoying the autumn colors, visit the Berkshires between October 1 and 14; the central part of the state October 5 to 18; and the coast, between October 15 and 24. The tourist and travel offices have compiled the following six drives for autumn touring.

Along the Mohawk Trail

On the Mohawk Trail, one of the first roads in the U.S. designed for automotive touring, there are 14 state parks and forests. Excellent "up-country" viewing sites include: the Whitcomb Summit; the hairpin turn before North Adams, with a pull-off for viewing the panoramas of rolling hills, valley farms and villages; the 10 mile drive to the **summit** of **Mount Greylock**; various sites off Rte 2; the French King Bridge, Millers Falls; the Bissell Covered Bridge, Charlemont; the **Natural Marble Bridge**, North Adams; and the Bridge of Flowers, **Shelburne Falls**.

The Berkshires

Follow Rte 7 north from Sheffield to Williamstown. Rte 8 runs from Sandisfield to Dalton and it's a beautiful route between two state forests. Rte 183, from Great Barrington to Lenox, follows the Housatonic River and passes small villages. Take Richmond Road, off Rte 183 just south of Tanglewood, and stop at the overlook for views of Stockbridge Bowl and the Southern Berkshire Hills. Rte 43 east, off Rte 7, is the lower road to Williamstown, and passes through lovely farmland. Rte 23, from Great Barrington to Monterey and then right onto Tyringham Road, takes you through the Tyringham Valley, and eventually to Lee.

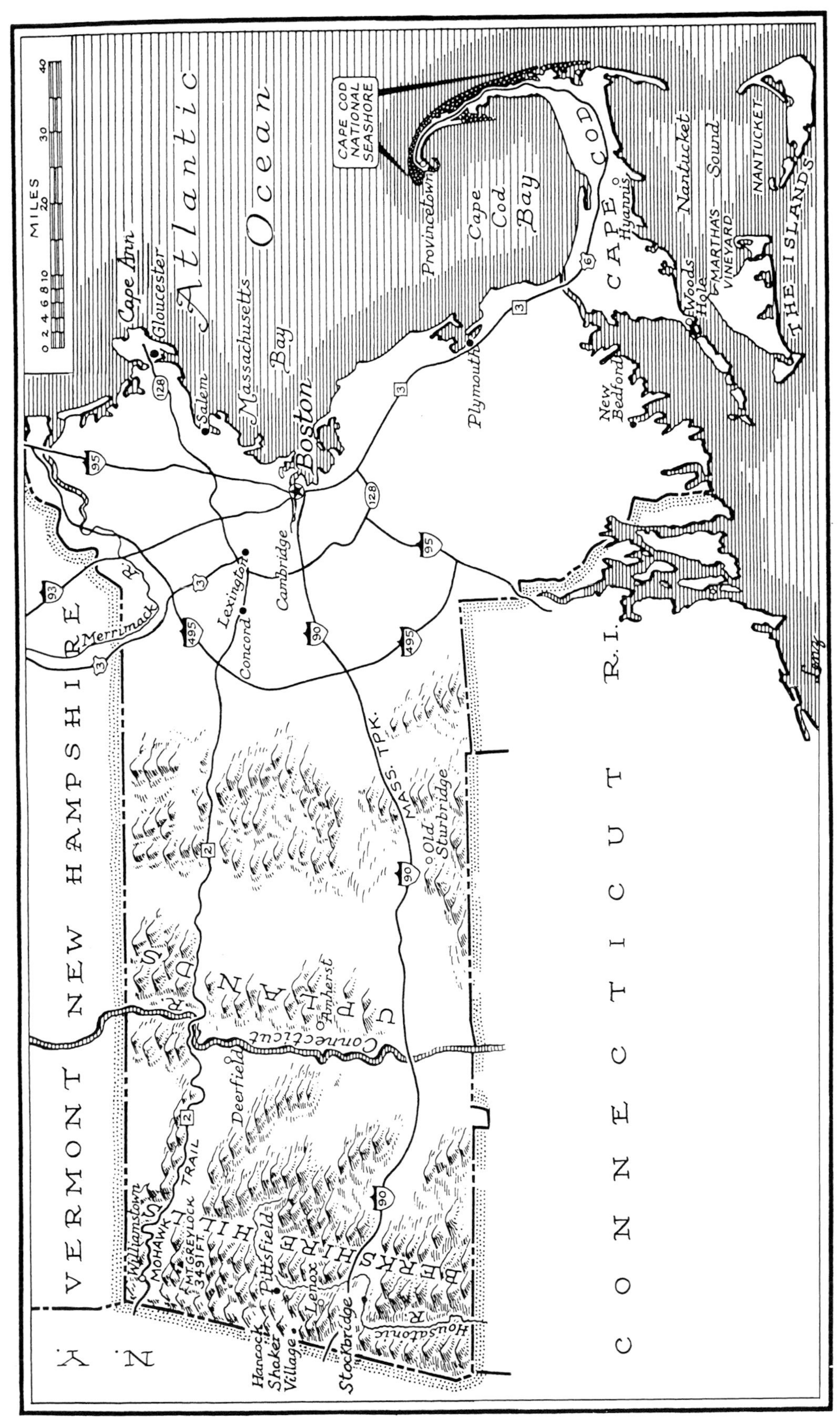

VERMONT
NEW HAMPSHIRE
N. Y.
CONNECTICUT
R. I.
Atlantic
Ocean
Massachusetts Bay
Cape Cod Bay
Nantucket Sound
CAPE COD
CAPE COD NATIONAL SEASHORE
THE ISLANDS
NANTUCKET
MARTHA'S VINEYARD
MILES
0 2 4 6 8 10 20 30 40
Cape Ann
Gloucester
Salem
Boston
Cambridge
Lexington
Concord
Plymouth
Provincetown
Hyannis
Woods Hole
New Bedford
Merrimack R.
Connecticut
Housatonic
Old Sturbridge
Amherst
Deerfield
Williamstown
MOHAWK TRAIL
MT. GREYLOCK 3491 FT.
Pittsfield
Lenox
Stockbridge
Hancock Shaker Village
BERKSHIRE HILLS
MASS. TPK.

Pioneer Valley

The secondary roads off Rte 116 and Rte 9 wind through rolling countryside and hill towns. Rte 116 passes through the picturesque towns of Conway and Ashfield, and, beginning in Pittsfield. Rte 9 leads through the village centers of Goshen and Cummington and the college towns of Amherst and Northampton.

Central Massachusetts

You'll find excellent color at a relaxed pace when you drive along the less frequently travelled routes to the Quabbin Reservoir: From Rte 128, follow Rte 117 to Stow, in the heart of apple country. At Stow, follow Rte 62 south and west to Princeton. Turn north on the unnumbered route to Wauchusett Mountain Reservation. There you can drive, hike, or take a "skyride" to the summit for a sweeping view of the countryside. Return to 62 and head west to Barre, then south on Rte 32 to Old Furnace. Follow the unnumbered road west to Hardwick. Turn north on Rte 32A which runs along the Quabbin Reservoir to Petersham. Turn left for a short drive to the Federation of Women's Clubs State Forest on the shores of the Quabbin. At Petersham, follow Rte 101 east through Templeton, Gardner and Ashburnhams to the junction of Rte 119. Head east on it through the Willard Brook State Forest in Ashby and Townsend where road and brook run parallel.

Day Trip from Boston

From Boston, follow Rtes 2 and 4 to Lexington. From Lexington to Concord, Rte 2A winds through brilliant autumnal countryside. Concord's famous Old North Bridge and Minuteman Monument are an ideal backdrop for foliage picture-taking. Pass through Concord Center and bear left at the fork on Sudbury Road. On the Sudbury line, the road becomes Concord Road and takes you through Sudbury Center and on to U.S. Rte 20. Return via U.S. Rte 20 through Waltham to Boston.

Southeastern Massachusetts

September and October are ideal in Plymouth County, Cape Cod and the islands of Martha's Vineyard and Nantucket. Days remain sunny and warm, offseason prices prevail, and an unusual foliage show awaits the autumn visitor. Rolling hills and heathland and, in particular, blueberry and blackberry bushes, turn a muted crimson color against the blue autumn sea. All this is best seen by foot or bicycle. Don't forget—autumn is also perfect for viewing cranberry bogs which turn ruby-red during wet-harvesting.

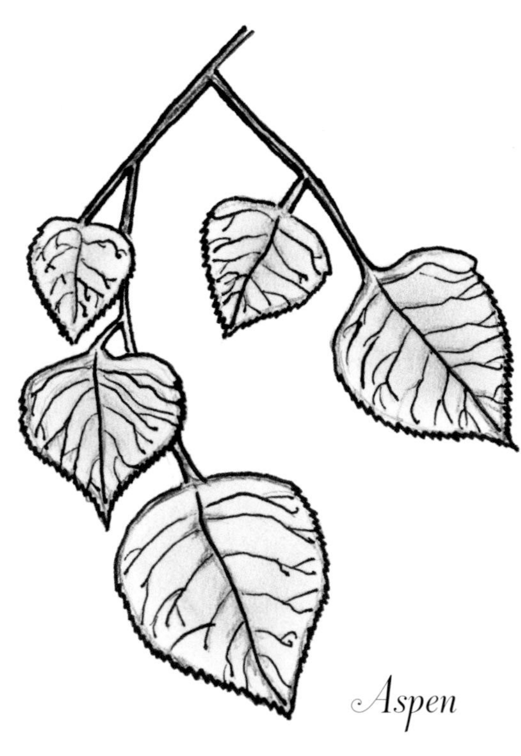

Aspen

Connecticut

The southern region of Connecticut is heavily industrialized and suburbanized, so the best place to do your fall touring is in the northwest corner of the state around the **Housatonic Valley**. Here you'll find quiet old villages and tranquil country roads, covered bridges, small farms and empty forests. Macedonia Brook State Park has streams and a rocky gorge, hiking and camping. Then there is Kent Falls State Park, and Housatonic Meadows State Park, whose 1,100 foot high Pine Knob (2 hr return hike) offers good valley views. The village of West Cornwall has a pretty covered bridge, and the town of **Litchfield** is one of the most favored for its blazing autumn leaves and 18th century houses.

Even if you are indifferent to sailboats and museums, you'll find a visit to **Mystic Seaport** in the northeast corner of the state worth a day's outing. It's a nicely reconstructed 19th century harbor, complete with an exceptionally preserved and rebuilt whaling ship, fishboats and sailboats of all description, a working smitty, a tavern, a watchmaker, a barrel maker, a vast sail loft, a figurehead carver, lighthouse, a complete ship's chandlery and fifty other buildings spread over the 17 acre site.

A couple of short—about 50 miles each—driving tours will take you through areas of colorful foliage.

East of the River Foliage Loop

Begin in Hartford. Take 1-84 east to Exit 60. Go left on Rte 44 toward East Hartford. Continue west on 44 to Rte 5. Turn right, north on Rte 5. Approximately 1 mile north of the Bissel Bridge turn left on Chapel Road. Turn right on Main Street through South Windsor to East Windsor Hill. Travel east on Rte 194 to Rte 74. Take Rte 74 to Rte 83 N. Take Rte 140 E to Crystal Lake (just past Rte 30 jct), Return to Rte 30 S to Rte 74 E to Tolland. Take 1-84 W to Exit 66, Rte 85. Travel south to Rte 94. Turn left (west) on Rte 94 to Rte 83. Travel on Rte 83 to Hartford Road. Turn left on Hartford Road to Keeney Street and entrance to Rte 384. Travel west on Rte 384 to Silver Lane and 1-84 to close loop.

Tobacco Valley Foliage Loop

Exit 1-91 in Enfield at Exit 47—east onto Rte 190. Go east on Rte 190, through Somers, to Stafford Springs. Intersect with Rte 140 W to East Windsor. Cross Warehouse Point Bridge. Turn south on Rte 159 in Windsor Locks and proceed into Windsor. Go west on Rte 75 to Rte 20. Continue west to East Granby. Go north on Rte 187 to Rte 168 in Suffield, east to Rte 159. Go north on Rte 159 to Rte 190. Turn right and cross bridge to 1-91 in Enfield to close loop.

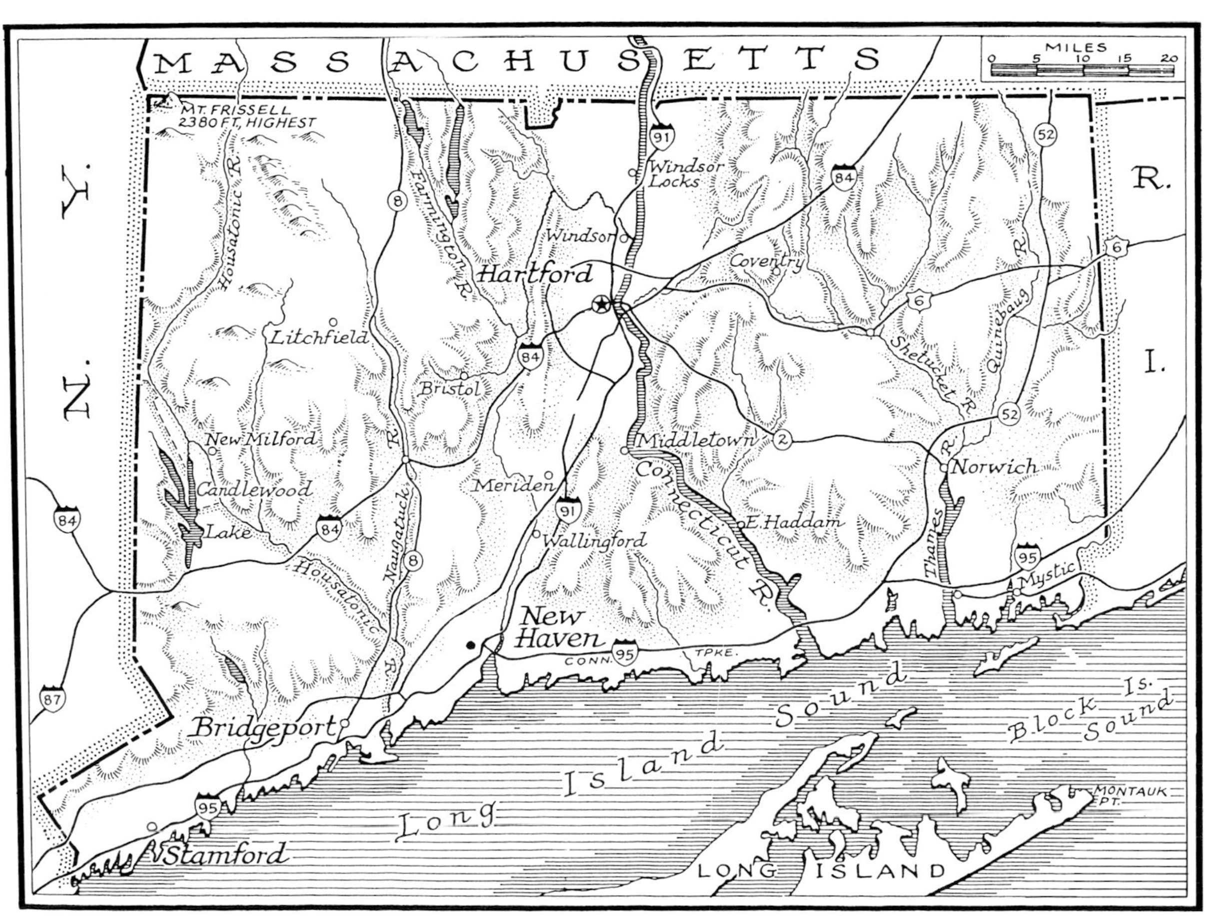

ACKNOWLEDGMENTS

Estate of Norma Millay Ellis. EDNA ST. VINCENT MILLAY, "Never May the Fruit Be Plucked," from *Collected Poems*, Harper & Row. Copyright 1923, 1951 by Edna St. Vincent Millay and Norma Millay Ellis. Reprinted by permission.

Farrar, Straus and Giroux, Inc. ELIZABETH BISHOP, excerpt from "At the Fishhouses" from *The Complete Poems 1927—1979* by Elizabeth Bishop. Copyright © 1979, 1983 by Alice Helen Methfessel. Reprinted by permission of Farrar, Straus and Giroux, Inc.

Harper & Row. SYLVIA PLATH, "Words" copyright © 1965 by the Estate of Sylvia Plath from her book *The Collected Poems of Sylvia Plath*. Reprinted by permission of Harper & Row.

Harvard University Press. EMILY DICKINSON, "As imperceptibly as Grief," "I reason, Earth is short," "This is my letter to the World." "To make a prairie," "Nature-sometimes sears a Sapling," "I died for Beauty." Reprinted by permission of the publishers and the Trustees of Amherst College from Thomas H. Johnson, editor *The Poems of Emily Dickinson*, Cambridge, Mass.: The Belknap Press of Harvard University Press. Copyright 1951, 1955 by The President and Fellows of Harvard College.

Henry Holt and Company, Inc. ROBERT FROST, "The Road Not Taken," "Stopping by Woods on a Snowy Evening," "Nothing Gold Can Stay," "Mending Wall," "After Apple-Picking," "An Old Man's Winter Night," "Dust of Snow," from *The Poetry of Robert Frost* edited by Edward Connery Lathem. Copyright © 1969 by Holt, Rinehart and Winston, Inc. Copyright © 1962 by Robert Frost. Copyright © 1975 by Lesley Frost Ballantine. Reprinted by permission of Henry Holt and Company, Inc.

Houghton Mifflin Company. ANNE SEXTON, "Ringing the Bells," from *To Bedlam and Part Way Back* by Anne Sexton. Copyright © 1960 by Anne Sexton. Reprinted by permission of Houghton Mifflin Company.

Liveright Publishing Corp. E.E.CUMMINGS. "nobody looses all the time" Reprinted by permission.

W.W.Norton & Co. Inc. works by SARAH ORNE JEWETT, MARY E. WILKINS FREEMAN, and JOHN GOULD. Reprinted by permission.